AQA Religious Studies A
Buddhism

GCSE

Kevin James
Nagapriya

Series editor
Cynthia Bartlett

OXFORD
UNIVERSITY PRESS

OXFORD
UNIVERSITY PRESS

Great Clarendon Street, Oxford, OX2 6DP, United Kingdom

Oxford University Press is a department of the University of Oxford. It furthers the University's objective of excellence in research, scholarship, and education by publishing worldwide. Oxford is a registered trade mark of Oxford University Press in the UK and in certain other countries

British Library Cataloguing in Publication Data
Data available

978-0-19-837032-1

(Kerboodle book: 978-0-19-837052-9)

10 9 8 7 6

Paper used in the production of this book is a natural, recyclable product made from wood grown in sustainable forests. The manufacturing process conforms to the environmental regulations of the country of origin.

Printed in India by Multivista Global Pvt. Ltd.

Approval message from AQA

This textbook has been approved by AQA for use with our qualification. This means that we have checked that it broadly covers the specification and we are satisfied with the overall quality. Full details of our approval process can be found on our website.

We approve textbooks because we know how important it is for teachers and students to have the right resources to support their teaching and learning. However, the publisher is ultimately responsible for the editorial control and quality of this book.

Please note that when teaching the AQA GCSE Religious Studies course, you must refer to AQA's specification as your definitive source of information. While this book has been written to match the specification, it cannot provide complete coverage of every aspect of the course.

A wide range of other useful resources can be found on the relevant subject pages of our website: www.aqa.org.uk.

Please note that the Practice Questions in this book allow students a genuine attempt at practising exam skills, but they are not intended to replicate examination papers.

Contents

PART TWO: THEMATIC STUDIES

Chapter 3: Relationships and families

Chapter 4: Religion and life

Chapter 5: The existence of God and revelation

Chapter 6: Religion, peace and conflict

Chapter 7: Religion, crime and punishment

Chapter 8: Religion, human rights and social justice

Introduction

This book is written specifically for GCSE students studying the AQA Religious Studies Specification A, 3.1.1 Buddhism and 3.2.1 Religious, philosophical and ethical studies.

Chapters 1 and 2 cover the beliefs, teachings and practices of Buddhism, including the Buddha's life and teachings, and the ways that Buddhists practise their faith, including worship and festivals. Chapters 3 to 8 cover religious, philosophical and ethical issues, including Relationships and families, Religion and life, the Existence of God and revelation, Religion, peace and conflict, Religion, crime and punishment, and Religion, human rights and social justice.

For the full course you must study two world religions, and four out of six of the philosophical and ethical themes. There are two examination papers, one on the religions and the other on the issues. For a short course qualification you must study the beliefs and teachings of Christianity and either Buddhism, Judaism or Islam. You must also study two themes: Relationships and families and Religion, peace and conflict. There is one examination paper on these topics. For the short course specification, please refer to the AQA website.

Where technical terms are used in this book, some are given in Pali and some in Sanskrit. We have followed the AQA specification in our choice of which terms to use.

Assessment guidance

Each chapter has an assessment guidance section that helps you to familiarise yourself with the AQA paper. There are multiple choice questions worth 1 mark, short-answer questions worth 2 marks, and longer questions worth 4 and 5 marks that test your ability to retell and explain facts. There are longer evaluation questions worth 12 marks that test your ability to analyse and evaluate different viewpoints.

Examination questions will test two assessment objectives, each representing 50 per cent of the total marks:

AO1: Demonstrate knowledge and understanding of religion and beliefs including:

- beliefs, practices and sources of authority
- influence on individuals, communities and societies
- similarities and differences within and/or between religions and beliefs.

AO2: Analyse and evaluate aspects of religion and belief, including their significance and influence.

For AO1 questions, the grid below gives guidance on how marks will be allocated:

Marks	Question type	Criteria
1 mark	Multiple choice	The correct answer chosen from 4 options
2 marks	Short-answer (asking for two facts)	One mark for each of **two** correct points
4 marks	Asking for two ways in which beliefs influence Buddhists today OR two contrasting ways in which religion is practised OR two contrasting beliefs in contemporary British society about an issue studied in the themes, including one from Christianity and one from another religion or in the case of theme C, non-religious perspectives	For each of the **two** ways / contrasts: • one mark for a simple explanation of a relevant and accurate way / contrast; • two marks for a detailed explanation of a relevant and accurate way / contrast
5 marks	Asking for two Buddhist beliefs or teachings OR two Buddhist practices OR two religious beliefs about a philosophical or ethical issue PLUS reference to scripture or sacred writings	For each of the **two** beliefs / practices: • one mark for a simple explanation of a relevant and accurate belief / practice; • two marks for a detailed explanation of a relevant and accurate belief / practice; **PLUS** one mark for a relevant, accurate reference to scripture or sacred writing

The grid below gives you some guidance on different levels for the 12 mark evaluation question (testing AO2).

Levels	Criteria	Marks
4	A well-argued response, reasoned consideration of different points of view Logical chains of reasoning leading to judgement(s) supported by knowledge and understanding of relevant evidence and information	10–12
3	Reasoned consideration of different points of view Logical chains of reasoning that draw on knowledge and understanding of relevant evidence and information	7–9
2	Reasoned consideration of a point of view A logical chain of reasoning drawing on knowledge and understanding of relevant evidence and information OR Recognition of different points of view, each supported by relevant reasons / evidence	4–6
1	Point of view with reason(s) stated in support	1-3
0	Nothing worthy of credit	0

For the latest mark schemes, please also refer to the AQA website.

In modern Britain, Buddhists practise their religion alongside people from many different faiths. The AQA GCSE specification requires that students understand Christian beliefs on three issues in each of the ethical and philosophical themes, and are able to compare these with other faith perspectives, including Buddhism (or between Christianity and non-religious viewpoints in the case of Theme C).

Theme	Students must be able to explain contrasting beliefs on the following:
A: Relationships and families	• Contraception • Sexual relationships before marriage • Homosexual relationships
B: Religion and life	• Abortion • Euthanasia • Animal experimentation
C: The existence of God and revelation	• Visions • Miracles • Nature as general revelation
D: Religion, peace and conflict	• Violence • Weapons of mass destruction • Pacifism
E: Religion, crime and punishment	• Corporal punishment • Death penalty • Forgiveness
F: Religion, human rights and social justice	• Status of women in religion • The uses of wealth • Freedom of religious expression

You should also bear in mind non-religious views such as atheism and humanism, and understand the influence of beliefs, teachings and practices on individuals, communities and societies.

Spelling, punctuation and grammar (SPaG) is also important so it will be useful to practise the 12 mark extended writing questions. There are 3 marks available for SPaG: 1 mark for threshold performance, 2 marks for intermediate performance and 3 marks for high performance. You should aim to write correctly using a wide range of specialist religious terms.

Examination grades will be awarded on a scale of 9–1 rather than A* to G. Grade 9 will be the equivalent of a new grade for high performing students above the current A*. Grade 4 will be the same as a grade C pass. The aim of the new grading system is to show greater differentiation between higher and lower achieving students.

Kerboodle book

An online version of this book is available for student access, with an added bank of tools for you to personalise the book.

Part 1: The study of religions

1 Beliefs and teachings

1.1 The birth of the Buddha and his life of luxury

■ The birth of the Buddha

There is a great variety of religious practices that are associated with the word Buddhism, but most take their source of inspiration to be Siddhartha Gautama, who lived and taught in northern India some 2500 years ago. After he was enlightened he became known as the Buddha, which is a title meaning 'the enlightened one' or 'the awakened one'. It is a title given to a being who has attained great wisdom and understanding through their own efforts.

There are many sources that tell us about the life of the Buddha. Some of these were written hundreds of years after his death, and so at times it is difficult to distinguish between fact and legend. Even so, for Buddhists these legends express important, spiritual truths.

It is believed that Siddhartha was born around 500 BCE in Lumbini in southern Nepal, close to the border with India. According to Buddhist tradition, Siddhartha was a prince: his father was King Suddhodana Tharu and his mother was Queen Maya Devi Tharu. The following traditional story is commonly told about Siddhartha's birth:

One night, Queen Maya had a dream that a white elephant came down from heaven and entered her womb. The elephant told her that she would give birth to a holy child, and that when he was born he would achieve perfect wisdom.

About ten months later, when the baby was almost due, Queen Maya began the journey home to her parents' house, where she had planned to give birth. On the way she stopped in the Lumbini Gardens to rest and here she gave birth to a son. According to legend, he could immediately walk and talk without any support. He walked seven steps and with every step he took, a lotus flower sprang up from the earth beneath his feet. He then stopped and said, 'No further rebirths have I to endure for this is my last body. Now I shall destroy and pluck out by the roots the sorrow that is caused by birth and death.' He was called 'Siddhartha', meaning 'perfect fulfilment'.

Shortly after Siddhartha's birth, a prophecy was made that he would become either a great king or a revered holy man.

> **Objective**
>
> - Examine some of the stories surrounding the Buddha's birth and his early life.

> **Key terms**
>
> - **Buddhism:** a religion founded around 2500 years ago by Siddhartha Gautama
> - **Buddha:** a title given to someone who has achieved enlightenment; usually used to refer to Siddhartha Gautama

▲ *The Buddha's first steps*

◼ Siddhartha's life of luxury

Siddhartha's mother died when he was just seven days old, and he was raised by his mother's sister, Maha Pajapati.

According to Buddhist tradition, Siddhartha grew up in a palace, surrounded by luxury. His father, Suddhodana, kept in mind the prophecy that was made about Siddhartha shortly after his birth. Suddhodana was determined that Siddhartha would follow in his footsteps and grow up to be a great king. So he decided to protect Siddhartha from any pain, sadness, disappointment or suffering that he might experience in his life. Suddhodana didn't want his son to seek religion and become a holy man.

▲ Most Buddhist traditions are inspired by the teachings of Siddhartha Gautama, who is known as 'the Buddha'

Suddhodana also thought that if his son became attached to a life of luxury, he would not want to leave the palace. Siddhartha was therefore supplied with everything he could possibly want. He wore clothes of the finest silk, ate the best foods, was surrounded by dancers and musicians, received an excellent education, and was generally cared for in every way.

Siddhartha later said of his upbringing:

> ❝ I was delicately nurtured … At my father's residence lotus ponds were made just for my enjoyment: in one of them blue lotuses bloomed, in another red lotuses, and in a third white lotuses … By day and by night a white canopy was held over me so that cold and heat, dust, grass, and dew would not settle on me. I had three mansions: one for the winter, one for the summer, and one for the rainy season. I spent the four months of the rains in the rainy-season mansion, being entertained by musicians, none of whom were male, and I did not leave the mansion. ❞
>
> The Buddha in the *Anguttara Nikaya*, vol. 1, p. 145

Research activity 🔍

Two traditional stories told about the Buddha's early life recall his visit to the ploughing festival, and his encounter with a swan. Research these two stories. Why did each event seem to have such a profound effect on Siddhartha?

Despite being spoilt and pampered while he was growing up, traditional stories say that Siddhartha was a good and kind person. At the age of 16 he married his cousin, Yasodhara.

Discussion activity 💬

Research online other accounts of the birth of the Buddha and his life as he grew up. Discuss with a partner some of the differences that you notice between the accounts. Why you think there are so many different accounts of the Buddha's birth and his life of luxury? What meanings do you think they have for Buddhists?

⭐ Study tip

Knowing about the extent of the luxury that the Buddha experienced while growing up is important for understanding his later teachings.

Activities

1 According to Buddhist tradition, what did Siddhartha do as soon as he was born?

2 How did the prophecy that was made about Siddhartha affect his upbringing?

Summary

You should now know some of the stories surrounding the Buddha's birth and his life growing up.

We have seen that Siddhartha grew up in a palace living a life of luxury, shielded from the rest of the world. However, Siddhartha grew curious and wanted to explore outside the palace walls. Traditional Buddhist stories say that one day at the age of 29, despite his father's orders, Siddhartha decided to leave the palace grounds and go with Channa (his attendant and chariot driver) to the nearby city. Siddhartha then encountered **the four sights**, which had a profound effect on his life. The story of the four sights is recorded in **Jataka** 075.

▲ *Siddhartha encountered four sights when he left the palace, which had a profound effect on his life*

The first sight: old age

Siddhartha and Channa may not have gone very far before Siddhartha saw a frail old man, something he had never witnessed before in his life. He was shocked by what he saw as it was his first real experience of old age.

The second sight: illness

Some stories say that Siddhartha asked Channa to take him back to the palace, and he saw the other three sights on separate visits to the city. Other stories say that Siddhartha saw all four sights on his first and only visit to the city. Whether he made a number of trips or just one to the city, Siddhartha also saw someone lying in the road in agony. This disturbed him as he had never seen sickness or illness before, and he began to understand that illness was a reality of life.

The third sight: death

Siddhartha then saw a dead man being carried through the streets in a funeral procession. Some say that this third sight struck Siddhartha even more deeply. It was, after all, the first time he had seen death.

Objectives

- Know the story of the Buddha's encounter with the four sights.
- Understand the effect this had on the Buddha.

Key terms

- **the four sights:** old age, illness, death, and a holy man; these four sights led the Buddha to leave his life of luxury in the palace
- **Jataka:** the Jataka tales are popular stories about the lives of the Buddha

Research activity

There are a number of different versions of the story of the Buddha's encounter with the four sights. Here are a few differences between the stories:

1 All the sights were seen on one trip, rather than on different trips.
2 Siddhartha's father actually gave permission for the trips to take place, rather than telling Siddhartha not to leave the palace.
3 Siddhartha never actually saw the four sights. They are just metaphors to show different forms of suffering.

Using the internet or a library, read different versions of this story and make a note of any other differences. Why do you think these differences have occurred? Do you think they change the overall message or importance of the story?

He realised that death came to everyone. If someone was born, they would go through a process which would involve growing older, illness, suffering and death. There was no escape, even for kings.

The fourth sight: a holy man

The fourth sight Siddhartha saw was quite different. Walking calmly through the city was a man dressed in rags and carrying an alms bowl. The peaceful expression on the face of this holy man impressed Siddhartha very much. He felt inspired to be like this holy man and to become a wandering truth seeker. This was perhaps the beginning of Siddhartha's quest to search for the answer to the problem of why people suffer, and how to stop that suffering.

▲ Monks use alms bowls to collect food or money from supporters

■ Leaving the palace

Finding the answer to the problem of suffering became the most important thing in Siddhartha's life. But he knew that if he stayed in the palace, he would find no answers. It is said that on the night his own son Rahula was born, he left the palace for good in search of an answer. He got up quietly, kissed his wife and newborn son, woke Channa, and they crept past the sleeping guards and silently rode away from the palace.

When they both reached the edge of a river, they dismounted from their horses. Taking his sword, Siddhartha cut off his hair and swapped his rich clothes for the clothes of a beggar. He gave all his rings and bracelets to Channa to take back to his father. Channa watched as Siddhartha crossed the river and disappeared into the forest on the other side.

By giving up his possessions and the symbols of his previous life, Siddhartha was letting go of the things that he thought were keeping him ignorant and thus resulting in his suffering. Later he was to teach that renunciation, a 'letting go', was important in reaching enlightenment.

Activities

1 How do you think you would feel on seeing each of the four sights for the first time in your life?

2 Explain what you think Siddhartha learned from seeing the four sights.

3 Describe how you think Channa, who was Siddhartha's charioteer and best friend, would have felt on seeing Siddhartha disappear into the forest.

Discussion activity

Discuss with a partner the effect you think that seeing the holy man would have had on Siddhartha, as he tried to search for the answer to the problem of suffering.

Summary

You should now know what the four sights are, and be able to explain the effect they had on Siddhartha.

⭐ Study tip

As you continue to learn about the Buddha's teachings, remember how they were influenced by his encounter with the four sights.

■ Living as an ascetic

After he left the palace, Siddhartha tried various methods to learn how to overcome the problem of suffering. He had been impressed by the sense of peace that he felt coming from the holy man – an **ascetic** – that he met before he left the palace, so he decided to follow ascetic practices for six years. He rejected anything that would give him pleasure and practised extreme self-discipline. He met and studied with various holy men. In particular, he began to practise meditation with two ascetics, Alara Kalama and Uddaka Ramaputta. They used pain and hardship to discipline their minds. It is said that the meditation gave Siddhartha a feeling of bliss, but did not offer him a permanent solution to the suffering that people experienced.

Siddhartha then began to ignore his appetite. He fasted for long periods of time, becoming increasingly hungry and weak. Stories say that his body became so thin that his legs were like bamboo sticks, his backbone was like a rope, his chest was like an incomplete roof of a house, and his eyes sank right inside his skull, like stones in a deep well. He looked like a living skeleton, and suffered from terrible pain and hunger.

Traditional stories also say that Siddhartha lived in dangerous and hostile forests, which were too hot during the day and freezing at night. He slept on a bed of thorns as part of his ascetic practices. He was frightened when the animals came but he never ran away.

▲ *Siddhartha ate very little as part of his ascetic lifestyle, becoming incredibly thin as a result*

Objectives

- Know how the Buddha lived as an ascetic.
- Understand why the Buddha wanted to follow ascetic practices, and why he later decided to reject them.

Key terms

- **ascetic:** living a simple and strict lifestyle with few pleasures or possessions; someone who follows ascetic practices
- **meditation:** a practice of calming and focusing the mind, and reflecting deeply on specific teachings to penetrate their true meaning

Discussion activity

Many people have found simplicity helpful in living a religious life. Discuss with a partner why some people have taken this further, ignoring the needs of the body. What are the dangers of this?

■ Turning away from asceticism

One day, Siddhartha was bathing in the River Nairanjana. When he got out of the water he saw a girl who was looking after a herd of cows for her father. The girl offered Siddhartha a bowl of milk and rice. He accepted the food because he had by this point become too weak even to meditate.

Siddhartha's strength was restored by the food and he decided to stop his ascetic practices, because he was no closer to the truth of why people suffer and how to get rid of this suffering. His ascetic practices taught him discipline and willpower, but they did not provide a cure for suffering. Neither luxury nor an ascetic lifestyle had given Siddhartha any real answers. This led him to develop a 'middle way' between the two extremes that he had experienced.

▲ *The Buddha stopped practising asceticism after he was offered a bowl of milk and rice*

Extension activity

Carefully read the quotation from the Jataka on this page. Rewrite the quotation in your own words, showing that you have understood what the Buddha did and why, after six years, he decided to give up his ascetic life.

> ❝ And the Bodhisattva ["One aspiring to Awakening"] himself, who was determined to practise austerities in their most extreme form began to subsist on one grain of sesamum or rice a day. He even took to complete fasting … When the Great Being was practising severe austerities for six years it was to him like a time of intertwining the sky with knots. Realising the practice of such austerities was not the path to Enlightenment he went about gathering alms in villages and townships in order to revert to solid food, and he subsisted on it. ❞
>
> The *Jataka*, vol. 1, p. 67

⭐ Study tip

When learning about the choices that the Buddha made during his life, consider why he made them, and how they helped him in his search for enlightenment.

Summary

You should now be able to explain what happened to Siddhartha after he left the palace and decided to live as an ascetic. You should also be able to understand why Siddhartha wanted to become an ascetic, and why he decided to stop following ascetic practices.

Activities

1 In your own words, explain what an ascetic is.
2 Give three different methods that Siddhartha tried in order to resolve the problem of suffering.
3 Explain why the meeting at the River Nairanjana was important for Siddhartha.

The Buddha's enlightenment

■ The Buddha's meditation

After rejecting his ascetic lifestyle, Siddhartha wondered if meditation might be a way of attaining the wisdom and compassion of **enlightenment**. Traditional stories say that he made himself a cushion of grass and found a suitable place to sit down and meditate, underneath a peepul tree. He sat with his face to the east and thought:

> 66 Let only my sin, sinews and bone remain and let the flesh and blood in my body dry up; but not until I attain the supreme Enlightenment will I give up this seat of meditation. 99
>
> The Buddha in the *Jataka*, vol. 1, p. 71

▲ *The peepul tree at Mahabodhi Temple in India is thought to be a direct descendant of the original peepul tree, and the place where Siddhartha gained enlightenment. It is a popular Buddhist pilgrimage site.*

Then Siddhartha began to meditate. Traditional stories tell how **Mara**, the evil one, appeared to try to stop him from achieving enlightenment. Mara tried a number of different tactics:

- he sent his daughters to seduce Siddhartha
- he sent his armies to attack Siddhartha
- he offered Siddhartha control of his kingdom
- Mara himself tried to attack Siddhartha.

Throughout it all, Siddhartha stayed focused on his meditation. He ignored the temptations of Mara's daughters. Arrows directed at him from the armies turned to flowers before they could hit him. Towards the end of his meditation, Mara claimed that only he had the right to

Objectives

- Know the story of how the Buddha became enlightened.
- Understand the three realisations that the Buddha made in order to achieve enlightenment.

Key terms

- **enlightenment:** the gaining of true knowledge about God, self or the nature of reality, usually through meditation and self-discipline; in Buddhist, Hindu and Sikh traditions, gaining freedom from the cycle of rebirth
- **Mara:** a demon that represents spiritual obstacles, especially temptation
- **the three watches of the night:** the three realisations that the Buddha made in order to achieve enlightenment
- **the five ascetics:** the Buddha's first five students; five monks who followed ascetic practices

▲ *Siddhartha sitting beneath the peepul tree*

sit in the place of enlightenment and his soldiers were witnesses to this. He claimed that without anyone to witness his enlightenment, Siddhartha would not be believed. Siddhartha then touched the earth and called upon the earth to witness his right to sit under the peepul tree in meditation. The earth shook to acknowledge his right.

There are different versions of the story of how Mara tried to stop Siddhartha from becoming enlightened. Most accounts are quite dramatic, but they all show that Siddhartha remained focused on his meditation, and that fear, lust, pride or other negative emotions were overcome with a disciplined mind.

▲ *Siddhartha being tempted by Mara*

■ Becoming enlightened

During the night that Siddhartha became enlightened, he experienced three important realisations. These realisations happened over three different periods (or 'watches') during the night, and so they are known as **the three watches of the night**:

- Firstly, Siddhartha gained knowledge of all of his previous lives.
- Secondly, he came to understand the repeating cycle of life, death and rebirth. He understood that beings were born depending on their kamma (their actions), and he realised the importance of anatta (there is no fixed self).
- Thirdly, he came to understand why suffering happens and how to overcome it.

After his enlightenment, Siddhartha became known as 'the Buddha', which means 'the enlightened one' or 'the fully awakened one'. The Buddha left the peepul tree and wandered back to the place where he had previously left **the five ascetics**, who were his first students. It is said that Mara still tried to tempt him further to keep his realisations to himself. But the Buddha was determined to teach about suffering and how to overcome it, to help others to achieve enlightenment. He asked anyone who would follow him to reject a life of extremism, which meant not having too many luxuries or living a very ascetic lifestyle.

Discussion activity

In achieving enlightenment, the Buddha chose between two extremes. Is it always best in life to avoid the extremes? Give reasons for your answer.

Research activity

Research traditional stories about the Buddha's enlightenment. In what different ways is he said to have been tempted? Consider whether it is possible for the Buddha to have concentrated his mind in such a way that he would not be distracted from achieving enlightenment by these temptations. If possible, discuss your thoughts with a partner.

Activities

1   The image of the Buddha meditating and achieving enlightenment is a focal point for many Buddhists. Why do you think this image is so important?

2   Have you ever been tempted by someone or something? What did you do to try to overcome the temptation?

3   What were the three realisations that the Buddha made during the night of his enlightenment?

4   When asked questions about his enlightenment, the Buddha often spoke in negative terms, describing what it is not rather than what it is (for example, it is *not* heaven, or it is *not* the end). Why do you think the Buddha spoke in this way?

★ Study tip

Learn the story of Siddhartha's enlightenment carefully. It will help you to understand Buddhism.

Summary

You should now know how Siddhartha became enlightened and became a Buddha.

1.5 The Dhamma

■ What does 'Dhamma' mean?

The term **Dhamma** (in **Pali**) or Dharma (in **Sanskrit**) has many meanings. It means the 'truth' about the nature of existence, as understood by the Buddha when he became enlightened. (His Four Noble Truths and the three marks of existence are examples of this.) It also means the path of training that was recommended by the Buddha for anyone who wishes to understand what he understood (for example, the Eightfold Path). It is sometimes translated as 'law', not in the sense of rules to be followed, but in the sense of a universal law such as Newton's law of gravity: a fact about the way things are.

Even though the Buddha described his insights into reality as the 'truth', he encouraged his followers to test his teachings against their own experience. He did not want people to follow his teachings unquestioningly because, for example, they were impressed with him as a teacher, or because he must be right if he had so many followers. In his book *Old Path White Clouds*, the Buddhist monk Thich Nhat Hanh recounts stories about the Buddha's life. In one of them, the Buddha explains his teaching to the ascetic Dighanaka like this:

> ❝ My teaching is not a philosophy. It is the result of direct experience …
>
> My teaching is a means of practice, not something to hold on to or worship.
>
> My teaching is like a raft used to cross the river.
>
> Only a fool would carry the raft around after he had already reached the other shore of liberation. ❞
>
> Thich Nhat Hanh (Vietnamese Buddhist monk)

Many Buddhists say that following the Buddha's teachings has relieved them of much suffering, giving them meaning, purpose and greater happiness or satisfaction in life. Becoming more aware, wise and compassionate is not only good for them, but also transforms their relationships with others and the wider world.

■ Dhamma as a refuge

The Dhamma is also the second of the three refuges (also known as 'treasures' or 'jewels') in Buddhism. The other two refuges are the Buddha and the Sangha. Depending on the context in which it is used, Sangha has three different meanings:

Objectives

- Examine what is meant by the Buddhist concept of Dhamma.
- Understand different meanings of Dhamma.

Key terms

- **Dhamma (Dharma):** the Buddha's teachings
- **Pali:** the language of the earliest Buddhist scriptures
- **Sanskrit:** the language used in later Indian Buddhist texts

Links

To read more about the three marks of existence and the Four Noble Truths, see pages 20–35.

▲ *The Buddha encouraged his followers to examine and question his teachings before accepting them*

1. all those who have become enlightened following the Buddha's teachings
2. monks and nuns
3. the community of all those who follow the Buddha's teachings, whether ordained or lay.

In many traditions, it is common to recite the three refuges at the start of a Buddhist event or meeting, and in ceremonies where people become Buddhists. They might say:

> " To the Buddha for refuge I go
> To the Dhamma for refuge I go
> To the Sangha for refuge I go "

▲ *By following the Buddha's teachings, Buddhists hope to eventually achieve enlightenment*

To 'go for refuge' means to seek safety. For Buddhists, this means looking for safety from suffering. The Buddha taught that, a lot of the time, people take refuge in things which are unreliable and cannot provide lasting safety (for example, you get the new mobile phone you really wanted and you feel great about it – until it breaks or a new model comes out). However, following the truths and path of training he discovered would give lasting safety from suffering. When Buddhists take refuge in the Buddha, Dhamma and Sangha, they are saying that they trust these things as lasting sources of safety from suffering. They are asking for the Buddha, Dhamma and Sangha to guide them in their development of wisdom and compassion. When Buddhists 'go for refuge', they are expressing their longing for enlightenment, and their commitment to following the path leading to enlightenment.

It is interesting to consider whether any of the three refuges could be said to be more important than the others. It could be argued that the Buddha is the most important because he provides an example for Buddhists to follow. If he had not discovered the Dhamma and then taught it, Buddhists might never have been able to understand the way out of suffering. On the other hand, it could be argued that the Dhamma is the most important because it describes the way things are. This 'truth' existed long before the Buddha recognised it (in the same way that the law of gravity is true whether anyone knows about it or not).

Finally, the Sangha is very important to a Buddhist's life. For an ordinary person following the Buddha's teaching, it is very encouraging to know that other ordinary people have reached the wisdom and compassion of enlightenment, not just the Buddha. Nuns and monks (and other experienced teachers) are essential as guides to less experienced Buddhists. In Buddhists' everyday lives, the Sangha around them can also provide support, encouragement and friendship.

Activities

1 Give two different meanings of the word 'Dhamma'.
2 In what circumstances might a Buddhist find (a) the Buddha, (b) the Dhamma, and (c) the Sangha the most useful refuge?

Discussion activities

Discuss the following questions with a partner:

1 Why do you think the Buddha wanted his followers to test and question his teachings? What were the potential benefits and disadvantages for the Buddha of his followers questioning his teachings?

2 Where do you 'go for refuge'? What experiences or things make you feel safe? Are they completely reliable?

Extension activity

Research meanings of 'Dharma' in Hinduism, and note some of the key differences between these and Buddhist meanings of 'Dhamma' or 'Dharma'.

⭐ Study tip

Remember that the word 'Dhamma' or 'Dharma' has significantly different meanings in other Indian religions.

Summary

You should now be able to understand the different meanings of the word Dhamma.

■ What is dependent arising?

Dependent arising (paticcasamuppada) expresses the Buddhist vision of the nature of reality. It says that everything arises, and continues, dependent upon conditions. Nothing is permanent and unchanging. Dependent arising is often expressed in this simple formula:

- when this is, that is
- from the arising of this, comes the arising of that
- when this is not, that is not
- when this ends, that ends.

This basically expresses the view that life is an interdependent web of conditions. For example, a tree depends on soil, rain and sunshine to survive. Everything else also depends on certain conditions to survive. Nothing is independent of supporting conditions, which means that nothing is eternal, including human beings. Everything is a constant process of change.

The Dalai Lama, the spiritual leader of the Tibetan people, explained dependent arising like this:

> ❝ All events and incidents in life are so intimately linked with the fate of others that a single person on his or her own cannot even begin to act. Many ordinary human activities, both positive and negative, cannot even be conceived of apart from the existence of other people. Because of others, we have the opportunity to earn money if that is what we desire in life. Similarly, in reliance upon the existence of others it becomes possible for the media to create fame or disrepute for someone. On your own you cannot create any fame or disrepute no matter how loud you might shout. The closest you can get is to create an echo of your own voice. ❞
>
> Tenzin Gyatso (the Dalai Lama)

■ The Tibetan Wheel of Life

The Tibetan Wheel of Life illustrates the process of dependent arising in relation to human life, death and rebirth. The outer circle of the wheel is made up of 12 links or stages (**nidanas**). The 12th link (old age and death) leads directly into the first link (ignorance). This represents the Buddhist teaching about rebirth: many Buddhists believe that when they die, their consciousness transfers to a new body. So the wheel shows the continual cycle of birth (and ignorance), death, then rebirth. This cycle is called **samsara**.

The type of world that a Buddhist is reborn into (for example, as a human, animal or heavenly being) is said to depend upon the quality of

Objectives

- Understand what is meant by the concept of dependent arising.
- Understand the Tibetan Wheel of Life as an example of dependent arising.

Key terms

- **dependent arising:** the idea that all things arise in dependence upon conditions
- **the Tibetan Wheel of Life:** an image that symbolises samsara, often found in Tibetan Buddhist monasteries and temples
- **nidanas:** 12 factors that illustrate the process of birth, death and rebirth
- **samsara:** the repeating cycle of birth, life, death and rebirth
- **kamma (karma):** a person's actions; the idea that skilful actions result in happiness and unskilful ones in suffering
- **nibbana (nirvana):** a state of complete enlightenment, happiness and peace

Activities

1 In your own words, explain what dependent arising means.

2 Analyse the existence of your school in terms of dependent arising. What conditions are necessary for it to continue?

3 How can kamma affect a person's future?

their actions (**kamma**) in their previous lives. The principle of kamma says that intentions lead to actions, which in turn lead to consequences. In the cycle of life, good intentions lead to good actions. Good actions can lead to a more favourable rebirth. Kamma is a specific example of dependent arising that explains how a person's actions create the conditions for their future happiness or suffering.

▲ *The Tibetan Wheel of Life*

For Buddhists, the ultimate aim is to break free of the cycle of samsara, because this is what causes suffering. The cycle is broken by following the Buddhist path but, more specifically, through breaking the habit of craving (tanha). For this reason, Buddhist practice focuses on the relationship between feeling and craving. When someone has an unpleasant feeling, they want to escape it, and when they have a pleasant feeling they become attached to it. Buddhism teaches that this kind of automatic response is what leads to suffering. Through breaking this response, and coming to understand the Buddha's teachings in other ways as well, Buddhists may achieve **nibbana**: a state of liberation, peace and happiness.

Extension activity

Research each of the 12 nidanas and find out how they are depicted on the Tibetan Wheel of Life. Does the image for each nidana help to illustrate what it means?

> ❝ Think of a wave in the sea. Seen in one way, it seems to have a distinct identity, an end and a beginning, a birth and a death. Seen in another way … you come to realize that it is something made temporarily possible by wind and water, and that it is dependent on a set of constantly changing circumstances. You also realize that every wave is related to every other wave. ❞
>
> Sogyal Rinpoche (Tibetan Buddhist teacher)

⭐ **Study tip**

The concept of dependent arising might seem complicated, but remember that in essence it means that all things change and all things are interconnnected, like a web.

Summary

You should now understand the concept of dependent arising and its relationship to kamma. You should also be able to explain how the Tibetan Wheel of Life is an example of dependent arising.

■ The three marks of existence

Buddhism teaches that there are three characteristics that are fundamental to all things. These are:

1. suffering (dukkha)

2. impermanence (anicca)

3. having no permanent, fixed self or soul (anatta)

For Buddhists, understanding these three characteristics as part of life is important for achieving enlightenment.

■ What is dukkha?

Dukkha is a fundamental concept in Buddhism. It has many different meanings but is best translated into English as suffering, dissatisfaction or unsatisfactoriness. Buddhists try to reduce suffering for themselves and others through right actions and intentions, and by gradually increasing their understanding of reality. Eventually they hope to break the cycle of samsara and achieve nibbana. The main reason why the Buddha left his life of luxury in the palace was to search for an answer to why people suffer.

After the Buddha became enlightened, he gave a sermon in the Deer Park at Sarnath (a city in India). He spoke of the seven states of suffering. The first four of these (birth, old age, sickness and death) refer to the suffering caused by samsara, while the other three refer to further types of suffering that people experience in their lives.

▲ The Buddha taught that there are seven states of suffering

- 1. Birth
- 7. Not getting what one wishes for
- 2. Old age
- 6. Contact with unpleasant things
- **The seven states of suffering**
- 3. Sickness
- 5. Sorrow, lamentation and despair
- 4. Death

> ❝ ... what I teach is suffering and the cessation of suffering. ❞
>
> The Buddha in the *Majjhima Nikaya*, vol. 1, p. 140

▲ *Illness can cause suffering by creating mental or physical pain*

Research activity

Find three examples from the Buddha's life of occasions when he suffered. What types of dukkha did he experience during these times of suffering?

■ Different types of dukkha

Suffering

The first type of dukkha (called dukkha-dukkhata) refers to ordinary pain or suffering. It is used to describe both physical and mental (emotional) pain. Examples might include breaking a leg, getting the flu, being separated from and missing someone you love, or being upset at not achieving a goal.

Change

Another type of dukkha (viparinama-dukkha) is produced by change. One of the Buddha's teachings is that nothing is permanent – things are always changing. These might be small changes (such as the weather turning cloudy), gradual changes (such as getting older), or larger changes (such as moving to a new city). When something changes and a sense of happiness is lost as a result, this is viparinama-dukkha. It refers to the sorrow and unhappiness that a person feels as a result of a change or losing something good.

Viparinama-dukkha can also be experienced *during* something good, as a subtle sense of unease and sorrow that comes from knowing the good thing won't last. Therefore, even happiness can be seen as dukkha.

▲ Change can cause suffering, such as when children grow up and leave home

Attachment

The third type of dukkha (samkhara-dukkha) is linked to the idea of attachment. Buddhism teaches that everyone is attached to other people, objects, activities and many other things. But when people crave and try to hold on to the things they are attached to, they suffer. This is perhaps the hardest form of dukkha to understand. It is often described as a more subtle dissatisfaction with life. Unlike dukkha-dukkhata and viparinama-dukkha, it may not arise due to specific events (such as twisting an ankle or ending a relationship). It is more to do with a general dissatisfaction with life that arises from many things, including the unhappiness that comes from change and from craving things that are not possible to have.

> **Discussion activity**
>
> With a partner, come up with as many examples as you can of the three different types of dukkha (dukkha-dukkhata, viparinama-dukkha and samkhara-dukkha). Do some of your examples fit into more than one category?

Activities

1 Give examples of some of the things that give people pleasure in their lives, and the ways in which they are only temporary.
2 Think of as many different words or phrases as you can for dukkha (such as 'suffering' or 'sorrow').

Summary

> You should now understand the concept of dukkha and be able to identify different forms of dukkha, with examples. You should be able to see how dukkha impacts on all aspects of life.

⭐ **Study tip**

Here is another example to show the differences between the three types of dukkha: you feel lonely because you miss your family, which is dukkha-dukkha. You eat a cake to cheer yourself up, which gives you temporary pleasure, but you then feel lonely again – this is viparinama-dukkha. You feel generally unhappy about life, which is samkhara-dukkha.

1.8 The three marks of existence: anicca

What is anicca?

Anicca is usually translated as impermanence. As we have already seen, the Buddha taught that everything is impermanent and continually changing.

Anicca can be thought of as affecting the world in three different ways:

1. It affects living things. For example, birth is followed by growth and then decay and finally death. Imagine for instance a small seed growing into a giant redwood tree.
2. It affects non-living things. For example, an iron nail that is left out in the rain will rust; a temple will eventually erode and turn into ruins if it is not repaired.
3. It affects our minds. Our thoughts, feelings, morals, longings and ideals change frequently throughout our lives.

Objective

● Understand the concept of anicca.

Key term

● anicca: impermanence; the idea that everything changes

How anicca and dukkha relate to each other

Even though things in the world change all the time, people often expect them to stay the same and the Buddha believed that this is one of the reasons why people suffer. He taught that when people expect things to remain unchanged, they become attached to them. Therefore when they do change (anicca) people experience suffering (dukkha).

Buddhists believe that accepting that all things change – including themselves – will lead to less suffering. For Buddhists, the ultimate goal is to break the cycle of samsara and achieve nibbana, a permanent state of no suffering.

▲ How might Buddhist teachings about anicca help a family come to terms with moving house?

▲ Buddhism teaches that attachment can lead to suffering when things change

Discussion activities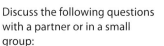

Discuss the following questions with a partner or in a small group:

1 Do you think you can understand dukkha without understanding anicca?
2 Is it important to understand the concept of anicca in order to suffer less in our lives?

Stories from Buddhist tradition

When Kisa Gotami had a child she at last found some happiness in her life. However, just when her little boy was old enough to begin to run about and play, he became ill and died. Gotami became almost crazy with sorrow, and refused to believe that he was dead. She took the corpse from house to house, asking for medicine to cure her child. 'Why are you asking for medicine?' everyone said. 'Can't you see that the child is dead? You are crazy.'

But one of her neighbours, who was wiser and kinder than the others, realised that Gotami's strange behaviour was due to the depth of her sorrow, and said: 'Why don't you go to the Buddha; perhaps he can give you the medicine you need.' So she took the dead body of her little boy and showed it to the Buddha, saying, 'Please, O Wise One, give me some medicine for my poor sick child.' The Buddha looked at Gotami and at her dead child, and he could see that deep down Gotami had enough wisdom and strength to understand her sorrow and gain comfort, even though her terrible loss had made her almost mad with grief. So he said to her, 'Go back to the town, knock on all the doors and wherever you find a household where no one has died, ask them to give you a little mustard seed. Then, in the evening, bring me all the mustard seed you collect and we will be able to make some medicine for your child.'

So Gotami went into the town, knocked on the door of the first house and said, 'If no one has died in your family, please give me some mustard seed: I need it as a medicine for my sick child.' The woman of the house looked at her sadly and said, 'Certainly I can give you some mustard seed, but I'm afraid that we have had many, many deaths in our family.' And Gotami looked sadly at the woman, saying, 'In that case, I'm sorry for you, but your mustard seed will be of no use as medicine for my little boy.' She went to the second house, and the same thing happened: yes she could have some mustard seed, but in that house also there had been many deaths and much sorrow. And at the third, fourth and fifth house it was the same. At every house where she knocked at the door the family told her that they also were in sorrow for the death of a dearly loved relative – a mother, or a father, or an uncle, or an aunt, or a son, or a daughter.

So by the evening, she still had no mustard seed for medicine for her child. However, something important had happened. As a result of sharing her sorrow with so many other people who had also lost a loved one, she found that her own sorrow was now different. She no longer felt agonised and almost mad with grief. Instead, although she still felt sorrow at the loss of her child, she also knew that everyone else in the town had experienced a similar loss and the same terrible sorrow. Suddenly she realised that sorrow and death are part of how life is, not only for her but for everyone. So she took her dead child to the cemetery outside the town and, sadly, lovingly, buried him.

Then she went back to the Buddha, who asked, 'Well, Gotami, have you got the mustard seed for the medicine?' Gotami answered, 'Thank you, O Wise One. No, I have not brought any mustard seed, but your medicine of the mustard seed has already worked, as you knew it would. Because I now see that my own sorrow is part of the sorrow of all people, and that the death of our loved ones is part of the pattern of life for everyone. That is the medicine I needed, and that is what you have helped me to understand.'

After this experience, Gotami became a follower of the Buddha and an Arhat (see page 40).

Activities

1 Think of as many words or phrases as you can for the term 'impermanence' (such as 'temporary' or 'not staying the same'). Use these words or phrases to write a definition of 'impermanence'.

2 Give an example of how anicca can affect non-living things.

3 Give an example of how anicca can lead to dukkha.

4 Read the story of Kisa Gotami. What did Gotami learn about suffering, and how did it help her?

⭐ Study tip

Being able to give examples of the different ways that anicca can affect the world will help you to explain the concept of anicca more effectively.

Summary

You should now understand the concept of anicca, and be able to explain how it relates to dukkha.

The three marks of existence: anatta

■ What is anatta?

In Buddhism, the concept of anatta was developed in contrast to the belief in a soul or unchanging self. Anatta is often translated as 'no self', but it does not mean that Buddhists believe there is no concept of 'I', 'me' or 'self', just that the self is not fixed or permanent. The Buddha taught that there is no fixed part of a person that does not change.

> ❝ If all the harm, fear, and suffering in the world occur due to grasping on to the self, what use is that great demon to me? ❞
>
> Shantideva (Indian Buddhist monk from the eighth century)

■ Nagasena and the chariot

A story that is often used to illustrate the concept of anatta is found in a text called 'The questions of King Milinda'. King Milinda was a Greek king who lived some 200 years or more after the Buddha. One day a monk called Nagasena arrived at the court of King Milinda. The king asked Nagasena what his name was. The monk replied that he was known as Nagasena, but that this was merely his name, without any reference to a real self or person. The king was confused by this and asked how there could be a person before him, who was standing in robes and was hungry for food, if Nagasena was just a name.

Nagasena replied in what might be seen as a strange way. He asked the king how he had arrived today. The king said that he had arrived by chariot. Nagasena asked him to point out what a chariot was, which the king did.

▲ A chariot does not have an independent 'self' that is separate from its parts; Nagasena said that people are just the same

Objective

- Understand the concept of anatta.

Key terms

- **anatta:** the idea that people do not have a permanent, fixed self or soul
- **the five aggregates:** the five aspects that make up a person

Discussion activity

Ask a partner to describe themselves to you and take notes of what they say. Read your notes back to them. Then ask them whether they have mentioned anything about themselves that will not change over time.

Nagasena then said that a chariot is not the wheels or the axle or the yoke, but is actually something separate to these things. So, the term 'chariot', like the term 'Nagasena', is merely a name used to refer to a collection of parts.

Nagasena said that people are made up of various body parts like liver, kidneys, lungs and so on, but only when these are put together in a particular order and given a name do we recognise the 'owner' of these parts. A chariot exists but only in relation to its parts; likewise a person exists but only in relation to the parts they are made up of. There is not a separate 'self' that is independent from these parts.

■ The five aggregates

The Buddha taught that people are made up of five parts. These are called the five aggregates (skandhas). They are:

1. Form (our bodies)
2. Sensation (our feelings)
3. Perception (our recognition of what things are)
4. Mental formations (our thoughts)
5. Consciousness (our awareness of things)

The Buddha said that these parts are constantly changing. Therefore the 'self' – which is the sum of all these parts – is also constantly changing.

On pages 18–19 we saw that according to Buddhist teaching, death is followed by rebirth. But if there is no fixed, independent 'self' or 'soul' then what is reborn? How is someone's identity taken forward into their new body? For Buddhists, the answer is that there is a continuation of kammic energy, which means that the energy that is a person's kamma passes on into another being.

▲ For Buddhists, a person's kamma determines their rebirth

Links

Learn more about the five aggregates on pages 36–37.

Activities

1 Explain why Buddhists believe there is no permanent self.
2 Explain the concept of anatta by using a more modern-day example than a chariot.
3 If there is no permanent, independent self, how is rebirth possible?

Summary

You should now be able to explain the concept of anatta. You should also understand the Buddhist view that people are all made up of five parts that are always changing.

★ Study tip

You could think of the Buddhist idea of the 'self' like a long-running football team. Many things about the team change over the years – new players come and go, as do new supporters, the team's position in the league changes, and so on. But the team itself still exists and has its own identity, even though it is made up of many changing parts.

■ What are the Four Noble Truths?

The Four Noble Truths are often said to contain the essence of the Buddha's teachings. They were discovered by the Buddha while he searched for enlightenment under the peepul tree. They were also the first teachings that he gave to the five ascetics, during his first sermon in the Deer Park at Sarnath.

▲ *Buddhists use meditation to help improve their understanding of the Four Noble Truths*

The Four Noble Truths are:

1. the truth of suffering (**dukkha**)
2. the truth of the cause of suffering (**samudaya**)
3. the truth of the end of suffering (**nirodha**)
4. the truth of the path leading to the end of suffering (**magga**).

Another way of thinking about these four truths is to say that:

1. suffering exists
2. suffering is caused by something
3. suffering can end
4. there is a way to bring about the end of suffering.

Therefore, the Four Noble Truths seek to explain why people suffer and how they can end that suffering.

■ The Four Noble Truths in practice

> 66 The truth of suffering is like a disease, the truth of origin is like the cause of the disease, the truth of cessation is like the cure of the disease, and the truth of the path is like the medicine. 99
>
> The *Visuddhimagga*, p. 512

In his teaching of the Four Noble Truths, the Buddha can be compared to a doctor. When a doctor establishes that you have an illness, he first finds the cause of the illness (the first two noble truths). He then tells you what the cure is (the third noble truth). He then prescribes the cure, and undergoing this treatment helps you to get better (the fourth noble truth).

> 66 Each of these truths entails a duty: stress [suffering] is to be comprehended, the origination of stress abandoned, the cessation of stress realized, and the path to the cessation of stress developed. When all of these duties have been fully performed, the mind gains total release … Thus the study of the four noble truths is aimed first at understanding these four categories, and then at applying them to experience so that one may act properly toward each of the categories and thus attain the highest, most total happiness possible. 99
>
> Thanissaro Bhikkhu (American Buddhist monk)

Discussion activity 💬

Some people think that Buddhism is a negative or pessimistic religion because it directs people's attention to suffering. Others think that Buddhism is a positive and uplifting religion because it provides a cure to suffering that relies on an individual's own actions rather than an external god. Discuss with a partner which of these viewpoints you agree with.

Buddhists aim to come to a complete understanding of these four truths through study, reflection, meditation and other activities. For Theravada Buddhists, understanding the four truths is the most important goal for achieving enlightenment. Mahayana Buddhists likewise believe the Four Noble Truths are very important, but they also emphasise other teachings, such as the development of compassion, as being central to the experience of enlightenment.

The Buddha taught that the 'cure' to overcome suffering is the Eightfold Path. This is a series of practices that Buddhists follow in order to achieve enlightenment. This is discussed in more detail on pages 34–35.

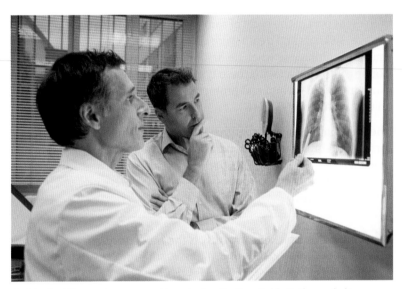

▲ *The Buddha can be compared to a doctor; the Four Noble Truths can help to 'cure' suffering*

Activities

1 Work in small groups to create a series of four posters to help your classmates understand the meanings behind the Four Noble Truths.

2 When you visit a doctor they will try to work out what the problem is and then come up with a way to cure it. The formula for helping a patient is basically: problem; cause; solution; treatment. Apply the same formula to the following problems:

  a an example of bullying

  b being worried about an exam

  c experiencing a very bad headache

  d falling out with a family member or good friend

3 Explain the connections between the Four Noble Truths and the other aspects of the Buddha's teachings that you have studied so far.

⭐ **Study tip**

Remember that it is helpful to consider how Buddhist teachings are linked. For example, the Four Noble Truths are an expression of dependent arising (see pages 18–19).

Summary

You should now have a basic understanding of the Four Noble Truths and know how they relate to each other. You should also understand why the Buddha can be compared to a doctor.

1.11 The first noble truth: the existence of suffering

■ What is the first noble truth?

We saw on pages 20–21 how dukkha (suffering) is one of the three marks of existence, and examined some of the different types of suffering that people experience. The first noble truth draws attention to the fact that suffering is a part of life and something that everyone experiences.

The Buddha taught that there are four unavoidable types of physical suffering: birth, old age, sickness and death. Everyone experiences these in the course of their life. Buddhism teaches that beings will experience these four types of suffering many times over a number of lives, as part of the cycle of samsara. Remember that old age, sickness and death were three of the sights that the Buddha saw when he first left the palace. Coming into contact with these types of suffering had a profound effect on him and prompted his search to find an end to suffering.

The Buddha also taught that there are three main forms of mental suffering: separation from someone or something you love; contact with someone or something you dislike; and not being able to achieve or fulfil your desires.

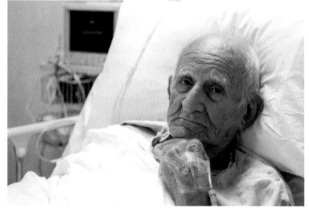

▲ *The Buddha taught that physical suffering is an unavoidable part of life*

> 66 Now this, bhikkhus [monks], is the noble truth of suffering: birth is suffering, aging is suffering, illness is suffering, death is suffering; union with what is displeasing is suffering; separation from what is pleasing is suffering; not to get what one wants is suffering; in brief, the five aggregates subject to clinging are suffering. 99
>
> The Buddha in the *Samyutta Nikaya*, vol. 5, p. 421

■ Suffering and happiness

Even though the Buddha taught that it is important to recognise that suffering is a part of life, he did not deny that happiness exists. He often acknowledged in his teachings that there are many different types of happiness that everyone can experience. However, as we saw on page 21, the Buddha taught that even though happiness is real it is also impermanent; it will not last and will therefore eventually give way to unhappiness.

Some people think that the Buddha's teaching that suffering is a part of life, and that happiness doesn't last, is a negative or pessimistic way to view life. Buddhists, however, would argue that it is simply realistic. They

▲ *Birth is one of the four main types of physical suffering*

would argue that everyone experiences pain and suffering at some point in their lives. It is a universal truth, meaning that it affects everybody. So dissatisfaction or suffering in life is a problem that everyone needs to overcome. Buddhists reflect on suffering not to make themselves miserable, but to be able to release themselves from that suffering.

Many people try to combat suffering with temporary pleasures. To take one simple example, imagine that you got a bad mark for an exam and feel miserable about it as a result. You eat a bar of chocolate to cheer yourself up, but the happiness that the chocolate creates only lasts until you get to the end of the bar. It doesn't solve the root cause of your unhappiness.

▲ *Because happiness is temporary, the Buddha thought it could not ultimately solve the problem of suffering*

Because happiness and pleasures are temporary, the Buddha did not believe they could be the ultimate answer to the problem of suffering. Instead he developed other teachings and advice to help prevent people from suffering because of their dissatisfaction with life. As part of this he taught that the first step to end suffering is to accept the first noble truth: that suffering is an unavoidable part of life.

Buddhism teaches that one of the ways in which suffering may be reduced is to not personalise it. Suffering simply happens, and the key to reducing it is to not become 'attached' to it. If a person puts themselves at the centre of the suffering, the suffering becomes worse because it is personalised. This is how Ajahn Sumedho wrote about suffering:

> 66 The ignorant person says, 'I'm suffering. I don't want to suffer. I meditate and I go on retreats to get out of suffering, but I'm still suffering and I don't want to suffer … How can I get out of suffering? What can I do to get rid of it?' But that is not the First Noble Truth; it is not: 'I am suffering and I want to end it.' The insight is, 'There is suffering' … The insight is simply the acknowledgment that there is this suffering without making it personal. 99
>
> Ajahn Sumedho (American Buddhist monk)

Research activity 🔍

Using the internet, find some examples of occasions when people have learned something from their suffering, and seen their suffering as being a positive experience as well as a negative one. Is it possible to avoid suffering? Do you think that it is important to experience some suffering during life? What benefits might suffering have?

⭐ Study tip

Remember that the Buddha did not deny the existence of happiness; instead he thought that happiness is real but only temporary, so it cannot permanently overcome suffering.

Summary

You should now understand the meaning of the first noble truth. You should also understand how the Buddha's teachings on suffering and happiness are viewed by Buddhists as being realistic and practical.

Activities

1 Explain why you think Buddhists feel it is important to understand and acknowledge that suffering is a part of life.

2 Do you think it is good to be optimistic in life, or does having expectations that are too high mean that you will always fail? Explain your answer.

3 What makes you the most happy? Write down five things and then discuss these with a partner. Is anything you have written permanent in your life?

4 In the quote above, the Theravada teacher Ajahn Sumedho advises people not to identify with suffering or make it personal. Explain what you think Ajahn Sumedho meant by these words. You may find it useful to give an example in your explanation.

1.12 The second noble truth: the causes of suffering

■ The concept of tanha

The second noble truth (samudaya) explores the origins of suffering. Buddhists believe that understanding *why* people suffer is important if suffering is to be reduced.

The Buddha taught that one of the main causes of suffering is **tanha**, which means 'thirst' or 'craving'. This refers to wanting or desiring things. The Buddha said that there are three main types of craving:

1. Craving things that please the senses, such as beautiful sights or pleasant smells. One example is drinking a hot chocolate not because you are thirsty, but because you like the taste of it.
2. Craving to become something that you are not, such as craving to become rich or powerful or famous.
3. Craving not to be, or craving non-existence. This refers to when you want to get rid of something or stop it from happening any more, such as not wanting to feel embarrassed after making a mistake, or not wanting to feel pain after twisting an ankle.

> 66 Now this, bhikkhus [monks], is the noble truth of the origin of suffering: it is this craving which leads to renewed existence, accompanied by delight and lust, seeking delight here and there; that is, craving for sensual pleasures, carving for existence, craving for extermination. 99
>
> The Buddha in the *Samyutta Nikaya*, vol. 5, p. 421

Objective

● Understand what causes suffering according to Buddhism.

Key terms

● **tanha:** craving (desiring or wanting something)
● **the three poisons:** greed, hatred and ignorance; the main causes of suffering

Buddhism teaches that the reason why people find life to be unsatisfactory and full of suffering is because they become attached to the things they like, and want to avoid the things they don't like. However, the concept of anicca (impermanence) teaches that everything changes. So if people become attached to things, when they lose them through change, they inevitably suffer. The temporary pleasures that people crave cannot last or make them feel consistently happy.

Links

Read more about the concept of anicca and how it causes suffering on pages 22–23.

■ Suffering and the three poisons

At the centre of the Tibetan Wheel of Life there are usually three animals that represent three different tendencies:

- a pig, representing ignorance
- a cockerel, representing greed and desire
- a snake, representing anger and hatred.

▲ *The three poisons in Buddhism are represented by a pig, cockerel and snake*

▲ *For Buddhists, trying to reduce anger and hatred is important for reducing suffering*

These are called **the three poisons** in Buddhism. They sit in the centre of the wheel because they are considered to be the forces that keep the wheel spinning, and the cycle of samsara turning.

The Buddha taught that craving is rooted in ignorance. This is not the sort of ignorance related to not knowing the location of a country or not knowing how to speak a language, but a deeper ignorance about people, the world and the nature of reality. Buddhists believe they will only achieve enlightenment by overcoming ignorance and finding wisdom. The Buddha also taught that craving leads to greed and hatred. It is these three poisons that trap humans in the cycle of samsara and prevent them from reaching nibbana.

Activities

1 Look at the three main categories of craving mentioned on page 30. Give two more examples of each of these types of craving.
2 Write a list of things that people commonly crave. Suggest the steps a person might take in order to get rid of these cravings.
3 Explain how letting go of craving and attachment in your own life might change you and your lifestyle.

Summary

You should now be able to explain how Buddhists believe that craving things can lead to suffering.

Discussion activity

Discuss with a partner how the three poisons could lead to suffering. Try to think of specific examples where greed, hatred or ignorance might cause someone to suffer.

❝ There is no fear for one whose thought is untroubled [by faults], whose thought is unagitated, who is freed from good and evil, who is awake. ❞

The Buddha in the *Dhammapada*, verse 39

⭐ Study tip

Remember that although the Buddha taught that craving for things results in suffering, this is not the same as saying that people should not have or experience those things. It is not the things themselves that are necessarily bad, but becoming obsessively attached to them.

■ What is the third noble truth?

The third noble truth (nirodha) is that there is an end to suffering. This means that Buddhism teaches it is possible to end a person's suffering through their own actions and efforts, and that this can lead to enlightenment. Buddhists believe that the Buddha achieved this, and that anyone else can achieve it too. This noble truth is important because it teaches that it is possible to achieve happiness, and that although suffering is an unavoidable part of life, it is also possible to overcome it.

■ Overcoming craving and ignorance

On the previous page we saw how the second noble truth teaches that one of the main causes of suffering is craving things. It follows then that if people stop craving things, their suffering will cease, and this is the message of the third noble truth.

The Buddha taught that when people desire things but don't get them – or can't hold on to them for long enough – they become frustrated and unhappy with life. So they have to let go of this craving in order to stop feeling dissatisfied with life.

The Buddha said that this does not mean that people should avoid the things they enjoy or crave. In fact, this might only make things worse, because they might end up craving something more if they can't have it at all. Instead, the Buddha taught that people should enjoy and take pleasure in things but recognise that they can't last. People should enjoy things without craving them or becoming too attached to them.

The Buddha also taught that the way to stop craving is to have an inner satisfaction with life and a total appreciation of what one has already got.

▲ Does a consumerist society encourage people to become attached to things?

> 　❝ Now this, bhikkhus [monks], is the noble truth of the cessation of suffering: it is the remainderless fading away and cessation of that same craving, the giving up and relinquishing of it, freedom from it, nonreliance on it. ❞
>
> 　　　　　　The Buddha in the *Samyutta Nikaya*, vol. 5, p. 421

Objectives

- Understand what the third noble truth means.
- Understand how Buddhists believe that suffering can be overcome.

Key term

- **nibbana (nirvana):** a state of complete enlightenment, happiness and peace

Research activity

How is it possible to stop craving or being attached to things? Research advice given online for Buddhists to follow, and write a short summary of the main points that are made.

Ajahn Sumedho's experience of how craving leads to suffering

Ajahn Sumedho, who was previously the abbot of the Amaravati Buddhist monastery in the UK, talks about his experience of how craving can lead to suffering:

'In my practice I have seen that attachment to my desires is suffering. There is no doubt about that. I can see how much suffering in my life has been caused by attachments to material things, ideas, attitudes or fears. I can see all kinds of unnecessary misery that I have caused myself through attachment because I did not know any better. I was brought up in America – the land of freedom.

It promises the right to be happy, but what it really offers is the right to be attached to everything. Like every materialist culture, America encourages you to try to be as happy as you can by getting things. However, if you are working with the Four Noble Truths, attachment is to be understood and contemplated; then the insight into non-attachment arises. This is not an intellectual stand or a command from your brain saying that you should not be attached; it is just a natural insight into non-attachment or non-suffering.'

Buddhists believe that it is important to overcome ignorance as well as craving in order to end suffering and achieve enlightenment.

The third noble truth, therefore, teaches that it is possible to end suffering, and that this can be achieved by overcoming ignorance and craving. The fourth noble truth gives specific steps to help Buddhists attain this goal.

■ Interpretations of nibbana and enlightenment

'Nibbana' literally means the 'extinction' or snuffing out of a flame – in this case, the extinction of the three poisons (or three fires) of greed, hatred and ignorance. The Buddha said after his enlightenment that he knew he was now entirely free of these three poisons.

'Bodhi' literally means 'knowing'. A Buddha is 'one who knows' the truth about the nature of existence. Such a person would know exactly what causes suffering, and have no expectations of permanence. Knowing this, they would naturally behave according to the five moral precepts, which are a description of the perfect wisdom and compassion of a Buddha.

But did the Buddha know everything? Buddhists have discussed this question over many centuries. Most Buddhists would probably say they believed the Buddha knew everything about the principles governing the nature of existence, such as the three marks of existence and Four Noble Truths. They would not say he knew absolutely everything, because that would mean believing he had supernatural powers.

Discussion activity

The third noble truth teaches that it is possible to stop craving things that cannot provide lasting satisfaction. However, the Buddha also said that some things offer deeper enjoyment and satisfaction than others: real friendship, for example, compared with a new pair of trainers. He said that enlightenment was the most satisfying experience of all, totally free of craving.

Discuss whether you have ever wanted something very much and then found it wasn't nearly as interesting or rewarding as you had expected. What sort of experiences are most deeply rewarding or satisfying, in your experience?

Activities

1 Read Ajahn Sumedho's thoughts about how attachment can cause suffering. Give an example of how attachment has led to suffering in your own life.

2 Recall the Buddha's childhood and the life of luxury that he had growing up. Write down a list of all the things you think the Buddha might have been attached to during his childhood in the palace.

⭐ Study tip

Think about the third noble truth as the start of trying to put things right. There is a clear change of direction from the first two truths – which identify the problem and cause of suffering – to the third truth, which tells Buddhists that they can overcome suffering by themselves.

Summary

You should now understand the meaning of the third noble truth, and understand how Buddhists believe suffering can be stopped by overcoming ignorance and craving.

1.14 The fourth noble truth: the cure for suffering

What is the fourth noble truth?

The fourth noble truth (magga) is the 'cure' to end suffering: a series of practices that Buddhists can follow to overcome suffering and achieve enlightenment. It is known as the middle path or middle way, because the Buddha taught that people should lead a moderate life between the two extremes of luxury and asceticism. He found that neither of these extremes was helpful in his search for enlightenment.

The fourth noble truth is the Eightfold Path, which consists of eight aspects that Buddhists can practise and follow in order to achieve enlightenment. These eight aspects are sometimes grouped into three different sections: ethics, meditation and wisdom. Together these three make up what is sometimes known as the threefold way.

> **"** But if any one goes to the Buddha, the Doctrine and the Order as a refuge, he perceives with proper knowledge the four noble truths: Suffering, the arising of suffering, and the overcoming of suffering, and the noble eightfold path leading to the cessation of suffering. **"**
>
> The Buddha in the *Dhammapada*, verses 190–191

The Eightfold Path

The Eightfold Path consists of the following eight practices, which are grouped below into the three different sections that make up the threefold way.

Wisdom (panna)

1. **Right understanding**: understanding the Buddha's teachings, particularly about the Four Noble Truths.
2. **Right intention**: having the right approach and outlook to following the Eightfold Path; being determined to follow the Buddhist path with a sincere attitude.

This section of the threefold way emphasises the importance of overcoming ignorance and achieving wisdom, to truly understand the Buddha's teachings and thus the nature of reality. For Buddhists, developing this understanding is essential for achieving enlightenment.

Ethics (sila)

3. **Right speech**: speaking truthfully in a helpful, positive way; avoiding lying or gossiping about others.
4. **Right action**: behaving in a peaceful, ethical way; avoiding acts such as stealing, harming others, or overindulging in sensual pleasures.
5. **Right livelihood**: earning a living in a way that does not harm others, for example not doing work that exploits people or harms animals.

Objectives

- Understand the meaning of the fourth noble truth.
- Understand the different sections on the Eightfold Path, and know how these can be grouped together to form the threefold way.

Key terms

- **the Eightfold Path:** eight aspects that Buddhists practise and live by in order to achieve enlightenment
- **the threefold way:** the Eightfold Path grouped into the three sections of ethics, meditation and wisdom
- **ethics (sila):** a section of the threefold way that emphasises the importance of skilful action as the basis for spiritual progress
- **meditation (samadhi):** a section of the threefold way that emphasises the role of meditation in the process of spiritual development
- **wisdom (panna):** a section of the threefold way that deals with Buddhist approaches to understanding the nature of reality

> **"** Bhikkhus [monks], abandon the unwholesome! It is possible to abandon the unwholesome. If it were not possible to abandon the unwholesome, I would not say: "[Monks], abandon the unwholesome!" **"**
>
> The Buddha in the *Anguttara Nikaya*, vol. 1, p. 58

This section of the threefold way is concerned with having good morals and behaviour, and living in an ethical way. It essentially requires Buddhists to act in ways that help rather than harm themselves and others.

Meditation (samadhi)

6. **Right effort**: putting effort into meditation, in particular thinking positively and freeing yourself from negative emotions and thoughts.
7. **Right mindfulness**: becoming fully aware of yourself and the world around you; having a clear sense of your own feelings and thoughts.
8. **Right concentration**: developing the mental concentration and focus that is required to meditate.

This section of the threefold way is concerned with how to meditate effectively, which for Buddhists is an important practice for developing wisdom and achieving enlightenment. Meditation is discussed in more detail on pages 52–57.

> ❝ Mental phenomena are preceded by mind, have mind as their leader, are made by mind. If one acts or speaks with an evil mind, from that sorrow follows him, as the wheel follows the foot of the ox ... If one acts or speaks with a pure mind, from that happiness follows him, like a shadow not going away. ❞
>
> The Buddha in the *Dhammapada*, verses 1–2

Despite being called a 'path', the Eightfold Path is often represented as a wheel with eight spokes. This emphasises the fact that the different steps do not need to be followed in a linear sequence, one after the other, but can be practised at the same time. Each of the different steps reinforces the others. For example, acting more ethically might include making the effort to meditate more regularly. This leads to a greater understanding of the Buddha's teachings, which in turn makes it easier to act more ethically and meditate more effectively, which further increases one's wisdom, and so on.

Research activities

1 Research the different parts of the Eightfold Path to make sure you understand what each part involves. Then give a specific example of how Buddhists might follow each of the eight practices. (For example, an example of right livelihood might be working for a charity.)

2 Using the internet, try to find links that are common between each of the three sections of the threefold way. Then draw a Venn diagram to illustrate which bits of the threefold way overlap with each other.

⭐ **Study tip**

To help you remember the information on this page, draw yourself a diagram showing the elements of the Eightfold Path, and how they divide into the threefold way.

Summary

You should now be able to explain the different steps on the Eightfold Path, and know how these are grouped together to form the threefold way.

Activities

1 Are there any steps of the Eightfold Path that you think you already follow? Why do you follow them? What does this tell you?
2 Look at the diagram below. Which of the images do you think is most helpful in trying to understand the Eightfold Path and why? Which is least helpful and why?

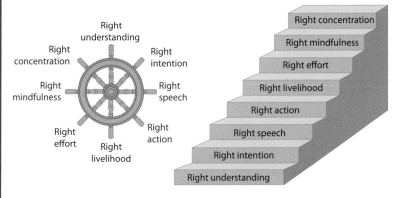

▲ *Three different ways of representing the Eightfold Path*

■ Theravada Buddhism

Theravada Buddhism is one of the oldest schools of Buddhism, and is known as 'the school of the elders'. (In Pali, which is the main language used in Theravada texts and chanting, 'thera' means 'elder' and 'vada' means 'school'.) Today, Theravada Buddhism is practised mostly in Thailand, Sri Lanka, Laos, Cambodia and Myanmar.

Theravada Buddhism is sometimes regarded as classical or orthodox Buddhism, with a high degree of uniformity in how it is practised. The school emphasises ordination in the monastic community. While some women have been ordained within Theravada Buddhism, full ordination is primarily reserved for men (see page 89).

The Buddha is seen as the main focus of commitment and is one of the three refuges. He is a guide, an example for others to follow and a teacher, but he is not considered to be a god.

Theravada monastics devote their whole lives to following the path of enlightenment, and promise to follow a number of rules, including not to own anything, not to have any sexual relationships, and never to be offensive to anyone.

Theravada monastics focus in particular on meditation. They believe that commitment to the Buddha and the Eightfold Path will bring good merit or kamma. Their goal is to achieve enlightenment and reach nibbana.

Some Theravada Buddhists believe it is possible to share their own good fortune with other people, by transferring the merit they have gained to someone else. This transfer of merit becomes particularly important when someone has died. When this happens, the family and friends may gather round whoever has died and transfer their merit to him or her, in the hope that this will help the dead person to have a favourable rebirth. (This practice is less common among Western Buddhists.)

■ The human personality in Theravada Buddhism

On page 25, we saw how the Buddha taught that people are made up of five parts, called the **five aggregates** (skandhas). Theravada Buddhists in particular believe that these five parts

Objectives

- Know the main features of Theravada Buddhism.
- Understand how the five aggregates make up the human personality.

Key terms

- **Theravada Buddhism:** 'the school of the elders'; an ancient Buddhist tradition found in southern Asia
- **the five aggregates:** the five aspects that make up a person

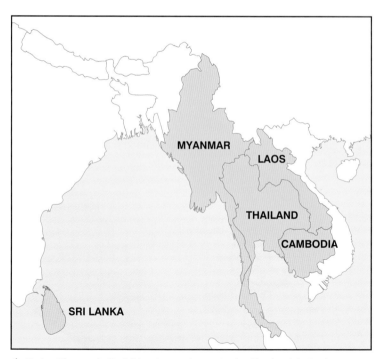

▲ *Today, Theravada Buddhism is mostly practised in Thailand, Sri Lanka, Laos, Cambodia and Myanmar*

▲ *Theravada monks at a temple in Thailand*

interact with each other to make up a person's identity and personality. The five aggregates are:

1. **Form:** this refers to material or physical objects (such as a house, an apple, or the organs that make up a person's body).
2. **Sensation:** this refers to the feelings or sensations that occur when someone comes into contact with things. They can be physical (such as a sensation of pain after tripping over), or emotional (such as a feeling of joy after seeing a friend).
3. **Perception:** this refers to how people recognise (or perceive) what things are, based on their previous experiences. For example, you might recognise what the feeling of happiness means because you have felt it before; you recognise what a car is because you have seen lots of other cars in the past.
4. **Mental formations:** this refers to a person's thoughts and opinions – how they respond mentally to the things they experience, including their likes and dislikes, and their attitudes towards different things.
5. **Consciousness:** this refers to a person's general awareness of the world around them.

Here is a simple example to show how the five aggregates interact (all of these things happen more or less at the same time):

- **Form:** you enter a room and see a slice of cake (a physical object).
- **Sensation:** seeing the slice of cake gives you a feeling or sense of anticipation.
- **Perception:** you recognise that it's a slice of cake, from having seen other slices of cake in the past.
- **Mental formations:** you form an opinion of the cake and decide whether you want to eat it or not.
- **Consciousness:** all of these things are connected by your general awareness of the world.

Mahayana Buddhism

Mahayana Buddhism is a term used to describe a number of different traditions that share some overlapping characteristics. A few of the main traditions that come under the Mahayana umbrella are Pure Land Buddhism, Zen Buddhism, Tibetan Buddhism and Nichiren Buddhism. Today, Mahayana Buddhism is mainly practised in China (including Tibet), Japan, South Korea, Vietnam, Mongolia and Bhutan.

Theravada Buddhists view the Buddha as a purely historical figure. They believe it is no longer possible to meet or interact with him in the world. In contrast, Mahayana Buddhists believe that the Buddha remains active and can influence the world. He can be encountered through visions and meditation, and he can manifest himself in many different forms, times and places.

Theravada and Mahayana Buddhists emphasise different beliefs and practices. One difference is how enlightenment can be achieved. Some of these differences are discussed on pages 40–41, and we will look at a few of the others below.

Sunyata

An important concept in Mahayana Buddhism is **sunyata**, which is often translated as 'emptiness'. For Mahayana Buddhists, understanding sunyata is essential for achieving enlightenment.

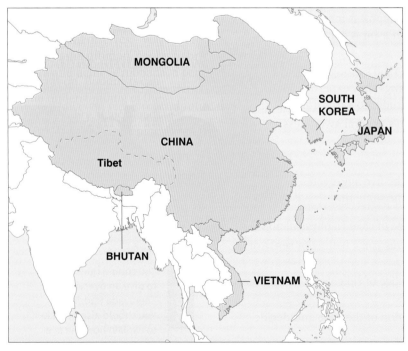

▲ Today, Mahayana Buddhism is mostly practised in China (including Tibet), Japan, South Korea, Vietnam, Mongolia and Bhutan

Objectives

- Know the main features of Mahayana Buddhism.
- Understand the concept of sunyata.
- Understand the idea of achieving Buddhahood by realising a person's Buddha-nature.

Key terms

- **Mahayana Buddhism:** an umbrella term to describe some later Buddhist traditions, including Pure Land Buddhism, Tibetan Buddhism and Zen Buddhism
- **sunyata:** emptiness; the concept that nothing has a separate, independent 'self' or 'soul'
- **Buddha-nature:** the idea that everyone has the essence of a Buddha inside them
- **Buddhahood:** when someone achieves enlightenment and becomes a Buddha

Activities

1 Using a different example to the one of the computer given on page 39, explain how the concept of sunyata teaches that everything is interdependent, interrelated and impermanent.

2 Use the internet to pick two contrasting images of a Buddha: one from China and one from India. What are the main differences between the images? Try to suggest reasons for the differences.

Sunyata could be understood as a restatement of anatta (see pages 24–25). It emphasises that not only do human beings not have a fixed, independent, unchanging nature, but that in fact all things are like that. Nothing exists independently but only in relation to, and because of, other things. A wave, for instance, cannot be separated from the sea.

The example of the chariot on page 24 helps to explain the concept of sunyata. For another example let's think about a computer. A computer does not have a 'soul' – a separate, independent bit that forms the essence of the computer. A computer is instead made up of lots of different parts, such as wires, a plastic case, a cooling fan, a graphics card and so on, which rely on each other and work together to form the whole computer. The computer relies on other people to make those parts and put them all together, and to keep them working. When the computer breaks down, it might be taken apart and bits of it reused to help repair other computers. This makes the computer interdependent and interrelated. It is also impermanent: the computer will eventually break down and stop working.

For Buddhists, realising that everything depends on, and interlinks with, everything else can lead to trust, compassion and selflessness. Realising that everything is impermanent is important for reducing the suffering that results in becoming too attached to things. These realisations are important for achieving enlightenment.

■ Buddha-nature and attaining Buddhahood

Buddha-nature is an important concept in some Mahayana traditions. At a basic level, it refers to the idea that everyone has the seed, even the essence (or nature) of a Buddha already inside them. Sometimes it is even said that, deep down, every person is *already* enlightened. But because a person's Buddha-nature is hidden by desires, attachments, ignorance, and negative thoughts, it is not realised. Only when people truly come to understand the Buddha's teachings – and therefore understand the nature of themselves and reality around them – do they experience the Buddha-nature that was always there.

One example given in traditional Buddhist scripture to help explain Buddha-nature is that of honey surrounded by many bees. The honey is sweet and tasty but as long as it is surrounded by bees, it isn't possible to get to the honey, even though it's been there all the time. The only way to experience the honey is to get rid of the bees.

Mahayana Buddhists aim to achieve **Buddhahood**: to become a Buddha (an enlightened being). They believe that everyone has the potential to do this and to become a Buddha because of their inherent Buddha-nature.

▲ *Zen Buddhist monks meditating*

Research activities

1 Look up the well-known Parable of the Burning House from the *Lotus Sutra*, an important Mahayana scripture. What is the message of the parable? What does it teach Buddhists?

2 Create a chart to show the differences between Theravada Buddhism and Mahayana Buddhism. Include the information you have learned from this chapter, then use the internet to find some further differences.

⭐ Study tip

Another example to illustrate Buddha-nature is a seed in an apple. The seed has the potential to become a great tree if all the right conditions for its growth are met.

Summary

You should now understand some of the main differences between Theravada and Mahayana Buddhism. You should also be able to explain the meaning of the terms sunyata, Buddha-nature and Buddhahood, and be able to say how they relate to each other.

■ Becoming an Arhat

For Theravada Buddhists, an **Arhat** is a 'perfected person' who has overcome the main causes of suffering – the three poisons of greed, hatred and ignorance – to achieve enlightenment. When someone becomes an Arhat, they are no longer reborn when they die. This means they are finally freed from the suffering of existence in the cycle of birth and death (samsara), and they can attain nibbana. This goal is achieved by following the Eightfold Path and concentrating on wisdom, morality and meditation.

▲ *Statues of Arhats at the Grand Temple of Mount Heng in China*

During the Buddha's lifetime, many of his disciples became Arhats. Among them were the first five monks the Buddha was with and the Buddha's own father, Suddhodana.

> **❝** I have no teacher, and one like me
>
> Exists nowhere in all the world …
>
> I am the Teacher Supreme.
>
> I alone am a Fully Enlightened One
>
> Whose fires are quenched and extinguished. **❞**
>
> The Buddha in the Majjhima Nikaya, vol. 1, p. 171

Mahayana Buddhists sometimes use the term Arhat to refer to someone who is far along the path of enlightenment but has not yet become enlightened. However, for Mahayana Buddhists the ideal is to become a **Bodhisattva** rather than an Arhat.

Objectives

- Consider two different goals of human destiny in Buddhism.
- Understand the differences between an Arhat and a Bodhisattva.

Key terms

- **Arhat:** for Theravada Buddhists, someone who has become enlightened
- **Bodhisattva:** for Mahayana Buddhists, someone who has become enlightened but chooses to remain in the cycle of samsara to help others achieve enlightenment as well

Links

To read about a person who became an Arhat, look at the story of Kisa Gotami on page 23.

Discussion activity

Look at the statements below and decide which ones you agree with and which ones you disagree with. Discuss as a whole class.

1 Bodhisattvas should not have a god-like status because that is not what Buddhism is all about.

2 Buddhists should not rely on others to help them because the Buddha said that people should seek out their own path for themselves.

3 Seeking enlightenment just for yourself shows vanity.

4 Arhats do not need to be compassionate and generous to others.

■ Becoming a Bodhisattva

A Bodhisattva is someone who sees their own enlightenment as being bound up with the enlightenment of all beings. Out of compassion, they remain in the cycle of samsara in order to help others achieve enlightenment as well. The ultimate goal for Mahayana Buddhists is to become Bodhisattvas.

Bodhisattvas combine being compassionate with being wise. Mahayana Buddhists believe that the original emphasis of the Buddha's teachings to his disciples was to 'go forth for the welfare of the many', and Bodhisattvas aim to do just this.

> ❝ However innumerable sentient beings are; I vow to save them. ❞
>
> A Bodhisattva vow

A person becomes a Bodhisattva by perfecting certain attributes in their lives. There are six of these that Mahayana Buddhists focus on (called the six perfections):

1. generosity – to be charitable and generous in all that is done
2. morality – to live with good morals and ethical behaviour
3. patience – to practise being patient in all things
4. energy – to cultivate the energy and perseverance needed to keep going even when things get difficult
5. meditation – to develop concentration and awareness
6. wisdom – to obtain wisdom and understanding.

Mahayana Buddhists believe there are earthly and transcendent Bodhisattvas. The 'earthly' ones continue to be reborn into the world, to live on Earth, while the 'transcendent' ones remain in some region between the Earth and nibbana as spiritual or mythical beings. However, they remain active in the world, appearing in different forms to help others and lead them to enlightenment. Mahayana Buddhists pray to these Bodhisattvas in times of need.

▲ The Bodhisattva Maitreya is considered to be the future Buddha, who will return to Earth at some point in the future to teach the Dhamma

Links

Read more about the six perfections on pages 72–73.

Research activity

Look up the Buddhist story of 'The Hungry Tigress'. Try to work out how this story shows compassion and wisdom in action.

★ Study tip

Try to remember the differences between what Theravada and Mahayana Buddhists believe about achieving enlightenment.

Summary

You should now understand what Theravada and Mahayana Buddhists believe are the goals of human destiny. You should be able to explain what an Arhat and Bodhisattva are, and how Buddhists aim to become one.

Activities

1   Read the statements below and decide whether you think they are true or false. Give reasons for your answers.

   a   An Arhat is someone who is close to enlightenment but has not yet achieved it.

   b   Arhats wish to stay in the cycle of samsara.

   c   There are five perfections that Bodhisattvas are trying to achieve.

   d   Bodhisattvas put off their own enlightenment to save others.

2   Give three differences between Arhats and Bodhisattvas.

1.18 Pure Land Buddhism

■ Pure Land Buddhism

Pure Land Buddhism is part of the Mahayana tradition of Buddhism. It began in China as early as the second century CE, then developed and spread throughout China and into Japan. Today, Pure Land Buddhism is the main type of Buddhism practised in Japan.

Pure Land Buddhism is based on faith in **Amitabha Buddha**, in the hope of being reborn in the paradise where Amitabha lives. Amitabha was a king who renounced his throne to become a monk. Mahayana scriptures tell how when he achieved enlightenment and became a Buddha, he created a pure land called **Sukhavati**, which is a land that can be found far to the west, beyond the boundaries of our own world. Amitabha created this perfect paradise out of his compassion and love for all beings. Pure Land Buddhists believe that if they are reborn into this land, they will be taught by Amitabha himself and will therefore have a much better chance of attaining Buddhahood (becoming a Buddha). In the pure land, there is no suffering, and none of the problems that stop people in our own world from attaining enlightenment.

▲ Amitabha Buddha in the pure land

Objectives

- Understand the main features of Pure Land Buddhism.
- Understand how Pure Land Buddhists believe they can reach Buddhahood.

Key terms

- **Pure Land Buddhism:** a Mahayana form of Buddhism based on belief in Amitabha Buddha
- **Amitabha Buddha:** the Buddha worshipped by Pure Land Buddhists
- **Sukhavati:** the paradise where Amitabha Buddha lives, and where Pure Land Buddhists aim to be reborn

> 66 [Sukhavati] is rich in a great variety of flowers and fruits, adorned with jewel trees, which are frequented by flocks of birds with sweet voices … And all the beings who are born … in this Buddha-field, they are all fixed on the right method of salvation, until they have won nirvana. For this reason that world system is called the 'Happy Land'. 99
>
> The *Larger Sukhavativyuha Sutra*, sections 16–24

■ How to reach the pure land

T'an-luan is considered to be the person who founded Pure Land Buddhism in China. He encouraged believers to follow five types of

▲ *Thousands of Pure Land Buddhists in Vietnam worshiping Amitabha*

religious practice: reciting scriptures, meditating on Amitabha and his paradise, worshipping Amitabha, chanting his name, and making praises and offerings to him. Of these five he taught that the most important is to recite Amitabha's name. If a person follows these practices, they will be reborn in the paradise of Sukhavati.

Pure Land Buddhism focuses on having faith in Amitabha, and believing that he will help Buddhists to be reborn in Sukhavati. Faith in Amitabha is more important than a person's own actions and behaviour. This is quite different to other schools of Buddhism. For example, Theravada Buddhism teaches that enlightenment can only be achieved through a person's own thoughts and actions, and they cannot rely on any outside help to achieve enlightenment. The fact that it is seen to be easier to reach enlightenment in Pure Land Buddhism, with Amitabha's help, has allowed this school of Buddhism to gain popular appeal.

> ❝ Even a bad man will be received in Buddha's land, how much more a good man? ❞
>
> Honen (twelfth century Japanese Pure Land teacher)
>
> ❝ Even a good man will be received in Buddha's land, how much more a bad man? ❞
>
> Shinran (a student of Honen)

Activities

1 Describe the land that Amitabha created when he became enlightened.

2 Why do Pure Land Buddhists believe it will be easier to achieve enlightenment in Sukhavati?

3 Imagine that a murderer was able to call on Amitabha's name and gain salvation in Sukhavati. Do you think this is fair? Should everyone be given the same chance to achieve enlightenment regardless of what they have done? Give reasons for your answer.

Discussion activity

Discuss with a partner whether you think Pure Land Buddhism sounds easier to follow than other types of Buddhism.

Research activity

Research Shinran, one of the most important figures in Pure Land Buddhism. Write a biography of him that explains his contributions to Pure Land Buddhism.

Extension activity

Honen and Shinran were two important figures in Japanese Pure Land Buddhism. Research their lives and note down some of the similarities and differences in their beliefs.

⭐ Study tip

Most traditions of Buddhism do not expect a Buddha to actively help people to achieve enlightenment. Pure Land Buddhism is different in that Pure Land Buddhists have faith that Amitabha Buddha will respond to their requests to be reborn in the pure land.

Summary

You should now have a basic overview of Pure Land Buddhism, and understand how Pure Land Buddhists believe they can achieve enlightenment.

The Dhamma (Dharma) – summary

You should now be able to:

✔ explain the concept of Dhamma (Dharma)

✔ explain the concept of dependent arising (paticcasamuppada)

✔ explain Buddhist teachings about the three marks of existence: suffering (dukkha), impermanence (anicca) and no fixed self (anatta)

✔ explain how the human personality is thought to be made up of five aggregates (skandhas) in Theravada Buddhism (form, sensation, perception, mental formations and consciousness)

✔ explain the concepts of sunyata, Buddha-nature and Buddhahood in Mahayana Buddhism

✔ explain the differences between Arhats and Bodhisattvas

✔ explain how Pure Land Buddhists believe they can attain Buddhahood and achieve enlightenment.

The Buddha and the Four Noble Truths – summary

You should now be able to:

✔ explain the circumstances of the Buddha's birth, and how his life of luxury growing up influenced his teachings

✔ explain the Buddha's encounter with the four sights (illness, old age, death and holy man), and its significance, including Jataka 075

✔ explain how the Buddha lived as an ascetic, how this later influenced his teachings, and how he achieved enlightenment

✔ explain the Buddha's teachings about the Four Noble Truths: suffering (dukkha); the causes of suffering (samudaya) including the three poisons; the end of craving (tanha); and the Eightfold Path (magga) or threefold way, made up of ethics (sila), meditation (samadhi) and wisdom (panna), including Dhammapada 190–191.

Sample student answer – the 4-mark question

1. Write an answer to the following practice question:

   Explain two ways in which learning about the four sights influences Buddhists today.
   [4 marks]

2. Read the following sample student answer:

   "Some Buddhists are reminded that all things are impermanent (which is called anicca) when they recall the four sights the Buddha saw. For example, when Buddhists remember the old man, it is a reminder that we will not stay young always as things change and people need to accept this change. When Buddhists recall the dead man, it makes them think that even our own lives are impermanent and we all die at some point. Also, remembering the holy man the Buddha saw as the fourth sight can influence Buddhists to follow the Eightfold Path, his major teaching, to hopefully reach enlightenment one day and a way out of the constant cycle of births, deaths and rebirths."

3. With a partner, discuss the sample answer. Is the focus of the answer correct? Is anything missing from the answer? How do you think it could be improved?

4. What mark (out of 4) would you give this answer? Look at the mark scheme in the Introduction (AO1). What are the reasons for the mark you have given?

5. Now swap your answer with your partner's and mark each other's responses. What mark (out of 4) would you give the response? Refer to the mark scheme and give reasons for the mark you award.

Sample student answer – the 5-mark question

1. Write an answer to the following practice question:

   Explain two Buddhist teachings about the causes of suffering.

   Refer to sacred writings or another source of Buddhist belief and teaching in your answer.
   [5 marks]

2. Read the following sample student answer:

   "Buddhists believe that there are many causes to suffering but craving (known as tanha) is one of the main causes. When people crave things they suffer because they cannot always have what it is they want. They are ignorant of the fact that nothing stays the same according to the Buddha's teaching, but their ego tells them that there are certain material things they must have in life because these material things will make them happy. The Buddha's teaching was that they would not make them happy. Some of the other causes of suffering are greed, hatred and ignorance, and these can be seen on the Tibetan Wheel of Life in the middle of the wheel itself. They are shown as a cockerel for greed, a pig for ignorance and a snake for hatred. Buddhists believe that they will always suffer if they do not get rid of these things from their lives."

3. With a partner, discuss the sample answer. Is the focus of the answer correct? Is anything missing from the answer? How do you think it could be improved?

4. What mark (out of 5) would you give this answer? Look at the mark scheme in the Introduction (AO1). What are the reasons for the mark you have given?

5. Now swap your answer with your partner's and mark each other's responses. What mark (out of 5) would you give the response? Refer to the mark scheme and give reasons for the mark you award.

Sample student answer – the 12-mark question

1. Write an answer to the following practice question:

'For Buddhists, dukkha is the most important of the three marks of existence.'
Evaluate this statement. In your answer you should:

- refer to Buddhist teaching
- give reasoned arguments to support this statement
- give reasoned arguments to support a different point of view
- reach a justified conclusion.

[12 marks]
[+ 3 SPaG marks]

2. Read the following sample student answer:

"Dukkha could be said to be the most important of the three marks of existence for Buddhists, as it is the first major teaching the Buddha gave and some Buddhists believe it to be the basis of the whole religion. It means suffering and everyone suffers so it is a universal teaching in that sense. We all experience suffering so it is a teaching that everyone can relate to. It is easy to understand, as there are so many different types of suffering such as birth, sickness, old age and death that people can easily relate to the Buddha's teaching. We all experience sadness too in life when things are not going our way or just don't feel right. All of this is part of dukkha and it affects all aspects of our lives.

On the other hand, the Buddha taught anicca which is that all things are impermanent, and unless we understand impermanence it may be hard for us to grasp aspects of dukkha, so maybe anicca is the most important of the three marks of existence. Everything changes and nothing is permanent and in theory if we understand this fact, we will suffer less. The Buddha also taught anatta which means that nobody has a permanent soul or self. If we understand this mark of existence then we will not be led by our ego; we will learn to let go and realise that only we, ourselves can make our situation better in this life. There is no God to ask for help and once we realise that we are just an ever-changing combination of mental and physical forces, impermanence and suffering become easier to understand. I do agree with the statement though as dukkha is so fundamental to everything the Buddha taught and is clearly the one thing Buddhists need to grasp and understand before everything else."

3. With a partner, discuss the sample answer. Consider the following questions:

- Does the answer refer to Buddhist teachings and if so what are they?
- Is there an argument to support the statement and how well developed is it?
- Is a different point of view offered and how developed is that argument?
- Has the student written a clear conclusion after weighing up both sides of the argument?
- What is good about the answer?
- How do you think it could be improved?

4. What mark (out of 12) would you give this answer? Look at the mark scheme in the Introduction (AO2). What are the reasons for the mark you have given?

5. Now swap your answer with your partner's and mark each other's responses. What mark (out of 12) would you give the response? Refer to the mark scheme and give reasons for the mark you award.

Practice questions

1 Which **one** of the following is a Buddhist school or tradition?

A) Sunyata   **B)** Asceticism   **C)** Theravada   **D)** Bodhisattva   **[1 mark]**

2 Give **two** of the four sights that the Buddha saw.   **[2 marks]**

>  **Study tip**
>
> If a question asks you to 'give' a piece of information, you do not need to give any explanation.

3 Explain **two** ways in which belief in the Buddha's enlightenment influences Buddhists today.   **[4 marks]**

4 Explain **two** Buddhist beliefs about the third noble truth.

Refer to sacred writings or another source of Buddhist belief and teaching in your answer.   **[5 marks]**

5 'The stories of the Buddha's birth have no relevance for Buddhists today.'

Evaluate this statement. In your answer you should:

- refer to Buddhist teaching
- give reasoned arguments to support this statement
- give reasoned arguments to support a different point of view
- reach a justified conclusion.   **[12 marks]**
    [+ 3 SPaG marks]

> ⭐ **Study tip**
>
> You should think carefully about the statement before you start writing. When you have finished writing, read what you have written to make sure you have included all that the question asks you to provide.

Buddhists can practise at home or in a communal space such as a temple. Pages 50–51 explore how Buddhists express devotion; here we will take a look at the different places and types of buildings that are used by Buddhists to practise their faith.

■ Temples

A **temple** is often at the heart of a Buddhist community. Buddhist temples can be found in many different shapes and sizes. Some consist of just one building, while the larger ones consist of a number of different buildings grouped together on one site.

Depending on its size and function, a Buddhist temple (or temple complex) may include the following:

- a main hall or building, where Buddhists practise together; this will contain a statue of the Buddha (Mahayana temples may also include statues of various Bodhisattvas)
- a meditation hall or building, which is a quiet space where Buddhists can meditate; in Tibetan Buddhism this is known as a **gompa**
- a study hall or building, for meetings and lectures
- a shrine or number of shrines dedicated to the Buddha (or, in Mahayana temples, to a Bodhisattva)
- a pagoda or **stupa**, which is a tiered tower or mound-like structure that is sometimes used to contain holy relics (items associated with the Buddha that are considered to be holy).

Pagodas and stupas are generally designed to symbolise the five Buddhist elements of earth, water, fire, air and wisdom. The base of the building symbolises the earth, then the building extends upwards with different segments stacked on top of each other to represent the other elements. These reach upwards to a point or spire that symbolises wisdom.

Temples are important centres of religious life where Buddhists can study, meditate and practise together. Buddhists may listen to talks given by members of the monastic community, and lay people may take offerings, including food, to support them.

■ Shrines

A Buddhist **shrine** is an area where the focus is a statue of the Buddha (a **Buddha rupa**), usually sitting cross-legged

Objective

- Understand what temples, shrines and monasteries are used for in Buddhism.

Key terms

- **temple:** a place where Buddhists come together to practise
- **gompa:** a hall or building where Tibetan Buddhists meditate
- **stupa:** a small building in a monastery that sometimes contains holy relics
- **shrine:** an area with a statue of a Buddha or Bodhisattva, which provides Buddhists with a focal point for meditation and devotion
- **Buddha rupa:** a statue of the Buddha, often sitting cross-legged in a meditation pose
- **monastery (vihara):** a place where Buddhist monks and nuns live

▲ Many temples are beautiful, peaceful places that are designed to support reflection and meditation

in a meditation pose. (In Mahayana Buddhism, there are also shrines where the focus is a statue of a Bodhisattva rather than the Buddha). Shrines can be found in a temple or in a home; they provide a focal point for Buddhists to meditate or practise.

Buddhists will also make offerings at a shrine, as a way of paying respect to the Buddha and expressing gratitude and thanks for his teachings. The offerings also remind Buddhists of the Buddha's teachings, because they symbolise different aspects of them. For example:

▲ Buddhists make offerings at a shrine to express thanks to the Buddha, and to remind them of his teachings

- An offering of light (such as a candle) symbolises wisdom, because the light of the candle drives away the darkness of ignorance.
- An offering of flowers (which will wilt and decay) reminds Buddhists that all things are impermanent.
- An offering of incense symbolises purity, reminding Buddhists of the importance of practising pure thoughts, speech and conduct.

> ❝ The time and effort required to keep the shrine clean and replenished with flowers and other offerings is considered a skilful activity to focus one's mind in the spiritual practices. ❞
>
> Lama Choedak Rinpoche (Tibetan Buddhist monk)

■ Monasteries

A **monastery (vihara)** is a building (or group of buildings) where a community of Buddhist monks or nuns live. These are Buddhists who have chosen to dedicate their lives full time to their spiritual practice; they spend their days studying, practising

▲ The Taktsang Palphug Monastery in Bhutan sits on the side of a cliff and is one of the least accessible Buddhist monasteries in the world

and meditating on the Buddha's teachings. Buddhist monks and nuns generally live a simple lifestyle, but the monastery still has to provide for all of their needs because it is where they live, eat, study and sleep. Some Buddhist monasteries are like small villages in themselves, while the smaller ones consist of one building only.

A stupa is a particularly important part of a monastery. When the Buddha died, his body was cremated and parts of his ashes are said to have been sent to different places. Stupas were then built to hold his ashes. Today, a stupa is a small, dome-shaped building that usually contains holy relics, such as the remains of monks and nuns or items associated with important Buddhists.

Activities

1 Explain why temples are important for Buddhists.

2 Explain the purposes of a Buddhist shrine.

3 Imagine that you have been asked to create a leaflet to attract people to go to a Buddhist temple that has just been built in your community. Design a leaflet that provides information about the types of activities that take place in a Buddhist temple, and explains why Buddhists might want to visit this one.

★ Study tip

Many Buddhists may feel a personal relationship with the Buddha. They may bow to a figure of the Buddha and make offerings to him in gratitude for his example and his teachings. However, it is important to remember that he is not a god. No Buddhist would ever claim that he had created them or the Earth.

Summary

You should now be able to describe the main features of a Buddhist temple, shrine or monastery. You should also understand why these places are important to Buddhists.

2.2 | How Buddhists worship

■ The purpose of worship

Worship (**puja**) allows Buddhists to express their gratitude and respect for the Buddha and his teachings. It gives them an opportunity to acknowledge how important the Buddha is in their lives. It also allows them to focus on their faith (their confidence in the path the Buddha taught), and to deepen their understanding of the Buddha's teachings.

Through performing puja and reciting verses of scripture, Buddhists acknowledge the Buddha's qualities and their commitment to following his example. They remind themselves of his teachings on the nature of existence and the way of life, leading to the wisdom and compassion of enlightenment. Through dwelling on these teachings, they may absorb them more deeply and find their lives changing for the better, as they become wiser and more compassionate towards themselves and others.

■ How Buddhists worship

Puja may include rituals and ceremonies carried out in groups, or private worship in the home. It often involves the following activities: meditation, making offerings, **chanting**, reciting **mantras**, and bowing.

Chanting

In the early days of Buddhism, before the invention of typewriters or computers, the only way to share Buddhist texts and teachings was to memorise them and pass them on orally. Monks would chant the texts in order to learn and remember them. Today, Buddhists still chant from sacred texts: written records of what the Buddha taught. Examples might include chanting the three refuges, the five moral precepts, or the Bodhisattva vows.

Chanting is a devotional practice: it may increase a Buddhist's receptivity towards the Buddha and his teachings. It can also be used to help calm and concentrate the mind.

Mantra recitation

A mantra is a sequence of sacred syllables that is usually chanted over and over, sometimes spoken, or experienced silently in the mind. Some Buddhists believe that mantras have transformative powers. They can be used in meditation to focus the mind.

Objective

- Understand how and why Buddhists worship.

Key terms

- **puja:** an act of worship
- **chanting:** in Buddhism, reciting from the Buddhist scriptures
- **mantra:** a short sequence of sacred syllables
- **mala:** prayer beads that are used to count the number of recitations in a mantra

Links

For more on Buddhist offerings, see page 49.

▲ *Buddhists making water offerings at a temple in Myanmar*

Mantras often call on the spiritual qualities of a Buddha or Bodhisattva. The most common mantra, used by Tibetan Buddhists, is *om mani padme hum*. This represents the sound of compassion, and is associated with the Bodhisattva of compassion, Avalokiteshvara. By chanting this mantra, Buddhists may hope to invoke the presence of Avalokiteshvara. They may feel that the mantra helps them to become more receptive to compassion, helping them to better express this quality in their lives.

▲ *Buddhists practising puja at a temple in New York, USA*

Buddhists may recite a mantra hundreds or even thousands of times, often using a mala (a string of prayer beads) in order to count the number of recitations. A mala usually has 108 beads.

Research activity 🔍

Find videos online of Buddhists performing puja in different traditions. (Search for 'Buddhist worship' or 'Buddhist puja' and 'Tibet' or 'Thailand', for example.) Write down some of the similarities and differences that you notice between how puja is carried out in the different videos.

Discussion activity 💬

Discuss with a partner whether the Buddhist practices described here are best described as 'worship' or something else.

Activities

1   Why do Buddhists recite the mantra 'om mani padme hum'?

2   Below are some of the main elements involved in Buddhist worship. Match up the correct elements with the correct definitions:

Offerings	Reciting a passage from a Buddhist text
Mala	A spiritual practice of reflecting deeply on the Buddha's teachings and the nature of reality
Bowing	Repeating 'om mani padme hum' over and over again
Chanting	A chain of beads used to count recitations
Sacred text	Bending the body three times in front of a shrine, to recall the three refuges
Reciting mantras	A text containing the Buddha's teachings
Meditation	Flowers and incense on a shrine

Links

Read more about meditation on pages 52–57.

⭐ Study tip

'Worship' (worth-ship) means to acknowledge what is truly valuable. Buddhist worship is not the worship of a creator God, but an acknowledgement of what is most valuable to a Buddhist.

Summary

You should now understand the significance of worship for Buddhists. You should also be able to explain some of the ways that Buddhists carry out worship.

We have seen that Buddhist worship includes a variety of practices such as chanting, making offerings, and reading from scriptures. Another important practice in most Buddhist traditions is **meditation**. This is a spiritual exercise that calms the mind and body, and leads to the development of insight into the nature of existence.

■ The practice of meditation

Before they begin meditating, Buddhists might recite verses praising the three refuges: the Buddha, the Dhamma and the Sangha. For Theravada Buddhists it is then customary to recite the five moral precepts (these are discussed on pages 70–71). Meditating itself usually involves the practice of mindfulness of the body and breath. The meditator settles their attention on these physical sensations, developing calm and stability. Whenever they notice their mind has wandered, they simply return to their physical experience.

> **❝** .... you should so train yourself that with respect to the seen there will be merely the seen, that with respect to the heard there will be merely the heard, that with respect to the sensed there will be merely the sensed, that with respect to the cognised there will be merely the cognised. **❞**
>
> The Buddha in the *Udana*, p. 8

There are many different forms of meditation. Theravada Buddhists often use samatha meditation to develop calm and positive emotion, and vipassana meditation to develop understanding and wisdom. Buddhists may focus on a variety of different objects, processes, character traits

▲ *Students meditating at a Buddhist monastery in Myanmar*

Objective

- Gain an overview of the Buddhist practice of meditation.

Key term

- **meditation:** a practice of calming and focusing the mind, and reflecting deeply on specific teachings to penetrate their true meaning

Links

You can learn more about samatha meditation on pages 54–55, and vipassana meditation on pages 56–57.

Extension activity

Some Buddhists believe that developing states of bliss (jhanas) is important in meditation. Research this online and write a brief summary about what the jhanas are.

▲ *Buddhists meditating at a retreat centre in the UK*

or emotions when they meditate, from a candle flame to the process of breathing to the quality of compassion.

In Tibetan Buddhism, students in the monastic community are sometimes given part of the Buddhist scriptures to learn by heart. They then go through two main stages of meditation: the analytical stage where they have to think carefully about the details of the teaching given in the text, followed by a more concentrated stage where they aim to fully understand the teaching.

Another common type of meditation in Buddhism is loving-kindness meditation, where the aim is to develop a sense of compassion towards oneself and others, and to let go of ill will and resentment. This helps to create a sense of calmness and positivity.

■ The purpose of meditation

Broadly speaking, meditation has two aims. The first is to develop a still, calm and focused mind. The second is to develop greater awareness and understanding of the Buddha's teachings in order to gain a deeper insight into the nature of reality. This deeper insight naturally brings about deeper compassion and less suffering, and leads eventually to enlightenment.

Although Buddhism does not include belief in a creator God, some forms of Mahayana Buddhist meditation involve visualising, and sometimes even praying to, the Buddha or other Buddhas and Bodhisattvas.

Activities

1 Explain why you think meditation is so important to Buddhists.

2 Describe the similarities and differences between prayer and meditation.

3 Find out about the Buddhist centre or vihara closest to your home or school. How does it help people to meditate? What else does it teach, and why?

> ❝ Even the gods envy those awakened and mindful ones who are intent on meditation, wise, delighting in the peace of the absence of desire. ❞
>
> The Buddha in the *Dhammapada,* verse 181

Discussion activity

Why do you think some schools and businesses offer meditation for their students and workers? Do you think this is a good thing to do? Discuss your thoughts with a partner.

Research activity

Divide a sheet of A3 paper into four quarters. At the top of each quarter add the following headings: 'Aims and purposes of meditation', 'Techniques and methods of meditation', 'Types of meditation' and 'Objects or things used to help meditation'. Do some research online or in a library to help you to start completing the chart. Continue to fill it in as you read pages 54–57.

⭐ Study tip

Try to understand why meditation is important for Buddhists; learn the 'aims and purposes of meditation' from your Research activity list.

Summary

You should now be able to discuss some of the different types of meditation, and understand the purpose of meditation.

2.4 Samatha meditation

■ What is samatha meditation?

Samatha meditation is an important meditation practice in Buddhism, and one of the two main types of meditation used in Theravada Buddhism. Samatha means 'calming'. Calming meditation can lead to a more tranquil, settled, restful mind, enabling deeper concentration. There are a number of different ways to do samatha meditation, but many Buddhists focus on the technique called **mindfulness of breathing**.

■ Mindfulness of breathing

Breathing is something most people do without paying any attention to it, but the idea in samatha meditation is to become more 'mindful', or aware, of your breathing. This means paying attention to the sensation of breathing, and all the tiny movements it brings about in your body: feeling your chest expand and contract, the air flowing in and out of your nose, feeling how your shoulders rise and fall, and so on.

Normally a person's attention is divided between many things at the same time, and when they meditate they may naturally find their mind wandering. When this happens they simply and gently return their attention to their breathing.

> **"** Breath is the bridge which connects life to consciousness, which unites your body to your thoughts. Whenever your mind becomes scattered, use your breath as the means to take hold of your mind again. **"**
>
> Thich Nhat Hanh (Vietnamese Buddhist monk)

Breathing is a popular focus of samatha meditation, but other objects may also be used, including kasinas. The Buddha mentioned ten kasinas: earth, water, fire, wind, blue, yellow, red, white, space and consciousness. For example, if a Buddhist wanted to meditate using

▲ *Different types of kasinas that could be used in samatha meditation*

Key terms

- **samatha meditation:** 'calming meditation'; a type of meditation that involves calming the mind and developing deeper concentration
- **mindfulness of breathing:** a meditation practice focusing on the experience of breathing

Research activities

1 Research some of the main postures used in samatha meditation. What do they have in common? State why you think it is important to have the right posture when you start to meditate.

2 The image on page 55 is a famous Tibetan painting that shows the process of samatha meditation. Research this painting online and write down some of the ways that it represents samatha meditation.

Discussion activity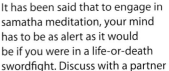

It has been said that to engage in samatha meditation, your mind has to be as alert as it would be if you were in a life-or-death swordfight. Discuss with a partner what you think this means.

'water' as a kasina, then they might focus on a bowl of water in front of them; if they wanted to use 'red' as a kasina then they might focus on a red circle. As with breathing, the object simply gives the person something to rest their attention on.

■ The purpose of samatha meditation

Learning to focus gently on one object helps to develop a calm and concentrated mind. This is a preparation for developing wisdom and understanding of the nature of reality. For this reason, samatha meditation is often seen as a preparation for vipassana meditation, which is discussed on the next page.

Buddhists emphasise that distraction is a normal aspect of meditation, and that it is important not to become discouraged or self critical. There is no question of failure – simply the need to keep practising.

> ❝ You must show energy. The Tathagatas [Buddhas] are [only] teachers. Those who have entered [on the path], meditative, will be released from Mara's fetter. ❞
>
> The Buddha in the *Dhammapada*,
> verse 276

▲ *This Tibetan painting shows the different stages of samatha meditation; a monk chases and finally gains control of an elephant, which represents the mind*

Activities

1 Describe how a Buddhist could use mindfulness of breathing to practise samatha meditation.

2 The Tibetan monk Dilgo Khyentse Rinpoche once said, 'Do not encumber your mind with useless thoughts. What good does it do to brood on the past or anticipate the future? Remain in the simplicity of the present moment.' Explain what you think Dilgo meant by these words. Are they good advice for someone trying to practise samatha meditation?

3 What is the main purpose of samatha meditation?

Summary

You should now be able to understand how Buddhists practise samatha meditation, and why it is important to them.

⭐ Study tip

Mindfulness meditation is becoming common in British schools, prisons, hospitals and other places, as a method of dealing with conditions such as stress, depression and anxiety. While many Buddhists are happy about this, they often point out that the Buddha taught that wisdom comes from a way of life that involves ethics as well as meditation.

2.5 Vipassana meditation

What is vipassana meditation?

Vipassana meditation is often called 'insight meditation', and it is the second main type of meditation practised in Theravada Buddhism. The idea of this type of meditation is to try to penetrate and gain insight into the true nature of reality – to see things as they really are. It may consist of reflecting on the three marks of existence: that all experience is characterised by impermanence, that nothing has an independent, unchanging identity, and that attachment leads to suffering.

The main difference between samatha and vipassana meditation is not in the techniques or methods used, but in the objects being studied. Like samatha meditation, vipassana also uses the technique of mindfulness: concentrating and focusing on specific objects, in a calm and detached manner, without letting the mind get distracted by other things. The difference is in what the meditator focuses on.

In samatha meditation, the meditator focuses on one neutral, simple object or process, such as a blue triangle, a candle flame, or the process of breathing. In vipassana meditation, everything can be explored objectively, including things that are more personal to the meditator. For example, they might reflect on the body and how people can become attached to their bodies. They might meditate on the more unattractive aspects of the body to help develop a detachment from their body. While meditating, they might feel an emotion such as nervousness or annoyance. Then they might try to consider this emotion with mindful kindness. They might hear a sound such as the rain falling outside, and concentrate solely on that sound.

In samatha meditation, the aim is to focus solely on one object for an extended period of time. This helps to develop powers of concentration. In vipassana meditation, the meditator might switch their attention between lots of different things one after the other. The aim is to give their full attention to whatever they are thinking about at any one particular time, to consider it mindfully, and to try to understand its true nature.

Vipassana meditation helps Buddhists to understand how all things are characterised by the three marks of existence, and to develop greater wisdom and awareness about the world. This makes

Objectives

- Understand the purpose and technique of vipassana meditation.
- Understand the practice of zazen meditation.

Key terms

- **vipassana meditation:** 'insight meditation'; a type of meditation that involves developing understanding of the nature of reality
- **zazen meditation:** a type of meditation in Zen Buddhism that requires awareness of the present moment

Links

Read about the three marks of existence on pages 20–25.

▲ *Buddhists practising walking meditation*

meditation an essential part of the Eightfold Path, with the goal of developing complete understanding and achieving enlightenment.

■ Zazen

Zazen is a Japanese word, literally meaning 'seated meditation'. It is a form of meditation practised in Zen Buddhism, which originated in Japan.

Zazen is intended to lead to a deeper understanding of the nature of existence. Though the method varies across the traditions within Zen Buddhism, it generally begins with sitting, relaxing and a period of mindfulness of breathing (see page 54). The meditator then simply sits with awareness of the present moment. Thoughts and experiences come and go, and the meditator returns again and again to the present moment.

▲ *A Buddhist meditating at the Sheffield Buddhist Centre in the UK*

How to practise walking meditation

Often Buddhists sit to meditate, but it is also possible to meditate while walking. Henepola Gunaratana, a Theravada Buddhist monk, explains one way to practise meditation while walking:

'The physical directions are simple. Select an unobstructed area and start at one end. Stand for a minute in an attentive position. Your arms can be held in any way that is comfortable – in front, behind your back, or at your sides. Then while breathing in, lift the heel of one foot. While breathing out, rest that foot on its toes. Again while breathing in, lift that foot, carry it forward and while breathing out, bring the foot down and touch the floor. Repeat this for the other foot. Walk very slowly to the opposite end, stand for one minute, then turn around very slowly, and stand there for another minute before you walk back. Then repeat the process. Keep your head up and your neck relaxed. Keep your eyes open to maintain balance, but don't look at anything in particular. Walk naturally. Maintain the slowest pace that is comfortable, and pay no attention to your surroundings. Watch out for tensions building up in the body, and release them as soon as you spot them. Don't make any particular attempt to be graceful. This is not an athletic exercise or a dance; it is an exercise in awareness. Your objective is to attain total alertness, heightened sensitivity and a full, unblocked experience of the motion of walking. Put all of your attention on the sensations coming from the feet and legs. Try to register as much information as possible about each foot as it moves. Dive into the pure sensation of walking, and notice every subtle nuance of the movement. Feel each individual muscle as it moves. Experience every tiny change in tactile sensation as the feet press against the floor and then lift again.'

Extension activity

Using the information given on these pages, and any extra research you might wish to do online, create a beginner's guide to Buddhist meditation. Include a series of basic steps that a person could follow to start meditating.

★ Study tip

Meditation is often mistakenly described as emptying the mind. It would be more helpful to see it as a method of calming, settling and focusing the mind.

Summary

You should now be able to describe how Buddhists practise vipassana meditation, and understand what they hope to achieve through vipassana meditation.

Activities

1 Give two differences between samatha and vipassana meditation.
2 Why is vipassana meditation important to Buddhists?

2.6 The visualisation of Buddhas and Bodhisattvas

What is visualisation?

Various Buddhist traditions will use **visualisation** as a part of meditation; it is particularly common in Tibetan Buddhism, but is also practised in other Mahayana traditions. It requires the meditator to visualise (imagine) an object in their mind.

Visualisation is a bit different to using a kasina in samatha meditation (see pages 54–55). When Buddhists meditate with a kasina, the kasina is physically present in front of them (for example, a Buddhist might place a bowl of water on the floor in front of them, to look at and focus on as they meditate). In contrast, visualising involves imagining the object in your mind.

The meditator might first look at an image of an object to gain inspiration. They will then get rid of the image and simply imagine or visualise that object in their mind. They will try to imagine the object with as much detail as possible, and examine in their mind all the tiny intricacies of the object. They will try to perceive the object as fully as they can, imagining and examining all the qualities and characteristics of that object. They will try to hold a detailed picture of the object in their mind for as long as possible.

Deity visualisation

Tibetan Buddhists will often visualise a 'deity' when they meditate. For Buddhists, a 'deity' is not a god but a being who has become fully enlightened, such as a Buddha or a Bodhisattva. The meditator will focus not just on what the deity looks like, but also on its qualities and characteristics. They might even imagine themselves as that deity, with its particular qualities, in order to gain those qualities and become more like that deity themselves. The idea here is that you imagine what you want to be, in order to understand it better and therefore become more like it.

Some Mahayana Buddhists also believe that visualising themselves as a Buddha helps them to stimulate and awaken their Buddha-nature.

Some of the Buddhas or Bodhisattvas that a Buddhist might focus on include:

- The 'Medicine Buddha': this Buddha is related to healing. Buddhists believe that visualising the Medicine Buddha will heal them and reduce their suffering, and may even increase their own healing powers.
- Avalokiteshvara: one of the most popular Bodhisattvas, who is related to compassion. Visualising

▲ A thangka of the Medicine Buddha

this Bodhisattva helps Buddhists to develop their own sense of compassion, which is considered to be an important quality to cultivate in order to achieve enlightenment.

- Buddha Amitabha: we saw on pages 42–43 that Pure Land Buddhists worship Buddha Amitabha in the hope that he will help them to be reborn in the pure land and achieve enlightenment quicker. Pure Land Buddhists might visualise Buddha Amitabha while meditating.

■ Using thangkas or mandalas

Sometimes Buddhists use paintings or patterns to help them visualise a deity. They might use a thangka: a detailed painting of a Buddha or Bodhisattva. Or they might use instead a mandala: an intricate, colourful, circle-shaped pattern. These patterns can symbolise different things; some symbolise the universe, others the Buddha, and others still a paradise or pure land. They are sacred diagrams that represent Buddhist principles or teachings. Buddhists who are highly skilled in visualisation can study a thangka or mandala and then imagine it in their mind, visualising all the tiny details and intricacies of the painting or pattern.

▲ A monk creating a mandala at a Tibetan Buddhist monastery in India

In Tibetan monasteries, monks often make mandalas out of brightly-coloured sand. It can take weeks to make a sand mandala, because many different colours of sand have to be delicately placed next to each other to form a complex, intricate pattern. Even though they may take a long time to compete, mandalas are always brushed away once they are finished, to try to encourage the monks to focus on the impermanence in life. They are never kept as a piece of art, as the attachment which that might lead to goes against the Buddha's teachings and one of the main aims of meditation, which is to see how everything is impermanent.

Links

For more on Buddha-nature, look back to page 39.

Discussion activity

Discuss with a partner why you think some Buddhists find it helpful to visualise certain Buddhas or Bodhisattvas as part of their meditation.

Extension activity

Research other Buddhas or Bodhisattvas that are often used by Buddhists for visualisation. (Examples could include Manjushri, Maitreya and Vajrapani.) Make some notes on each of their particular characteristics, and why Buddhists meditate on them.

Activities

1 Explain how using a kasina in samatha meditation is different to the practice of visualisation.

2 Why do Tibetan monks brush away their sand mandalas once they are finished?

 Study tip

Learn the definition of the key term 'visualisation'.

Summary

You should now be able to explain the practice of visualisation, and understand why some Buddhists visualise Buddhas or Bodhisattvas when they meditate.

Ceremonies and rituals associated with death and mourning

■ Buddhist beliefs about death

Buddhist tradition teaches that when a Buddhist dies, their kammic energy leaves their body and is reborn in a new one. Death therefore is not seen as an end, only a transition from one form to another. While Buddhists will naturally grieve the loss of people they loved, they also bear in mind what the Buddha taught about impermanence being a natural part of life. Funerals are a valuable reminder of this teaching of impermanence. Nothing lasts, and people suffer less if they are able to accept this fact.

Funeral customs differ between the various Buddhist traditions and from one country to the next. Some funerals can be very elaborate and even noisy rituals, while others are simple, reflective and calm.

■ Theravada funerals

In Theravada communities, very little money is usually spent on a funeral. Instead the family and friends may donate to a worthy cause and transfer the merit to the deceased. (We saw on page 36 how some Theravada Buddhists believe it is possible to transfer the kamma created by your own good actions and deeds to someone else. In this case, the good kamma that is created by donating to a worthy cause is transferred to the dead person, to help them have a more favourable rebirth.)

Rituals that transfer merit to the deceased may also be performed by family members or other mourners. For example, they might offer cloth to make new robes to a senior monk of a nearby monastery on behalf of the deceased person.

> 66 At the hour of death, the king and the beggar are exactly equal in that no amount of relatives or possessions can affect or prevent death. But who is the richer at the time of death? If the beggar has created more merits, then although he looks materially poor he is really the rich man. 99
>
> Thubten Zopa Rinpoche (Nepalese Buddhist monk)

A shrine may be set up to display the deceased's portrait, along with offerings to the Buddha of candles, incense and flowers. An image of the Buddha is usually placed beside or in front of the shrine. Monks will often attend a funeral of a lay person. They may give a sermon and perform Buddhist rites.

The deceased may be cremated or buried, although cremation is traditional and more common. Monks will perform the last rites before the casket containing the dead person is sealed. Family members may assist in lifting the casket as a final act of service, while others present observe a moment of respectful silence. During the funeral procession,

Objectives

- Understand Buddhist teachings about death.
- Know about different Buddhist ceremonies and rituals associated with death and mourning.

▲ A Buddhist funeral in Thailand with a shrine to the deceased person

family members may walk behind the hearse. All mourners should be sending good thoughts to the family and contemplating the impermanence of life.

▲ *Tibetan monks at a funeral*

■ Ceremonies and rituals in Tibet and Japan

Ceremonies and rituals associated with death differ greatly between the various Tibetan and Japanese traditions, and between geographical areas. One of the best-known Tibetan traditions is that of 'sky burial', in which the body is left in a high place as a gift to the vultures. In a mountainous country short of firewood and often too frozen for grave-digging, giving away one's body was seen as both a practical and generous act. However, it is increasingly customary to burn the body instead. Revered teachers have always been cremated, and the remains placed in a chorten (a memorial structure also known as a stupa) to become a site of worship. In all cases, ceremonies involving prayers and offerings of yak-butter lamps may be made every seven days for 49 days after the death.

In Japanese Pure Land traditions, the coffin may be placed with the head pointing west, while those assembled chant 'Namo Amida Bu' as they process around it. Nichiren Buddhist funerals include readings from the *Lotus Sutra.* It is common across all Japanese traditions for relations to gather after the cremation and pick out the bones from the ashes, using chopsticks. As in Tibet, these remains may be kept for 49 days and prayers offered every seventh day.

Discussion activity

Do you think that Buddhist teachings about the naturalness of impermanence could make it easier to accept the fact that someone you love has died?

Extension activity -🔅-

Research what Buddhists believe happened to the Buddha when he died. How did he die, and what was his view of an afterlife?

⭐ **Study tip**

Buddhism is enormously diverse across and within traditions and countries. One can never say that all Buddhists believe or do exactly the same thing.

Activities

1 Read the following statements. Which do you think Buddhists would agree with and which do you think Buddhists would disagree with? Give reasons for your answers.

 a 'There is no life but this one. When you die, that's it. What is important is making the most of this life because it's all you've got.'

 b 'I believe life is the same as all energy; it never ends but rather passes from one living thing to another.'

 c 'My Nan died five years ago but somehow I feel that she is still with me at times. Your spirit has to live on after death.'

 d 'I know that I believe in a heaven. I want to go there when I die. I can pray to God and he will take me there at my death.'

2 Some Theravada Buddhists believe they can transfer merit to another person. Explain what this means, and how this belief can be seen in a Theravada funeral.

3 Write out a script for a radio interview with a Buddhist monk. What questions about death and mourning would you like to put to this monk, and what answers do you think he would give?

Summary

You should now have some understanding of Buddhist teachings about death and impermanence. You should also have some idea of the variety of rituals and ceremonies associated with death and mourning in Tibet, Japan, and Theravada communities.

2.8　Wesak and Parinirvana Day

■ Buddhist festivals and retreats

Buddhist **festivals** are usually a time for joy and celebration, although some festivals (such as Parinirvarna Day) are more solemn occasions. They give Buddhists an opportunity to remember and celebrate the Buddha's life and his teachings, and an opportunity to meet and practise together.

▲ *Monks lighting candles at a temple in Thailand for Wesak*

Objectives

- Understand what festivals and retreats mean to Buddhists.
- Understand the origins, celebrations and importance of Wesak and Parinirvana Day.

Key terms

- **festival:** a day or period of celebration for religious reasons
- **retreat:** a period of time spent away from everyday life in order to focus on meditation practice
- **Wesak:** a Theravada festival that celebrates the Buddha's birth, enlightenment and passing away
- **Parinirvana Day:** a Mahayana festival that commemorates the Buddha's passing away

Some festivals are specific to a certain tradition or country. For example, Mahayana Buddhists might celebrate the birthdays of certain Bodhisattvas. Most of the major festivals celebrate significant events in the Buddha's life, such as his first sermon after his enlightenment (celebrated by Theravada Buddhists as Asalha Puja Day).

Retreats are popular in the West. There are many places in the UK, for example, that offer Buddhist retreats. Many of them give an opportunity to spend a weekend or week away from everyday life, with a group of people who are similarly interested in the religion. They might be held in a monastery or Buddhist centre. Retreats vary in structure and focus on different aspects, but they generally give people an opportunity to deepen their understanding of Buddhist practice. They might involve meditation, talks and study groups, workshops, and taking part in rituals.

In Theravada communities, monks observe Vassa, an annual retreat that lasts for three months during the rainy season. During these three months, monks only leave their temples when necessary, and dedicate more time to meditation and study.

■ Wesak

Wesak (also known as Vesak or Buddha day) is probably the best known and most important of all the Buddhist festivals. It is celebrated on the full moon during the month, of Vesak (which usually falls in May). The festival commemorates three major events in the Buddha's life: his birth, his enlightenment and his passing into parinirvana (the final state of nibbana). All three of these events are said to have happened on a full moon. Wesak is a festival to honour and remember the Buddha and his teachings. It has been celebrated since at least the early twentieth century, although only became a public holiday in the 1950s.

▲ *Thousands of lanterns are lit at the Maha Vihara temple in Malaysia for Wesak*

To celebrate Wesak, Buddhists may light up their homes with candles, lamps or paper lanterns, and put up decorations. They will make offerings to the Buddha, and may give gifts such as food, candles and flowers to the monks in the local monastery. In return, the monks may lead some meditation, chant from the Buddhist scriptures, or give sermons about the Buddha's teachings. These will focus on the Buddha's life, in particular his enlightenment.

Wesak celebrations vary from country to country. In some places, such as Singapore, there are ceremonies where caged birds and animals are released as a symbol of liberation, and to signify the release from past troubles and wrong-doings. In countries such as Indonesia, giant paper lanterns are lit to float up into the night sky. Light is an important symbol during this festival, and is associated with a number of different meanings: the idea that light can be used to overcome darkness or ignorance, the fact that the Buddha showed people how to become enlightened, and as a symbol of hope.

■ Parinirvana Day

Parinirvana Day is a Mahayana festival that is celebrated during February to remember the Buddha's passing into parinirvana. As might be expected, the festival is a more solemn occasion than Wesak. For Buddhists, it is a chance to reflect on the fact of their own future death, and to remember friends or relatives who have recently passed away. The idea that all things are impermanent, which is central to Buddhist teaching, has a real focus for the day.

The *Mahaparinirvana Sutra* is an important Buddhist scripture that describes the Buddha's last days, and passages from it are often read on Parinirvana Day. Buddhists might spend the day reading this text and meditating at home, or joining others in temples and monasteries for puja and meditation.

Some places will organise retreats, because the day is seen as a suitable occasion for quiet reflection and meditation.

Parinirvana Day is also a traditional day for pilgrimage, and many Buddhists will visit the city of Kushinagar in India, which is where the Buddha is believed to have died.

Discussion activity

Discuss with a partner why you think festivals might be important to many Buddhists.

Extension activity

Research the history behind Wesak Day and Parinirvana Day, and make your own notes on how the festivals started and then developed.

▲ *'The reclining Buddha' is a type of statue that shows the Buddha lying down during his final illness, about to enter parinirvana*

Activities

1 Explain the difference between a festival and a retreat.

2 Light is an important symbol in Wesak celebrations. Think about the properties of light and explain why light is used as a symbol during this festival.

3 Do you feel it might be helpful to spend a day focusing on the topic of death and impermanence? Give reasons for your answer.

4 'Religious festivals are just an excuse for people to have a good time and nothing more.' Evaluate this statement. Remember to include more than one point of view, and refer to Buddhist teachings in your answer.

★ Study tip

There is not a single festival that is common to all Buddhist traditions worldwide. The festivals described here are just some examples.

Summary

You should now be able to explain why festivals and retreats are important to Buddhists. You should also be able to describe what happens during Wesak and Parinirvana Day, and explain the significance of these festivals.

■ The concept of kamma in Buddhism

It is sometimes said that **kamma (karma)** means 'actions have consequences', but its meaning is more precise than that. It is a principle that explains how the ethical impulses behind a person's actions lead in the direction of either suffering or happiness. Buddhism speaks of '**skilful**' actions, which are rooted in generosity, compassion and understanding, and '**unskilful**' actions, which are rooted in their opposites: craving, hatred, and ignorance. Put basically, skilful actions lead to happiness and unskilful actions lead to suffering.

The consequences of a person's actions can be understood in different ways. First, through repeated actions people develop habits. For example, if someone regularly acts with anger, they become an angry person. Anger is not a pleasant state and so this leads to suffering. In addition, a state of mind leads to action: angry people shout, break things, beep their horn when driving and create a situation where no one wants to be around them. This is kamma. Kamma shows not that people are punished or rewarded *for* their actions, but rather *by* them.

According to Buddhist tradition, a person's actions in this life will not only impact on their happiness and suffering right now, but will also sow the seeds for a future rebirth. Depending on a person's kamma, they may be reborn in one of six realms: the realm of the gods, the realm of the angry gods, the realm of the animals, the realm of the tormented beings, the realm of the hungry ghosts, or the human realm. The human realm is said to be the best realm within which to reach enlightenment.

For Buddhists the idea of kamma is empowering, because it means they can

▲ *Buddhism teaches that the human realm is the best realm in which to achieve enlightenment*

Key terms

- **kamma (karma):** a person's actions; the idea that skilful actions result in happiness and unskilful ones in suffering
- **skilful:** good, ethical actions or behaviour
- **unskilful:** bad, unethical actions or behaviour

Activity

Imagine you are trying to teach a young child about the concept of kamma.

Write a short story that illustrates how a Buddhist's actions cause either suffering or happiness, and how this affects their rebirth.

▲ *Helping those in the local community is one way that Buddhist monks can act ethically*

change the future through their own actions. By cultivating skilful mental states and actions, they can not only live a happier life but can lay the ground for a favourable rebirth.

■ Buddhist ethics

We saw on page 34 that 'right action' is one of the eight practices in the Eightfold Path. Acting morally and ethically – choosing to do the right things – is therefore very important for Buddhists, both in order to reduce suffering in this life for themselves and others, and to eventually achieve enlightenment. A few of the many ways that they might do this is in acting compassionately towards others, not taking part in any work that harms animals, showing patience in their teachings, and helping the poor in the local community.

The concept of kamma is central to Buddhist ethics. The fact that a person's own behaviour causes their happiness and suffering is an incentive to cultivate a more skilful way of life. This means that not only does the person benefit (because they experience greater happiness as a result of their skilful behaviour), but also that others benefit (because they will experience a person's generous, kind and wise actions rather than their greedy, hateful and ignorant ones).

Extension activity

Kamma is represented in the Tibetan Wheel of Life. Research which bit of the wheel illustrates the concept of kamma, and what it teaches Buddhists.

⭐ Study tip

Remember that in Buddhist ethics, the motivation behind any action is very important.

Summary

You should now be able to explain what kamma means, and understand how it is an important part of Buddhist ethics.

Activities

1 Do you think the motivation behind an action matters the most, or are the consequences of that action more important? Give reasons for your answer.

2 Explain how believing in kamma might affect the way a Buddhist lives their life.

Compassion (karuna)

■ What is karuna?

After the Buddha became enlightened, he faced the question of what to do next. Should he keep the knowledge and understanding he had discovered about enlightenment to himself? Or should he share what he had found with the rest of the world, by teaching it to others? He would have known that some people would have difficulty accepting his teachings and might even ridicule his beliefs. The Buddha was asking people to accept concepts that might be seen as difficult, such as the idea of anatta (no self or soul). However, the Buddha could see there was much hardship in the world, and he wanted to share his knowledge of how to overcome it out of compassion for everyone who was suffering.

This compassion is called **karuna** by Buddhists. Karuna refers to the compassion that Buddhists show for the sufferings of everyone in the world. For Buddhists it means feeling concern for the suffering of others, almost as if it were their own suffering. It means wanting others to be free of suffering and being moved to do whatever is possible to relieve the suffering of others. It also means recognising when you yourself are suffering and acting with compassion towards yourself. Above all, it means recognising that a person cannot be truly happy while there are others in the world who are still suffering.

■ The importance of karuna in Buddhism

Karuna is one of **the four sublime states** in Buddhism, which are: loving-kindness, compassion, sympathetic joy (being happy for others) and equanimity (maintaining stability and calm in the face of both happiness and suffering). These are four qualities that the Buddha taught were important for all Buddhists to develop. Together, they explain how Buddhists should act towards themselves and others. Compassion is an important quality for all Buddhists to develop. In Mahayana Buddhism it is a crucial quality required to become a Bodhisattva.

> **Objective**
>
> - Understand the concept of compassion (karuna) in Buddhism.

> **Key terms**
>
> - **karuna:** compassion; feeling concerned for the suffering of other people and wanting to relieve their suffering
> - **the four sublime states:** the four qualities of love, compassion, sympathetic joy and equanimity which the Buddha taught that Buddhists should develop

▲ *The Bodhisattva Avalokitesvara, who represents compassion*

> **❝** I believe that at every level of society, the key to a happier and more successful world is the growth of compassion. We all share an identical need for love and on the basis of this commonality, it is possible to feel that anybody we meet, in whatever circumstances is a brother or sister. If we are to protect this home of ours, each of us needs to experience a vivid sense of universal compassion. **❞**
>
> Tenzin Gyatso (the Dalai Lama)

> **Discussion activity**
>
> Discuss with a partner how people in your school could show more compassion to each other. What sort of things could they do in an ordinary school day to help others?

Buddhists believe that wisdom and compassion should be developed together, and it is not really possible to have one without the other. To take one example, a very clever scientist might develop a new type of explosive, but without the wisdom to understand the power and potential of his invention, and without a sense of compassion for others, he might sell the formula to someone who can turn it into a deadly weapon. For Buddhists it is therefore important to develop the wisdom for how to help others, along with the compassion to want to help others.

Extension activity

Research how Brahma Sahampati convinced the Buddha to show karuna and teach others what he had discovered. Write a brief summary of your findings.

ROKPA

The Tibetan word 'rokpa' means 'help' or 'friend', and it is the name given to an international charity that was set up in 1980 based on the premise of showing compassion to others. ROKPA is involved in projects in Zimbabwe, Nepal, and Tibet. The charity helps to run schools and provide education to thousands of children each year. The aim is to help families out of poverty through better education, but also to teach children about the value of compassion. ROKPA believe that learning how to be kind and developing a desire to help others is the way to bring about real and lasting change.

▲ ROKPA helps to provide education for orphans and children whose families are too poor to pay for their schooling

Activities

1 Why do Buddhists believe it is important to develop wisdom *and* compassion?

2 Have you ever done something to help someone you didn't know? If so, why do you think you did this? Did this change the way you felt about yourself? Explain your thoughts.

3 Pick any two of the following topics. Imagining you are writing for a Buddhist newspaper, create a headline and write a short news story about each one, based on a compassionate response to the world:

   a world poverty   **d** asylum seekers

   b racism   **e** hunting foxes or deer

   c homelessness

4 Do you agree with what the Dalai Lama says in the quotation on page 66? Give reasons for your answer.

⭐ Study tip

Compassion in Buddhism is not just a good way to live. According to the Buddha, compassion is inseparable from wisdom. The more a person understands suffering and the nature of existence, the more compassion they will feel.

Summary

You should now be able to explain what karuna means and why it is important to Buddhists.

What is metta?

We saw on the previous page how karuna (compassion) is one of the four sublime states. These are four ideal qualities that Buddhists try to develop over their lifetimes. Another one of these states is **metta** or 'loving-kindness'. Buddhists try to develop a loving, kind, friendly attitude towards themselves and all other beings. It is a wish for all beings to be happy and free from suffering, without expecting anything in return. It does not even depend on the goodness of others; metta is cultivated even towards people who act unskilfully.

Metta and karuna might seem like the same thing but they are in fact a little different. One way to think about it is that metta is a general desire to want people to be happy. It is an attitude of warmth and kindness that Buddhists try to cultivate towards all people in general. Karuna arises when metta comes into contact with a specific person who is suffering. For example, a person might wish for their friend to be happy: this is an example of metta. However, if the friend has an accident, the person's goodwill towards them transforms into compassion – the urge to alleviate their suffering.

The importance of developing metta

Buddhists cultivate loving-kindness towards themselves and others in order to dissolve away the tendency to act out of greed, hatred, jealousy or any other negative emotions. We saw on pages 30–31 that greed and hatred are two of the three poisons, which the Buddha taught were the main causes of suffering. Therefore, developing metta helps Buddhists to overcome suffering and to eventually achieve enlightenment.

Buddhism teaches that someone who has cultivated metta will not be so easily angered. They will be more caring, more loving, and more likely to love unconditionally (without expecting anything in return). Buddhists believe that those who cultivate metta will feel at peace because they see no need to possess any ill will or hostility towards others. Radiating metta is thought to contribute to a world of love, peace and happiness.

Loving-kindness meditation

Loving-kindness meditation is a common form of meditation in Buddhism. Its aim is to help the meditator develop an attitude of metta, firstly towards themselves and then towards everyone else in the

▲ Metta means showing a kind and friendly attitude towards all people

> ### Objective
> - Understand the concept of loving-kindness (metta) in Buddhism.

> ### Key term
> - **metta:** loving-kindness; showing a benevolent, kind, friendly attitude towards other people

> **❝** Just as a mother would protect with her life her own son, her only son, so one should cultivate an unbounded mind towards all beings, and loving-kindness towards all the world. **❞**
> The *Sutta Nipata*, verses 149–150

▲ *Metta can be developed through loving-kindness meditation*

Discussion activity

Discuss how you think the Buddha showed metta after he became enlightened.

Research activity

Buddhist scriptures say that there are eleven benefits or advantages of practising metta. Find out what these eleven benefits are and make a list of them.

> ❝ Just as compassion is the wish that all sentient beings be free of suffering, loving-kindness is the wish that all may enjoy happiness. As with compassion, when cultivating loving-kindness it is important to start by taking a specific individual as a focus of our meditation, and we then extend the scope of our concern further and further, to eventually encompass and embrace all sentient beings. ❞
>
> Tenzin Gyatso (the Dalai Lama)

world. It often consists of five steps, which involve cultivating loving-kindness towards:

1. yourself
2. a good friend
3. a 'neutral' person (someone you come into contact with on a regular basis, but who does not give rise to strong positive or negative emotions)
4. a 'difficult' person (someone you dislike)
5. all four of these people, gradually followed by everyone else in the world.

The meditator might visualise or imagine one of these people looking happy. They might reflect on the positive qualities of the person and any acts of kindness they have done. They might start by saying phrases such as, 'May I be happy. May I be well. May I be safe. May I be peaceful.' Then they will apply these phrases to other people as part of their meditation.

⭐ Study tip

Cultivating metta is not just about being 'nice' and avoiding conflict or difficulty. For example, in the fourth step of loving-kindness meditation, the meditator is simply remembering that whatever the person has done, they are still a suffering human being who needs love and care, just like everyone else.

Activities

1 Explain how metta is different to karuna.
2 'Metta is impossible to show towards everyone in the world.' Do you agree? Evaluate this statement, showing that you have thought about more than one point of view.
3 In loving-kindness meditation, the aim is to develop an attitude of loving-kindness first towards yourself, then a good friend, then a neutral person, then a difficult person, then everyone in the world. Why do you think this order is used?
4 Explain how, if you practised metta in your life, it could affect you and those around you. Give examples to help explain what you mean.

Summary

You should now be able to explain what metta means and why Buddhists think it is important to cultivate it. You should also be able to give an overview of loving-kindness meditation.

2.12 The five moral precepts

■ What are the five moral precepts?

Most religions have their own code of ethical behaviour, and Buddhism is no different. Most Buddhist traditions have a set of precepts. The most common list of precepts found across the Buddhist world is that of **the five moral precepts**: a series of five commitments that Buddhists undertake. The five precepts are:

1. to abstain from taking life

2. to abstain from taking what is not freely given

3. to abstain from misuse of the senses or sexual misconduct

4. to abstain from wrong speech

5. to abstain from intoxicants that cloud the mind.

Objective

● Understand what the five moral precepts are.

Key term

● **the five moral precepts:** five principles that Buddhists try to follow to live ethically and morally

Let us look at these in a little more detail. The first precept means that Buddhists undertake not to harm or kill any living being, including animals. It is for this reason that many Buddhists, particularly in the West, are vegetarian or vegan.

The second precept means that Buddhists undertake not to take things that have not been given to them. As well as not stealing, this means they wish to avoid manipulating or exploiting other people (i.e. taking advantage of others by taking more from them than they are giving freely).

The third precept means that Buddhists undertake not to abuse or overindulge in sensual pleasures, or to use sex harmfully. For example, they should not engage in sexual activity that causes harm to others, such as adultery, rape or incest.

▲ *The fifth moral precept recommends that Buddhists should not drink alcohol*

The fourth precept means that Buddhists undertake not to lie or gossip about other people. Buddhists aim to speak truthfully, kindly, helpfully and at the right time.

The fifth precept – not taking alcohol or drugs – is important for Buddhists who have committed themselves to developing calm, clear awareness.

■ Following the five moral precepts

Some religions have laws or commandments from a god which, if broken, are believed to result in punishment by the god. However, Buddhism does not include belief in a god who rewards or punishes. The five precepts are principles that Buddhists voluntarily practise more and more deeply as the progress.

> **❝** Whoever destroys a living creature, and speaks untruth, takes what is not given in the world, and goes to another's wife, and whatever man applies himself to drinking liquor and intoxicants, that person digs up his own root here in this very world. **❞**
>
> The Buddha in the *Dhammapada*, verses 246–247

▲ *The first moral precept teaches that Buddhists should not harm any living beings, including animals*

The precepts need to be applied sensitively. Sometimes Buddhists have to balance one precept against another. For example, what if being truthful may lead to harm? Sometimes it could be more ethical to lie, if this is motivated by genuine kindness.

The root precept is the first one – not to cause harm. The others are all expressions of this. The precepts can be practised on ever deepening levels, especially at the level of the mind (for example, wanting to hurt someone is still unskilful even if you don't actually hurt them).

This attitude links in with the Buddhist belief in kamma. Intentions and the reasons for doing things are very important in Buddhism. Good or skilful intentions lead to good or skilful actions, which have positive consequences in this life and (according to tradition) in future lives. Therefore the first step in following the five precepts is to *want* to follow them. Over time, this will enable a Buddhist to practise the precepts at ever deeper and more subtle levels. This will purify their mind of greed, hatred and ignorance, as they move towards the wisdom and compassion of enlightenment.

 We just keep on working, we are patient with ourselves, and on and on it goes. Little by little our life comes more into alignment with the wisdom that gives rise to the precepts. As our minds get clearer and clearer, it's not even a matter of breaking or maintaining the precepts; automatically they are maintained. 🙶

Jan Chozen Bays
(Zen meditation teacher)

Discussion activity

Discuss with a partner whether or not you think that a person's intentions behind an action are as important as the action itself.

Extension activities

1   Research the concept of ahimsa. It is an ancient Indian idea that was further developed within Buddhism. How does this concept apply to the five moral precepts?

2   Novice monks and nuns in Theravada Buddhism agree to live by the five moral precepts and an extra five rules, which together form the ten moral precepts. Find out what the extra five precepts are.

⭐ Study tip

The five moral precepts apply to the way a Buddhist treats him or herself, as well as others.

Summary

You should now be able to explain what each of the five moral precepts is, and understand how Buddhists view them more as a series of guidelines rather than strict rules.

Activities

1   Which of the five moral precepts do you think most Buddhists in the West would find hardest to follow? Give reasons for your answer.

2   'The five moral precepts should be treated as strict rules that Buddhists should always obey.' Do you agree? Give reasons for your answer. Think about more than one point of view.

3   The five moral precepts are usually written as a series of principles about what Buddhists should *not* do, for example they should *not* harm others or *not* tell lies. Rewrite the five moral precepts as a series of positive guidelines telling Buddhists what they *should* do.

■ What are the six perfections?

The six perfections are six qualities that express how a Bodhisattva lives, according to Mahayana Buddhists. In contrast to the five precepts, which are concerned with avoiding doing unskilful things, the six perfections define the qualities that ought to be developed in order to live in an enlightened way. For Mahayana Buddhists, spiritual life consists of the cultivation of these qualities.

The six perfections are:

1. generosity or giving
2. morality
3. patience
4. energy
5. meditation
6. wisdom.

We will look at these in a bit more detail below.

Generosity

The first perfection is concerned with the cultivation of giving or generosity. Tibetan Buddhists talk about three main types of giving. The first is to give material goods such as food, clothes and money. This helps to give immediate relief to people's suffering, but does not present a long-term solution. The second is to give protection from fear. They should help somebody if they are in trouble or in a situation that is making them afraid. The third is to give the Dhamma, the Buddha's teachings. This is seen as a gift that helps the recipients to help themselves, and therefore has a longer-lasting impact.

▲ *For monks, sharing and explaining the Buddha's teachings is one way to show generosity*

For Buddhists, the intention behind giving is very important. Buddhists should give without expecting anything in return. It is therefore not only important to give, but also to develop awareness of the motives behind giving, and to gradually purify these motives in order to give more freely.

Morality

The second perfection concerns the cultivation of morality. Most Buddhists try to follow the five moral precepts: not to kill or harm others; not to steal; not to abuse or misuse sex; not to lie; and not to abuse alcohol and drugs. Mahayana Buddhists try to follow a further five precepts: not to talk about other people's errors or faults; not to praise

Extension activity

Theravada Buddhism also has the idea of perfections. There are ten perfections in Theravada Buddhism, some of which are the same. For example, both sets have generosity as the first perfection.

Use the internet to find out about the ten perfections in Theravada Buddhism. What are the similarities and differences between these and the six perfections in Mahayana Buddhism?

oneself and speak badly of others; not to be stingy; not to be angry; and not to speak badly of the three refuges.

In trying to develop this perfection, a Buddhist might begin by feeling as if they have to restrain themselves from doing immoral things, and it may require a great deal of self-discipline. However, the aim is to stop feeling that behaving morally is a restraint, and to feel that it is something that one genuinely wants to do out of compassion and concern for others. Buddhists use meditation and the practice of mindfulness to help with this.

Patience

A Bodhisattva embodies patience, which is expressed through tolerance and endurance. This means that Buddhists should learn to endure personal hardship or suffering, to practise compassion towards those who show them anger, and to have patience with others.

An important first step for developing this perfection is to accept the first noble truth, the existence of suffering. Understanding that suffering is an intrinsic part of life helps Buddhists to cultivate the patience needed to endure it.

Energy

The fourth perfection consists of the cultivation of mental energy and strength. Buddhists should put as much effort and enthusiasm into their practice of the Dhamma as possible. They should cultivate the courage and energy needed to strive for enlightenment over many years (or indeed lifetimes).

A Buddhist can develop this perfection in different ways. They might look after their own health, decide to deepen different aspects of their practice (such as meditation), or study the Buddha's teachings.

Meditation and wisdom

The fifth perfection is concerned with meditation. We have already seen on pages 52–53 how important meditation is to Buddhists. It helps them to develop the concentration and awareness needed to achieve the sixth perfection, which is wisdom.

All of the first five perfections contribute to the development of the sixth one. Through meditating and studying the Buddha's teachings, and through living morally and ethically, Buddhists aim to develop a full understanding of the nature of reality. Mahayana Buddhists believe that the Bodhisattva, who is the ideal Buddhist, combines wisdom with compassion.

Summary

You should now understand what each of the six perfections is, and be able to explain some of the ways that Buddhists aim to develop these perfections during the course of their lifetime.

Discussion activity

Discuss with a partner what qualities or virtues you would like to perfect in your lives. Do you think it is possible to perfect them during your lifetimes?

Activities

1 Which of the six perfections do you think might be easiest for Buddhists to develop? Which do you think might be the hardest? Give reasons for your answers.

2 Describe the three different types of generosity.

3 Read this story and then explain which of the six perfections you think it demonstrates, and why.

'A group of people were travelling through a burning hot desert. Two of them strayed away from the others and got lost. As they walked on they became desperate to find water, and were eventually delighted to come across a well. They both rushed over to it. The first man to arrive drank his fill of the beautiful clear water. He drank so much that he could no longer move, and sank down on the ground beside the well. The second man looked at the well, turned around and then went off in search of his fellow travellers, to guide them back to the well.'

⭐ **Study tip**

The Buddha's teaching of the six perfections and five moral precepts indicates that every single person (whether Buddhist or not) has the potential to make progress in wisdom and compassion. This is an expression of his teaching of anatta: that nothing has any fixed essence or self, and therefore people have limitless potential for change for the better. This is useful to remember when learning about Buddhist attitudes towards crime and rehabilitation.

Worship and festivals – summary

You should now be able to:

✔ explain the nature, use and importance of Buddhist places of worship, including temples, shrines, monasteries (viharas), halls for meditation or learning (gompas) and their key features including Buddha rupa, artefacts and offerings

✔ explain how Buddhists perform puja in the home and in the temple, including chanting, mantra recitation, and the use of malas

✔ explain the aims, methods and significance of different types of meditation, including samatha meditation, vipassana meditation, and the visualisation of Buddhas and Bodhisattvas

✔ explain the practice and significance of different ceremonies and rituals associated with death and mourning in Theravada Buddhism, and in Japan and Tibet

✔ explain how Buddhists celebrate the festivals of Wesak and Parinirvana Day, including their origins and significance; understand the importance of festivals and retreats to Buddhists in Great Britain today.

Buddhist ethics – summary

You should now be able to:

✔ explain Buddhist teachings about kamma (karma) and rebirth, compassion (karuna) and loving-kindness (metta)

✔ explain Buddhist teachings about the five moral precepts

✔ explain Buddhist teachings about the six perfections in the Mahayana tradition.

Sample student answer – the 4-mark question

1. Write an answer to the following practice question:

   Explain two contrasting types of Buddhist meditation.   [4 marks]

2. Read the following sample student answer:

   "Some Buddhists practise samatha meditation, which is all about focusing on one thing, like your breathing. The purpose is to clear the mind of emotions and thoughts and just focus your attention on one thing. This helps Buddhists to learn how to concentrate, and also to calm the mind.

   A different type of meditation is called metta or loving-kindness meditation, where a Buddhist will try to think loving thoughts firstly to family, then acquaintances, then strangers and even enemies, which would be very hard to do."

3. With a partner, discuss the sample answer. Is the focus of the answer correct? Is anything missing from the answer? How do you think it could be improved?

4. What mark (out of 4) would you give this answer? Look at the mark scheme in the Introduction (AO1). What are the reasons for the mark you have given?

5. Now swap your answer with your partner's and mark each other's responses. What mark (out of 4) would you give the response? Refer to the mark scheme and give reasons for the mark you award.

Sample student answer – the 5-mark question

1. Write an answer to the following practice question:

   Explain two reasons why temples are important in Buddhist worship.

   Refer to sacred writings or another source of Buddhist belief and teaching in your answer.
   [5 marks]

2. Read the following sample student answer:

   "Buddhists can worship at home with a personal shrine, or they can go to a temple where they can be with fellow Buddhists. This is one of the reasons why temples are important for Buddhist worship, because all the focus is there with the right atmosphere for worship with like-minded followers.

   Another reason is so that a lay Buddhist can meet a monk and ask for help and guidance with their meditation. They might feel that they can only gain this specialist help at a Buddhist temple."

3. With a partner, discuss the sample answer. Is the focus of the answer correct? Is anything missing from the answer? How do you think it could be improved?

4. What mark (out of 5) would you give this answer? Look at the mark scheme in the Introduction (AO1). What are the reasons for the mark you have given?

5. Now swap your answer with your partner's and mark each other's responses. What mark (out of 5) would you give the response? Refer to the mark scheme and give reasons for the mark you award.

Sample student answer – the 12-mark question

1. Write an answer to the following practice question:

    'The most important religious festival for Buddhists is Parinirvana Day.'

    Evaluate this statement. In your answer you should:
    - refer to Buddhist teaching
    - give reasoned arguments to support this statement
    - give reasoned arguments to support a different point of view
    - reach a justified conclusion.   **[12 marks]**

2. Read the following sample student answer:

    "Parinirvana Day is a very popular festival in the Mahayana tradition of Buddhism. It remembers the death of the Buddha and although it may seem odd to celebrate someone's death, for Buddhists this day is very important as they believe that when the Buddha died he entered nibbana and became free from all sufferings in the world, and they want to achieve this too. The fact that the Buddha managed to do this gives Buddhists hope that the same thing can happen for them.

    On Parinirvana Day, passages are read from the Nirvana Sutra and Buddhists visit monasteries and temples. It is a social occasion and presents are bought for family and friends, and people can reflect on death and remember those who have already died.

    On the other hand, the most important festival for Buddhists is probably Wesak. This is usually in May when there is a full moon, and remembers the birth of the Buddha, without which there would be no Buddhism. This festival remembers his enlightenment too and the day he died, so there are many aspects to this day which make it more important for Buddhists than Parinirvana Day.

    Buddhists will visit the temple where they live and listen to monks and nuns giving talks, where they can think about the Buddha's message. Everybody who attends meditates and they decorate the shrine rooms. They put candles and flowers on the Buddha shrine too.

    I don't think there is too much difference between the two days but the festival of Wesak celebrates more about the Buddha so I think that this one is the most important." .

3. With a partner, discuss the sample answer. Consider the following questions:

    - Does the answer refer to Buddhist teachings and if so what are they?
    - Is there an argument to support the statement and how well developed is it?
    - Is a different point of view offered and how developed is that argument?
    - Has the student written a clear conclusion after weighing up both sides of the argument?
    - What is good about the answer?
    - How do you think it could be improved?

4. What mark (out of 12) would you give this answer? Look at the mark scheme in the Introduction (AO2). What are the reasons for the mark you have given?

5. Now swap your answer with your partner's and mark each other's responses. What mark (out of 12) would you give the response? Refer to the mark scheme and give reasons for the mark you award.

Practice questions

1 Which **one** of the following is the Buddhist word for compassion?

    A) Metta   **B)** Karuna   **C)** Kamma   **D)** Anicca   **[1 mark]**

2 Give two of the six perfections in the Mahayana tradition.   **[2 marks]**

> **Study tip**
>
> This question only requires the naming of two of the six perfections. Do not waste time by answering in sentences.

3 Explain **two** contrasting Buddhist rituals associated with death and mourning.   **[4 marks]**

> **Study tip**
>
> Do not forget to develop the points you are making. This may be done by referring to examples and giving detailed information.

4 Explain **two** ways that Buddhists can perform puja in the home.

Refer to sacred writings or another source of Buddhist belief and teaching in your answer.

    [5 marks]

5 'Meditation is the most important practice for Buddhists.'

Evaluate this statement. In your answer you should:

- refer to Buddhist teaching
- give reasoned arguments to support this statement
- give reasoned arguments to support a different point of view
- reach a justified conclusion.   **[12 marks]**

> **Study tip**
>
> You should aim to refer to Buddhist teaching in your arguments, for example scripture, religious writings or the teaching of modern Buddhists.

Part 2: Thematic studies

3 Relationships and families

3.1 Human sexuality

Human sexuality refers to the way that people express themselves as sexual beings. A **heterosexual** relationship is a sexual relationship with a member of the opposite sex; that is, between a man and a woman. A **homosexual** relationship is a sexual relationship with a member of the same sex, either between a man and another man or a woman and another woman.

■ Buddhist attitudes towards sex

Within the lay community

Buddhist views on sex differ greatly from country to country, perhaps in particular between Buddhists in Asia and the West. Buddhism teaches that sex is not wrong, shameful or embarrassing. It acknowledges that everyone has passions and that these should not be avoided or denied. For example, Roshi Robert Aitken (a Zen Buddhist teacher) once said:

> 66 For all its ecstatic nature, for all its power, sex is just another human drive. If we avoid it just because it is more difficult to integrate than anger or fear, then we are simply saying that when the chips are down we cannot follow our own practice. This is dishonest and unhealthy. 99

> ### Objectives
>
> - Examine Buddhist attitudes towards sex and homosexuality.
> - Consider different religious and non-religious views about sex and homosexuality.

> ### Key terms
>
> - **human sexuality:** how people express themselves as sexual beings
> - **heterosexual:** sexually attracted to members of the opposite sex
> - **homosexual:** sexually attracted to members of the same sex

> 66 There is a middle way wherein sexuality is fully acknowledged and regarded compassionately without the need to indulge in actions which lead to suffering. 99
>
> Daishin Morgan (the abbot of Throssel Hole Abbey in Northumberland, UK)

◀ *Many Buddhists, particularly in the West, think that the way a relationship is conducted is much more important than the gender of the people involved*

However, as sexual attraction generally involves craving (tanha), which is one of the main causes of suffering in Buddhism, it is important for Buddhists to approach sex ethically. Buddhists believe that their sexual behaviour, as in other areas of life, should be guided by kindness, generosity, honesty and awareness, not causing harm to oneself or others.

Within the monastic community

Most Buddhist monks and nuns take a vow of celibacy when they become ordained. This means they choose to avoid sexual activity as one aspect of a simple life devoted to meditation and study.

▲ *Buddhism teaches that sexual relationships should be guided by kindness, generosity, honesty and awareness*

■ Buddhist approaches to homosexuality

The Buddha did not give teachings related to same-sex relationships. Many Buddhists, particularly in the West, would say that the five moral precepts apply as much to same-sex relationships as to opposite-sex relationships. What matters is that there is consent and respect, regardless of the gender of the people involved.

■ Contemporary British attitudes

Many people in Britain today, whether religious or not, agree with the Buddhist viewpoint that sexual acts should be loving and respectful, and that sex which is purely driven by physical desire may cause emotional harm to those involved. Many people in Britain believe this approach should apply equally to homosexual and heterosexual relationships, and to sexual relationships within or without marriage.

However, there are a wide range of views in British society about how sexuality should be expressed. Some people, including many Christians, believe that sex expresses a deep commitment that should be reserved for marriage. Some people wait to find someone they love before having sex, while others think that casual sex is fine, providing it doesn't cause any harm.

There has been considerable debate in the UK about whether Christian Churches should carry out same-sex marriages or not. Currently, same-sex marriage is legal in the UK, but same-sex couples are not allowed to get married in most churches. The Catholic Church teaches that homosexual acts are sinful and that homosexuals should refrain from having sex. This contrasts with the widely held view in British society that homosexuals should be entitled to the same rights as anyone else, including the right to marry and the right to have sexual relationships.

> ### Discussion activity
>
> Discuss with a partner why refraining from any type of sexual activity might help some Buddhists to achieve enlightenment.

> ### Contrasting beliefs
>
> Find out more about Christian beliefs about homosexual relationships. Do Christian beliefs agree or contrast with Buddhist beliefs about this issue?

> ### ⭐ Study tip
>
> Buddhism does not teach that sex is better or worse within marriage. It teaches the importance of kindness, generosity, contentment, honesty and awareness in all relationships. Therefore a marriage could be ethical or unethical, depending on the behaviour of the couple. So too could an unmarried relationship.

> ### Activities
>
> 1 Explain Buddhist attitudes towards same-sex relationships.
> 2 Describe how Buddhist attitudes towards sex differ between those in the lay community and those in the monastic community.

> **Summary**
>
> You should now be able to explain Buddhist attitudes towards human sexuality, including homosexual relationships.

■ Marriage in contemporary Britain

Marriage is a serious, lifelong, public commitment. It is a legal contract that brings security to a relationship and protects the rights of each partner. Until recently, marriage in the UK was defined as the legal union of a man and a woman. In 2004, same-sex couples were allowed to register their union in a **civil partnership** which gave them the same legal rights as married couples. **Same-sex marriages** became legal in England, Wales and Scotland in 2014, and in Ireland in 2015.

A growing number of couples in Britain choose to live together without getting married. This is called **cohabitation**.

■ The purpose of marriage for Buddhists

Buddhism does not view marriage as a religious duty or sacred act. This does not mean that Buddhism is against the idea of marriage, just that marriage is regarded as a social contract and not a religious rite. Marriage is a personal choice that a couple make for themselves. Buddhist weddings are secular, not religious, occasions – the couple are expected to follow the civil laws for marriage for whichever country they are getting married in. Monks may bless the marriage after the wedding ceremony, but they cannot conduct the ceremony itself.

Unlike some religions, having children is not viewed as an important purpose of marriage in Buddhism. Buddhists are not expected to feel any religious obligation or pressure to have children; it should purely be the personal choice of the couple. This contrasts with Christianity for example, and particularly Catholicism, where marriage is seen as the starting point for raising a family.

Buddhism teaches that everything is interrelated and interdependent. Buddhists believe this is true for people as well, and that strong, trusting relationships are important for the wellbeing of a community and society as a whole. Marriage is seen to play an important part in this, and for Buddhists it helps to cement the relationships that provide support, protection and happiness for the community.

■ Sex before and outside marriage

Sex before marriage is not forbidden in Buddhism. Individual Buddhists may believe in waiting until marriage to have sex, but this is more likely to be for personal reasons rather than religious ones, and is likely to be influenced by local customs and traditions. For many Buddhists

▲ *Monks may bless the couple in a Buddhist wedding, although they cannot conduct the ceremony itself*

the most important thing is to live by the five moral precepts, and to make sure that sexual acts are respectful and loving, with the full consent of both people involved. Likewise, views on cohabitation vary between Buddhists and in some societies it is not seen as acceptable, but this is not something that Buddhism teaches is wrong.

In contrast, religions such as Islam and Christianity teach that people should wait until marriage to have sex. They teach that sex expresses a deep, lifelong union that first requires the commitment of marriage, and that sex is part of the loving, trusting relationship that should be developed within a marriage. However, more liberal Christians sometimes accept that sex before marriage is a valid expression of a couple's love.

▲ In a traditional Thai wedding a white thread may be used to connect the couple together, symbolising the fact they are now united

Most Buddhists would regard **adultery** as unskilful, because it generally involves dishonesty, and does not show kindness towards or awareness of the feelings of the person being cheated on.

■ Same-sex marriage

Legally recognised same-sex marriage is a fairly recent development. It was first legalised in 2011 in the Netherlands, and only a minority of countries around the world have so far followed suit (including the UK). It is currently illegal in Asia. However, Buddhist teachings are not against same-sex marriage, and traditional Buddhist cultures that might have condemned same-sex marriage some years ago now seem to be changing slowly. In places such as Hong Kong, Taiwan, South Korea and Japan, there have been recent challenges to the law, to promote the view that the right to marriage should be equally available for heterosexual and homosexual couples.

> **Discussion activity**
>
> Discuss why Buddhists are generally accepting of same-sex relationships.

> **Activities**
>
> 1 'Religion is not important in a marriage ceremony.' Evaluate this statement. Include more than one point of view, and refer to Buddhist teachings and beliefs in your answer.
> 2 What do Buddhists believe about sex before marriage?
> 3 What does Buddhism teach about adultery?
> 4 Write a letter to the leader of a Buddhist country expressing the reasons why you think they should *or* should not legalise same-sex marriage.

> **Contrasting beliefs**
>
> Find out more about Christian teachings on sexual relationships before marriage. Do Christian beliefs agree or contrast with Buddhist beliefs on this issue?

> ⭐ **Study tip**
>
> Remember that Buddhist beliefs are likely to be influenced by local traditions and social norms. This means that a Buddhist in the UK might think differently to a Buddhist in China, because they were brought up in a different culture and environment.

> **Summary**
>
> You should now understand Buddhist attitudes towards marriage, sex before and outside marriage, cohabitation, and same-sex marriage.

■ What is contraception?

Contraception is a way of preventing pregnancy when a couple have sex. There are a range of different types of contraception available in Britain today, which prevent pregnancy from happening through various methods. These include:

- the pill, which stops the woman from producing an egg in the first place
- the diaphragm and the condom, which stop the sperm from meeting the egg
- the morning-after pill, which stops a fertilised egg from implanting in the womb – some people consider this method to be a form of abortion
- natural contraception, which involves only having sex at certain times in the woman's menstrual cycle, when she is less likely to conceive
- sterilisation, which involves a surgical operation and is more permanent.

■ Buddhist attitudes towards contraception and family planning

Buddhist traditions differ in their thinking about when consciousness arises in a new life. Some might say that it begins at conception (when the egg meets a sperm). Others might say that consciousness is continuous, from life to life. (We saw on pages 18–19 that Buddhism teaches the cycle of samsara: the repeating cycle of birth, life, death and rebirth.)

Most Buddhists believe it is fine to use forms of contraception that prevent fertilisation from taking place. Some Buddhists would consider contraception that works by preventing a fertilised egg from implanting in the womb (such as the morning-after pill) to be less acceptable. This is because they might see it as a form of killing, which breaks the first moral precept.

▲ Having children is not considered to be a sacred duty in Buddhism

On the other hand, if giving birth to a child might cause serious harm, for example by threatening the mother's life, or if she already has children she struggles to feed, then a Buddhist might decide to choose the morning-after pill as the lesser of two harms.

Although the Buddha taught all kinds of people, including parents, according to the early scriptures he did not recommend family life as the best path by which to reach enlightenment. Unlike in most other religions, having children is not regarded as a sacred duty for Buddhists. They are free to make their own choices about whether or not to have a family, but Buddhist teachings suggest that they should plan a family responsibly, and only have children if they can bring them up in a happy and safe environment.

■ Contrasting views

In Britain today there is widespread acceptance of the use of contraception in **family planning**. Many people think it is responsible to use contraception to prevent unwanted pregnancies, to control population growth, and to prevent the spread of sexually transmitted diseases.

▲ *Many different types of contraception are available in the UK today*

Some Christians – particularly Catholic and Orthodox Christians – oppose any artificial methods of contraception but accept natural ones. Catholics, for example, believe that one of the main purposes of sex is to create new life, therefore using artificial contraception cannot be accepted because it completely goes against this purpose. Other Christians accept the use of contraception. For example, the Church of England teaches that it is fine to use contraception to limit the number of children in a family.

Some people in Britain, including some Christians, believe that human life is created at the moment of conception. As a result they agree with the view of some Buddhists that contraception which prevents conception from taking place is acceptable, but contraception which prevents a fertilised egg from implanting in the womb is not.

Contrasting beliefs

Find out more about Christian teachings on contraception. Do Christian beliefs agree or contrast with Buddhist beliefs on this issue?

Discussion activity

Discuss with a partner how you think Buddhist views on contraception relate to Buddhist teaching.

Activities

1 Some Buddhists think that birth control is appropriate when additional children would place a burden on the family or their environment. Explain whether or not you agree with this, giving reasons why.

2 'Buddhists do not believe in a soul so should agree with all forms of contraception.' Evaluate this statement. Include more than one point of view, and refer to Buddhist beliefs and teachings in your answer.

3 How far do you agree with the view that sexual desire, like all desire, needs to be understood and controlled to avoid causing suffering to others?

Summary

You should now be able to explain Buddhist attitudes to contraception and family planning. You should also be able to contrast this with other religious and non-religious views on the same topic.

★ Study tip

Remember that Buddhists' views about contraception stem from their belief in the cycle of samsara and the first moral precept.

3.4 Divorce

Divorce in Britain

In 2012, it was estimated that 42 per cent of all marriages in England and Wales end in **divorce**. Divorce is allowed after one year of marriage if the marriage cannot be saved. A legally recognised civil divorce must be obtained through a court. **Remarriage** is allowed as many times as people wish, to a different partner or to their original spouse.

Why do couples get divorced? There are many different reasons why a marriage can fail. One of the most common causes of divorce is adultery. People can also change, grow apart and fall out of love. One partner may become ill, disabled or become addicted to alcohol, drugs or gambling. Work and money pressures can wear people down. A couple's inability to have children may put a strain on their marriage. Domestic violence or abuse can also cause the complete breakdown of a relationship.

Buddhist attitudes towards divorce

In Buddhism, there is no law stating that a husband and wife cannot be separated if they cannot live together harmoniously. However, Buddhism also teaches an approach to life that includes implied duties and responsibilities between a husband and wife. If followed, these are hoped to lead to a long and healthy relationship together.

Divorce rates are typically much lower in Buddhist countries than they are in the UK. One reason for this is that people in these countries more commonly get married later in life, when they tend to be more mature and more certain about what they want from a relationship. Another reason is that divorce is traditionally not approved of by society as a whole. This means that couples tend to put more effort into trying to mend a relationship, supported by the help of their family, friends and local community, because divorce is very much seen as a last resort.

Most Buddhists agree with this view of divorce. Through the help of Buddhist teachings – such as developing loving-kindness (see pages 68–69) and following the five moral precepts (see pages 70–71) – they would work hard to try to improve the marriage. Buddhists would only consider divorce when it is no longer possible to reconcile the relationship, and so divorce is preferable to living together and suffering. Most Buddhists would argue that clinging to an attachment that produces suffering goes against the Buddha's teaching. Divorce is an acceptable solution if it is seen to be the only way to reduce a couple's suffering.

Buddhism teaches that the best way to deal with divorce is to go about it sensibly and sensitively. It is likely that people will suffer as part of the process, but the couple should try to avoid anger and unkindness towards one another. Buddhism teaches that hurting another person

Objectives

- Examine Buddhist attitudes towards divorce.
- Understand contrasting views on divorce.

Key terms

- **divorce:** legal ending of a marriage
- **remarriage:** when someone marries again, after a previous marriage or marriages have come to an end

▲ Divorce rates are typically much lower in Buddhist countries than they are in the UK

Extension activity

Research the divorce rates in two Buddhist countries, and try to find views from people in both countries about divorce.

in the process of divorce can never make the person who is causing the hurt to be happy or satisfied.

As with divorce, views on remarriage vary between Buddhists in different countries and traditions, but it is not something that Buddhist teachings are against. For many Buddhists, remarriage can be seen as an opportunity for someone who has divorced to commit to a new relationship, creating happiness for themselves and their partner, and thus reducing people's suffering.

Discussion activity

Consider the reasons for divorce. Discuss with a partner what actions a couple could take to try to prevent a divorce from happening.

■ Other religious and non-religious viewpoints

Most non-religious people in Britain accept divorce and remarriage from a practical point of view. They argue that if a couple end up in a situation where they are causing each other (as well as any children they have) great emotional pain, divorce may be the best and most compassionate solution.

Some people in Britain argue that it is too easy to get divorced, and this means that people do not always try hard enough to make their marriage work.

▲ Many Buddhists think that divorce is preferable to living together and suffering as a couple

Religions differ in their approach to divorce. For example, within Christianity, the Catholic Church is strongly against divorce because of its beliefs in the sanctity of marriage. The Catholic Church teaches that because the marriage promises are made before God, they are sacred and should never be broken. If a Catholic gets divorced, they are not allowed to remarry in a Catholic church while their original partner is still alive. A Catholic who has remarried is not allowed to receive Holy Communion in a Catholic church.

Other Christian Churches, such as Anglicans and Methodists, do sometimes allow people who have been divorced to remarry, and do not stop them from receiving Holy Communion.

For most religious believers, divorce is seen as a last resort because it breaks the sanctity of the marriage vows, but it is sometimes the most compassionate solution if the relationship is causing harm and suffering to those involved.

⭐ Study tip

In addition to knowing Buddhist attitudes towards divorce, it is helpful to know what other religions say about divorce and whether they contrast with Buddhist views.

Activities

1 Explain how Buddhist beliefs about the following concepts might influence a Buddhist couple who are considering a divorce. Give reasons for your answers.

   a Dukkha   **b** Anatta   **c** Anicca

2 'Buddhists do not agree with divorce'. Evaluate this statement. Include more than one point of view, and refer to Buddhist beliefs and teachings in your answer.

Summary

You should now understand Buddhist attitudes towards divorce. You should also be aware of contrasting religious and non-religious viewpoints on this topic.

The nature of Buddhist families

Buddhism is not an especially **family**-centred religion. For Buddhists, there are no religious pressures or expectations to get married or to **procreate**. Both of these decisions should be a personal choice, although they may be influenced by the customs and traditions in the person's country.

Buddhist family life usually reflects what is normal for the family's country. For example, in Buddhist countries such as Thailand and Sri Lanka, **extended families** are very common. Parents, children, grandparents and other relatives may all live together, helping to raise the children and supporting one another in a large family unit. In the West, **nuclear families** are more common, consisting of a mother, father and their children living together.

The Buddha did not forbid **polygamy**, but he did suggest that it would probably cause suffering to those involved. The implication is that while polygamy is tolerated in Buddhism, it is not the favoured family model. However, the Buddha taught that if a family is built on respect and love for each other then it does not matter who it consists of, as long as it respects the laws of the family's country.

A similar approach can be taken to the issue of **same-sex parents**. Buddhist teachings suggest that the values, morals and love shown in a family are more important than the gender of the parents.

> **"** Social life begins with our parents; the intellect is cultivated through our teachers; family life is adjusted through experience; the world is appreciated through friends and relations; interdependence is realised through our employment and our final goal is achieved through spiritual guides. **"**
>
> Medagama Vajiragnana Nayaka Thera
> (former Head of the London Buddhist Vihara)

The purpose of Buddhist families

The Buddha gave no explicit rules about how family life should be conducted, but he did give advice on how families can live happily together, based on respect and love for one another. In Buddhist families, husbands and wives are expected to respect and honour each other, to cultivate love and trust towards each other, and to remain faithful to each other.

▲ *Buddhist parents teaching their children how to make offerings at a shrine*

Buddhist parents should love and care for their children, and provide a stable and safe environment in which they can grow up. They should try to practise the four sublime states (loving-kindness, compassion, sympathetic joy and equanimity) when raising their children. They are responsible for teaching their children good morals and values, and for giving them a good education. They should be able to support their children and make sure they are provided for in the future.

Parents are also responsible for ensuring their children are taught Buddhist beliefs and practices. Families usually have a shrine dedicated to the Buddha in their home, and they teach children how to show respect and gratitude to the Buddha in front of the shrine. Parents should also involve their children in the local religious community, attending services and participating in festivals.

Children are expected to be obedient and to respect their parents and other relatives. As they grow up, they are expected to preserve the traditions of the family. Later in life, they should support their parents when old age or illness become an issue.

◼ The family in contemporary British society

In the UK today the nuclear family is still the most common type, although approximately 25 per cent of children now live in single-parent families. There are also more stepfamilies, where divorced people with children marry new partners with children of their own. Same-sex couples may have children from previous relationships, legally adopt children, conceive through in vitro fertilisation (IVF), or use surrogates.

Many of the values and responsibilities that Buddhists aim to uphold within the family – such as love, respect, trust, and providing a good education – are similarly respected by many families in Britain today, regardless of their faith. There are some differences though between the values of Buddhism and other faiths. For example, greater emphasis is placed by Catholic Christians, Muslims and Sikhs on having children.

▲ *A young Buddhist performing puja in front of a family shrine*

Discussion activity

With a partner or in a small group, discuss what society would be like if families did not exist. How might newborn babies be cared for? Who would protect and raise children?

★ Study tip

Remember that the Buddha wanted his followers to think for themselves, rather than blindly follow religious rules. This is why Buddhism rarely dictates what people should do, but instead gives advice and suggestions on how to live happily without causing harm to others.

Summary

You should now understand the nature and purpose of families in Buddhism.

Activities

1 Do you think the following statements are true or false? Give reasons for your answers.

   a Buddhist parents are expected to have children.

   b Buddhism teaches that polygamy is OK if it does not cause any suffering to those involved.

   c Buddhism teaches that an extended family is a better environment to bring up children than a family with same-sex parents.

2 'Educating children in a faith is just brainwashing them.' Evaluate this statement. Include more than one point of view, and refer to Buddhist beliefs and teachings in your answer.

3.6 | Gender equality

■ Gender equality, prejudice and discrimination

Gender equality means that men and women should be given the same rights and opportunities as each other. Many people in Britain today agree with the idea of gender equality, but there are also many examples where it does not happen.

Gender prejudice is the attitude that women are not as good as men, or that men are not as good as women. It assumes that men or women should behave in a certain way, or have certain strengths or weaknesses because of their gender.

Gender discrimination turns this attitude into action and affects how people treat others. For example, an office manager might be prejudiced against women because he does not think they are as reliable as men. If he decides not to employ any women as a result, this is an example of gender discrimination.

■ Gender equality in Buddhism

In early Buddhism

During the time of the Buddha in ancient India, women were generally seen as inferior to men and had a very low position in society. They were not allowed to participate in religious life, had very limited freedom, were usually not allowed an education, and were primarily expected to act as housewives.

It is difficult to know what the Buddha's attitude was towards women because the scriptures containing his teachings are inconsistent. Historians are not sure whether these inconsistences come from the Buddha himself or those who later wrote down his teachings.

For example, although the scriptures show him teaching that women and men have equal potential for enlightenment, they also portray him as having originally refused to ordain women as nuns, saying that doing so would mean that his teachings would die out twice as fast. However, he did eventually agree to ordain women, having been asked again, this time by his aunt, who brought him up after the death of his mother. At the time, giving women this amount of religious freedom was very unusually liberal, and it can be argued that his initial reluctance stemmed from his understanding that, given women's low status, his teachings would be taken less seriously if associated with women.

The Aparimitayur Sutra suggests women must be reborn as men before they can achieve enlightenment. Some Buddhists still believe this today. In contrast, the Lotus Sutra teaches that men and women are equal in their ability to practise Buddhism and attain enlightenment.

Objectives

- Understand the differences between gender equality, prejudice and discrimination.
- Examine gender equality in Buddhism.

Key terms

- **gender equality:** the idea that people should be given the same rights and opportunities regardless of whether they are male or female
- **gender prejudice:** unfairly judging someone before the facts are known; holding biased opinions about an individual or group based on their gender
- **gender discrimination:** acting against someone on the basis of their gender; discrimination is usually seen as wrong and may be against the law

▲ In Thailand, women are more likely to work in low-paid, low-skilled jobs than men

In Buddhism today

There have been nuns in Mahayana Buddhism for many centuries. In contrast, in many parts of the Theravada tradition, the lineage for ordaining nuns has died out.

According to Buddhist monastic rules, a woman must be ordained by a certain number of monks and nuns from an unbroken line of ordained monks and nuns. This lineage has died out in some traditions. More conservative monks, particularly in the Theravada tradition, argue that women can therefore no longer be ordained.

Today things are changing. A growing number of Buddhists are challenging this situation or finding ways around it, and some women have been ordained within the Theravada tradition. Women are being ordained equally with men in some Asian traditions, by assembling the required number of senior nuns from other traditions. However, in general, nuns in Theravada Buddhism are still seen as being subservient to monks, and are not given the same respect and recognition.

In the UK, the Order of Buddhist Contemplatives (a Soto Zen tradition, founded by a British woman in 1978) ordains both women and men as 'monks'. The Triratna Buddhist Order (a neither lay nor monastic order) has also ordained women and men equally since its foundation in London in 1968. Moreover, many Western Buddhist organisations have recognised women as senior teachers without ordination. In 2015, the Dalai Lama (the most senior Tibetan Buddhist leader) said he believed there was no reason why a future Dalai Lama could not be a woman.

Many Buddhists today believe that men and women should and can have equal status within Buddhism. Where gender inequality still exists, it is mainly in more conservative traditions and countries, where it tends to reflect local belief and custom.

▲ *The Dalai Lama, the spiritual leader of Tibetan Buddhists, said there was no reason why his successor could not be a woman*

Research activities

1 Research the Buddha's attitudes and behaviour towards women. To what extent did the Buddha challenge the social customs of his time?

2 Research the status of women in a Buddhist country such as Thailand or Cambodia. What roles are women expected to fulfil in society?

▲ *In Theravada Buddhism, nuns who are not fully ordained wear white or pink robes*

★ Study tip

Make sure you can give examples of gender prejudice and discrimination as well as general explanations.

Activities

1 Explain the difference between gender prejudice and gender discrimination.

2 Explain Buddhist attitudes to gender equality.

3 Give an example of gender discrimination within Buddhism.

Summary

You should now be able to explain the terms gender equality, gender prejudice and gender discrimination. You should also be able to explain Buddhist attitudes towards these issues.

Sex, marriage and divorce – summary

You should now be able to:

✔ explain Buddhist teachings about human sexuality, including heterosexual and homosexual relationships

✔ explain Buddhist teachings about the nature and purpose of marriage

✔ explain Buddhist teachings about sexual relationships before and outside marriage

✔ explain Buddhist attitudes to family planning and the use of different forms of contraception

✔ explain reasons for divorce in Britain today, and Buddhist teachings about divorce and remarriage

✔ explain Buddhist attitudes to same-sex marriage and cohabitation.

Families and gender equality – summary

You should now be able to:

✔ explain Buddhist beliefs and teachings about the nature of families, the role of parents and children, and extended and nuclear families

✔ explain Buddhist attitudes to contemporary family issues, including polygamy and same-sex parents

✔ explain Buddhist beliefs and teachings about the purpose of families, including procreation, stability and protection of children, and educating children in a faith

✔ explain Buddhist teachings and attitudes towards gender equality, gender prejudice and discrimination, including examples

✔ explain similar and contrasting perspectives in contemporary British society to all the above issues

✔ explain similar and contrasting beliefs in contemporary British society about the three issues of homosexual relationships, sexual relationships before marriage and contraception, with reference to the main religious tradition in Britain (Christianity) and one or more other religious traditions.

Sample student answer – the 4-mark question

1. Write an answer to the following practice question:

   Explain two contrasting beliefs in contemporary British society about homosexuality.

   In your answer you should refer to the main religious tradition of Great Britain and one or more other religious traditions.   **[4 marks]**

2. Read the following sample student answer:

   "Buddhists seem to have no problem with homosexuality as it is never mentioned in the Buddha's teachings. The third moral precept is to abstain from sexual misconduct, but where there is mutual consent and as long as it does not involve adultery, Buddhists would say that homosexuality does not break the third precept. The Bible in Christianity though teaches that to engage in homosexual activity is wrong, so some Christians think that homosexual practice is wrong because of this."

3. With a partner, discuss the sample answer. Can you identify two contrasting points? Is there reference to the main religious tradition in Great Britain (Christianity) and at least one other religious tradition? Can it be improved? If so, how?

4. What mark (out of 4) would you give this answer? Look at the mark scheme in the introduction (AO1). What are the reasons for the mark you have given?

5. Now swap your answer with your partner's and mark each other's responses. What mark (out of 4) would you give the response? Refer to the mark scheme and give reasons for the mark you award.

Sample student answer – the 5-mark question

1. Write an answer to the following practice question:

   Explain **two** religious beliefs about divorce.

   Refer to sacred writings or another source of religious belief and teaching in your answer. **[5 marks]**

2. Read the following sample student answer:

   "Most people think it is fine to get a divorce as a last resort. They would say that it is better for people to split up than to make each other miserable by fighting and arguing all the time. This could affect the children and make them sad. However, if you are a Buddhist the important thing is to get rid of any suffering, so if the couple being together is causing suffering for the children, then Buddhists would suggest a divorce is the better option. Buddhism teaches that there are certain duties a husband has towards his wife and a wife has towards her husband, and if this is not working, then it would be better not to cause any more dukkha but to separate."

3. With a partner, discuss the student answer. Can you identify two religious beliefs about divorce? If so, are they simple or detailed? How accurate are they? Is there a clear reference to scripture or sacred writings? Is there anything important missing from the answer? How can it be improved?

4. What mark (out of 5) would you give this answer? Look at the mark scheme in the Introduction (AO1). What are the reasons for the mark you have given?

5. Now swap your answer with your partner's and mark each other's responses. What mark (out of 5) would you give the response? Refer to the mark scheme and give reasons for the mark you award.

Practice questions

1. Which **one** of the following is the name given to the practice in some religions of having more than one wife or husband?

   A) Procreation   **B)** Contraception   **C)** Stability   **D)** Polygamy   **[1 mark]**

2. Give **two** religious beliefs about the purpose of families. **[2 marks]**

3. Explain **two** contrasting beliefs in contemporary British society about sex before marriage.

   In your answer you must refer to one or more religious traditions. **[4 marks]**

4. Explain **two** religious beliefs about the nature of marriage.

   Refer to sacred writings or another source of religious belief and teaching in your answer. **[5 marks]**

5. 'Same-sex parents are just as good at bringing up children as other parents.'

   Evaluate this statement. In your answer you:
   - should give reasoned arguments to support this statement
   - should give reasoned arguments to support a different point of view
   - should refer to religious arguments
   - may refer to non-religious arguments
   - should reach a justified conclusion.   **[12 marks]**
   [+ 3 SPaG marks]

> ### ⭐ Study tip
>
> You should aim to develop two different points of view. Contrasting viewpoints can show differences between those who think that same-sex couples can fulfil the same purposes of family life for their children as other couples, and those who think that same-sex couples will not be able to fulfil some of those purposes.

4 Religion and life

4.1 The origins of the universe

■ The Big Bang theory

The **Big Bang** theory is currently the leading scientific explanation for how the universe began. This theory suggests that around 13.8 billion years ago, all matter was compressed into an incredibly small, hot and dense collection of mass. A massive expansion of space suddenly took place and the condensed matter was flung in all directions. It has been expanding ever since, forming the cosmos as we know it today. As the universe expanded and cooled, the matter that had been flung in all directions became stars grouped into millions of galaxies. The size of the universe is so enormous that, even with the most advanced telescope, astronomers are unable to see its end and see for certain if this theory is correct. Much of what scientists understand about the Big Bang theory comes from mathematical theory and models.

▲ Did the universe start with a massive expansion of space?

Objectives

● Understand the Big Bang theory.

● Explore Buddhist teachings about the origins of the universe.

Key term

● **Big Bang:** a massive expansion of space which set in motion the creation of the universe

■ Buddhist teachings about the origins of the universe

Buddhist teachings neither explicitly support nor deny the Big Bang theory. Buddhism teaches that all things are dependent upon conditions (this teaching is known as 'dependent arising' and is explained on pages 18–19). Buddhism also teaches about the cycle of samsara, which is the repeating cycle of birth, life, death and rebirth. Both of these teachings are relevant to Buddhist thinking about the origins of the universe.

Buddhism does not include belief in a God or creator. In fact, it does not teach that the universe has any origin – a point in time when the universe suddenly came into being from nothing without any cause. Instead, Buddhist teachings view the universe a bit like the cycle of life. They suggest that universes come into existence, expand and evolve, and then wither and die, over and over again without beginning or end. One universe simply replaces the next one.

This means that Buddhists can accept the Big Bang theory, which does not necessarily state that there was nothing before the Big Bang happened. Scientists are unsure about what caused the Big Bang. Some scientists believe that there might be a number of universes, creating one giant multiverse, where one universe grows out of another one. This idea is very similar to Buddhist teachings.

■ The story of the poisoned arrow

Buddhism does not view the origins of the universe as an important question. The Buddha himself declared it to be an unanswerable question. He said he taught only the way out of suffering, and wondering about the origins of the universe was not relevant to this. To illustrate his point he told the following story:

One day a man was hit by a poisoned arrow and would only live if a doctor removed it quickly enough. His friends found a doctor to remove the arrow, but the man refused the doctor's help. He first wanted to find out who had shot the arrow. He wanted to know what type of person they were, where they came from, and what sort of bow they were using. But before the man could find out the answers to these questions, the poison took effect and the man died.

Another way of thinking about this is to imagine what you would do if you were walking along a street and someone shot you in the leg. Would you first want to find out who shot you? Or would you want to find a way to stop the bleeding?

Summary

You should now understand Buddhist beliefs about the origins of the universe, and be able to explain how these relate to the Big Bang theory.

Discussion activity

Discuss with a partner whether you think it is important to try to answer questions about the origins of the universe. Do you think the Buddha should have been more concerned with finding out the answers to questions like this one?

Activities

1 In your own words, explain the Big Bang theory.

2 'Belief in the Big Bang theory goes against Buddhist teachings.' Evaluate this statement. Refer to Buddhist teachings and beliefs in your answer.

3 Explain the meaning of the story of the poisoned arrow.

★ **Study tip**

Remember that Buddhism is not anti-scientific, and there are plenty of Buddhist scientists. The Buddha's point was that wondering about the origins of the universe will not lead to the wisdom and compassion of enlightenment.

■ The theory of evolution

The theory of evolution is the leading scientific theory explaining how life began and then developed. It was first brought to the public's attention in 1859 when the scientist Charles Darwin published a book called *On the Origin of Species*. In this book Darwin suggested that all life in the world has gradually developed over billions of years from the first single-celled organisms. These organisms originally appeared in the sea. Over a long period of time they gradually evolved (changed) into other species.

Darwin argued that the earliest forms of life developed into more complex ones through the process of adaptation. In a population of animals, one animal might have slightly different characteristics that give it a better chance of survival than the rest. It will be more likely to reproduce and pass on those characteristics to its offspring. Over a very long period of time, these characteristics will gradually spread throughout the population and the species will change into a new one.

According to the theory of evolution, humans evolved from ape-like ancestors over a period of about six million years. Some Christians in England were outraged by this idea when Darwin first proposed it, because to them it seemed to go against Christian teachings about God creating the world and human life.

■ Buddhist views on the origins of life

Though early Buddhist scriptures do contain creation stories, most Buddhists would regard these as mythological and not to be taken literally. Instead they accept current scientific thinking about how the Earth and life on it came into existence.

The Buddha said that anything can come into existence when all the necessary conditions are there. When those conditions change, so do the things they give rise to. For example, seeds germinate and grow into plants when light, oxygen and moisture are present, and they die when any of those conditions are removed. This just happens. No creator or God makes it happen. This means that Buddhists do not use the terms 'creator' or 'creation'.

It is the same with the Earth and life on it. Buddhism teaches that it is not possible to identify a beginning or end to the Earth as we know it. We don't know what came before it, but at some point atmospheric conditions caused it to come into being. Then when the conditions were right on Earth, plants and animals came into being. Life on Earth has continued to evolve ever since. Today, conditions continue to change, and we can see the effect on plant and animal life. As with everything else, Buddhists would say the Earth is not a fixed thing. It is in a constant process of change, millions of years old.

Objectives

- Understand Buddhist teachings about the origins of life.
- Understand Buddhist teachings about the sanctity of life and quality of life.

Key terms

- **the theory of evolution:** the theory that higher forms of life have gradually developed from lower ones
- **adaptation:** a process of change, in which an organism or species becomes better suited to its environment
- **sanctity of life:** the belief that all life is holy or deeply valuable, and should not be misused or abused
- **quality of life:** the general wellbeing of a person, in relation to their health and happiness; also, the theory that the value of life depends upon how good or how satisfying it is

▲ *Buddhism teaches that Earth is in a constant process of change*

> ❝ For here there is no Brahma God,
> Creator of the round of births,
> Phenomena alone flow on –
> Cause and component their condition. ❞
>
> The *Visuddhimagga,* p. 603

Activities

1 Explain the main ideas of Darwin's theory of evolution.

2 What do you think the Buddha would have said about Charles Darwin's theory if he had known about it?

3 Why do Buddhists view human life as being more valuable than other types of life?

■ Buddhist views on the sanctity and quality of life

Sanctity of life

Sanctity of life is not really a Buddhist term. It comes from Christianity, which regards all life as holy and valuable because it is created by God. Although Buddhism does not see things as having been created by a god, it certainly teaches the importance of acting with kindness, compassion and wisdom towards all living things. Buddhists are especially careful about how they act towards 'sentient beings', things that have consciousness and feelings, and can therefore suffer.

Discussion activity

Discuss with a partner what you think is needed for a good quality of life. Would Buddhists agree or disagree with your views?

A traditional Buddhist view is that every sentient being is valuable because it has the potential to be reborn with an ever-more sophisticated consciousness, eventually being born as human with the potential to attain enlightenment. Buddhism teaches that human life is the most valuable because humans are more self-aware. They are more able than any other species to reflect on their behaviour and make choices about how to live. This means that humans have greater potential to develop the perfect wisdom and compassion of enlightenment, like the Buddha.

▲ *Buddhism teaches that human life is the most valuable because humans have the greatest potential to develop compassion and wisdom*

Quality of life

Buddhist tradition says that a good **quality of life** has nothing to do with being rich and having whatever you want. It is about living with awareness of oneself, others and the world. This has an effect on people's relationships with others, and the way they see themselves in relation to society. Buddhism teaches that feeling a connectedness with others and being aware of all the beautiful things in life can give people a sense of meaning.

Of course, without basic needs such as shelter, clothing and food, it is hard to have a good quality of life. However, beyond those things, Buddhists believe that wellbeing comes from accepting the fact that suffering is a normal part of life, and from doing one's best to live by the values in the five moral precepts.

⭐ Study tip

Buddhist teachings about dependent arising (see page 18) can help to explain Buddhist views on the origins of life.

Summary

You should now be able to explain the theory of evolution, and say why most Buddhists accept this. You should also be able to explain Buddhist views on the quality and sanctity of life.

■ Why the world is of value to Buddhists

The world is where we live, and it provides and sustains life. We need its resources in order to provide food, shelter, clothing and other basic necessities for ourselves. Buddhism teaches that the world is a valuable thing that belongs to nobody, but is everybody's **responsibility**.

There are two further reasons why Buddhists might consider the world to be so valuable:

- The world provides Buddhists with all the conditions (challenges and help) that are needed in order to develop perfect wisdom and compassion, to become enlightened, and to free oneself from suffering.

- The Buddha taught that there are other worlds into which it is possible to be born. Buddhist tradition teaches that to be born a human, in this particular world, is enormously fortunate, and follows many lives in other, less conscious forms. Humans are able to make ethical choices not available to other species, and thus move towards enlightenment. In this world, there was once a Buddha who explained the origins of suffering and the way to end it. Had people been born in another time and world, they might never have heard this teaching.

Of course, some people in this world are much more fortunate than others. Buddhist tradition says that anyone who lives in a country free from war, where most people have enough to eat, where there is education and healthcare for everyone – and where it is possible to hear the teaching of the Buddha – is among the world's most fortunate people, even if they are not rich. For all these reasons, and because they live in a society in which people are free to follow whichever faith they prefer (or none), Buddhists in Britain often say they are among the world's most fortunate people.

▲ Are people living in Britain among the world's most fortunate people?

> ❝ Where shall I find such favourable circumstances again?
>
> The arising of a Buddha,
>
> Faith, the human state itself,
>
> The capacity to practise skilful deeds,
>
> Health and this day
>
> With food and freedom from disaster. ❞
>
> The *Bodhicaryavatara*, chapter 4, verses 15–16

■ Stewardship and responsibility

Sometimes people of other religions talk about **stewardship** of the Earth, but this is not a Buddhist term. Traditionally a steward was someone who was paid to take care of land on behalf of its owner. Christians, for example, see the Earth as belonging to God, who has **dominion** over it and who has trusted them to look after it for him. Buddhism, however, does not involve belief in a creator God to whom all things belong. In the Buddhist view, nobody owns the Earth.

The Buddha never talked of how the world came into being, or who owned it. He said it is just a fact that it is here and so are we. Knowing this, it is people's responsibility to develop more and more wisdom and compassion to move towards enlightenment. Buddhists also accept that humans need to take responsibility for protecting the environment and caring for all living beings.

■ Awe and wonder

We live in a universe that is complex and mysterious. There is plenty to **wonder** at, even if nobody created it. In fact, Buddhists might say it was even more amazing that such a thing just happened without being created by anyone.

The Buddha's teaching of dependent arising is also very mysterious: if absolutely everything happens because of other things, they must be interconnected in millions of ways that nobody can even imagine. For Buddhists, this means that humans live in a vast web of interconnectedness with nature, people and all sorts of things, through time and space.

Buddhists often talk about the importance of developing 'mindfulness' – appreciative, non-judgemental awareness. Buddhists believe that this appreciative awareness of every passing moment can bring people deep enjoyment of the beauty and mystery in ordinary life, as well as helping people to be calm and less shaken by life's difficulties.

▲ *Through practising mindfulness and meditation, Buddhists can learn to better appreciate the beauty and mystery in the world*

Discussion activity

Imagine a world owned by nobody, in which nobody is in charge. With a partner, discuss what kind of problems and advantages this might have. Which Buddhist teachings could help people live together in this world in such a way as to make it enjoyable for the greatest number of people?

Activities

1 Give two reasons why the world is valuable to Buddhists.

2 Do you think everyone should take equal responsibility to look after the Earth? Or should some people take more responsibility than others? Explain your opinion.

3 Explain how mindfulness can help Buddhists to enjoy the world more.

Extension activity

How do the actions of people in the past still affect you today? Thinking about the history of the area where you live, identify three things local people did in the past that still affect you and your community now. They may be to do with architecture or services such as your library, or industry or government.

★ Study tip

It is important to understand that while Buddhism does not teach about the concept of stewardship, Buddhists accept that humans need to take responsibility for protecting the environment and caring for all living beings.

Summary

You should now be able to explain why Buddhists think the world is valuable.

4.4 The use and abuse of the environment

The use and abuse of the environment

The rapid growth in the world's population is putting the **environment** under extreme pressure. Two of the major environmental problems facing people today are the increase in **pollution** and the increase in the consumption of **natural resources**.

Pollution damages the environment and contributes to global warming. It can come in many forms. Fumes from factories and vehicles can contribute to global warming and acid rain. Waste that is dumped into the sea can have a devastating effect on marine life. Chemicals that get into the ground can poison wildlife and contaminate people's food. Despite laws to limit pollution and attempts to clean up the environment, it continues to be a problem as technology advances and the world's population grows.

Earth's growing population also means that natural resources are being used up more quickly. These are materials that are found in nature which can be used by people to make more complex products. Many natural resources are non-renewable. This means that the world cannot produce them as quickly as people are using them up. For example, oil is a very valuable natural resource that takes millions of years to form in the ground. At the rate of current consumption, it is estimated that there is enough oil left for about 50 years. After this the world may have to adapt considerably in order to live without it.

Buddhist reasons for protecting the environment

Many Buddhists are aware of the importance of avoiding damage to their environment. Here are some of the reasons why:

1. The concept of dependent arising teaches that everything depends on other things. We live in a complex network of people, animals and plants, all of whom depend in various ways on a healthy planet to survive.

2. The second noble truth is that suffering is caused by greed. The Buddha encouraged people to practise contentment, having just as much as they need for a simple but dignified life. Taking too much from the environment goes against this teaching.

3. The first of the five moral precepts is to avoid causing harm to any living being. This means looking after the Earth so that other people and living things, and those who come after us, can have a planet worth living on.

> **Objective**
> - Understand Buddhist beliefs about the use and abuse of the environment.

> **Key terms**
> - **environment:** the natural world; the surroundings in which someone lives
> - **pollution:** making something dirty and contaminated, especially the environment
> - **natural resources:** materials found in nature – such as oil and trees – that can be used by people

> 66 I believe that not only should we keep our relationship with our other fellow human beings very gentle and non-violent, but it is also very important to extend that kind of attitude to the natural environment. 99
>
> Tenzin Gyatso
> (the Dalai Lama)

▲ *Buddhists in Cambodia ordaining trees, to help protect the forest from those who want to cut it down*

4. Making efforts to care for others is part of the Buddhist path of training that leads people gradually towards enlightenment. This includes caring for the Earth and everything that depends on it.

> ❝ In order to protect the environment we must protect ourselves. We protect ourselves by opposing selfishness with generosity, ignorance with wisdom, and hatred with loving kindness. Selflessness, mindfulness, compassion and wisdom are the essence of Buddhism. We train in Buddhist meditation which enables us to be aware of the effects of our actions, including those destructive to our environment. ❞
>
> *Faith in Conservation* (Palmer and Finlay)

The Holy Isle Project

Holy Isle is a small island off the west coast of Scotland. Lama Yeshe Rinpoche, a Tibetan Buddhist, set up a centre on the island called the Centre for World Peace and Health, which is used to hold Buddhist retreats and courses.

Taking care of the island's natural environment is very important to the Buddhists who live and work there. The centre itself has been built with the environment in mind. For example, all the insulation materials are environmentally friendly, and a lot of the furniture was made using oak from a sustainable forest source. Buddhists have also been looking after the environment of the island in other ways, for example:

- 35,000 trees have been planted on the island to create a woodland habitat that will provide shelter for wildlife and encourage biodiversity.
- Local resources such as seaweed and manure are being used to restore the soils on the island.
- Water conservation is encouraged, particularly during the summer, and all the water that supplies the centre is collected from rain-fed natural springs.
- The east coast of the island has been turned into a nature sanctuary to help protect local animals, birds and sea life.

Activities

1 Explain why the growth in the world's population is putting the environment under more pressure.
2 Give three reasons why Buddhists think it is important to look after the environment.

Discussion activities

1 Look at the quote to the left from the book *Faith in Conservation*. Do you agree that getting people to develop qualities such as generosity, compassion and wisdom is the best way to protect the environment?

2 The Buddha taught that greed, hatred and ignorance are the main causes of suffering. How might this belief affect the way a Buddhist interacts with their environment?

Research activity

Around the world many Buddhists are working on environmental issues, including Buddhists in Britain. Use the internet to find out about the following:

- Buddhist Action Month (June) – an annual British festival of Buddhist social action which began in 2012 and is spreading to other countries
- the Dharma Action Network on Climate Engagement (DANCE)
- the Sarvodaya movement in Asia.

⭐ Study tip

Remember that the Buddha taught that all things are impermanent, meaning it is natural for things to change all the time. The Earth has been through many climate changes already. So a Buddhist approach to climate change might focus not so much on the fact that the climate is changing, but on the fact that this change (which will cause enormous suffering to many living things, including people) appears to be caused by avoidable human greed.

Summary

You should now understand Buddhist attitudes towards looking after the environment, and be able to give examples of Buddhist environmental projects.

Buddhist attitudes towards animals

The kind treatment of animals has always been important in Buddhism. Most Buddhists will try to show loving-kindness (metta) and compassion (karuna) in all their dealings with animals. Some of the reasons for this include the following:

- The first moral precept teaches that Buddhists should not kill or harm any living beings, including animals.
- The Eightfold Path teaches that Buddhists should not make a living from work that harms others, including animals.
- Treating animals cruelly is unskilful and will lead to suffering. Treating animals with kindness and compassion is skilful and will lead to happiness, and even a favourable rebirth.
- Many Buddhists believe they could be reborn as animals. This means that any animal may have been a Buddhist in a past life.
- The lives of humans and animals are so closely related and interwoven that it makes no sense to treat animals cruelly, because this could have a negative effect on society as a whole.

▲ Buddhists try to treat animals with kindness and compassion

Buddhism and animal experimentation

Scientists conduct experiments on animals to check that new products, such as medicines, cosmetics and additives used in processed foods, are safe to use on humans. Testing cosmetics on animals was banned in the UK in 1998, and other types of animal testing have been reduced as scientists have developed alternative methods using computers or cell culture (cells that are grown artificially). Most animal experiments that still occur are on mice or rats that have been specially bred for the purpose.

Buddhists differ in their opinions about animal testing. Some argue against it because of the reasons given above for why Buddhists believe

Objectives

- Examine Buddhist beliefs about the use and abuse of animals.
- Understand Buddhist attitudes towards animal experimentation and the use of animals for food.

Key terms

- **vegetarian:** a person who does not eat meat or fish
- **vegan:** a person who does not eat animals or food produced by animals (such as eggs); a vegan tries not to use any products that have caused harm to animals (such as leather)

Contrasting beliefs

Some Christians agree with animal experimentation because the Bible teaches that humans have more value than animals, therefore if animal testing can help to save human lives then it is worth it. Other Christians disagree with animal experimentation because all animals are made by God and should be respected. They argue that there are better methods for testing medicines and (in particular) cosmetics.

Find out more about Christian teachings on animal experimentation. Do Christian beliefs agree or contrast with Buddhist beliefs on this issue?

in the kind treatment of animals. They feel there are alternative methods that scientists can use which do not result in animal cruelty. Others argue for it because they are aware that using animals to develop new drugs may benefit millions of people and save many lives. They believe that animal experimentation is important for developing medicines that help to reduce people's suffering, without causing any lethal side effects. Many Buddhists adopt an approach that animal testing is acceptable where it is absolutely necessary (i.e. there is no other safe alternative), and it is carried out as caringly as possible.

Discussion activity

Discuss with a partner whether you think a Buddhist might agree with animal experimentation if it meant that a cure could be found for a disease that badly affected humans, such as cancer.

Buddhism and vegetarianism

There are differing views in Buddhism about whether eating meat should be allowed. These seem to stem from inconsistencies in the Buddhist scriptures. For example, a number of scriptures include references to the Buddha and his monks eating meat. In Theravada Buddhism, the rules that monks and nuns have to follow (the Patimokkha) state that monks and nuns who rely on the donations and generosity of others to live – including gifts of food – should not be picky about what type of food they accept. Meat is fine to eat as long as the animal has not been killed on the monk or nun's behalf.

▲ *Many Buddhists are vegetarian or vegan*

In contrast, various Mahayana scriptures, including the Lankavatara Sutra and Mahaparinirvana Sutra, state that the Buddha insisted his followers should not eat any meat or fish, and that eating meat has negative effects. These scriptures argue that eating meat does not show compassion (an essential quality for achieving enlightenment), and that it spreads an atmosphere of fear among all living beings.

> ❝ All tremble at violence; all fear death. Comparing [others] with oneself, one should not kill or cause to kill. ❞
>
> The Buddha in the *Dhammapada*, verse 129

In practice, many Buddhists are **vegetarian** or **vegan**, particularly those in the Mahayana tradition. Buddhists who do eat meat might argue that:

- the Buddha would have been clearer about his views on eating meat if he thought that vegetarianism was important for achieving enlightenment
- a person's diet is not an important factor in spiritual enlightenment
- when a person eats meat, they are not directly responsible for the animal's death (unless they have actually killed the animal they are eating themselves, which almost all Buddhists would refuse to do).

Activities

1 Give three reasons why many Buddhists think it is important to treat animals kindly.

2 What do Buddhist scriptures say about eating meat?

⭐ **Study tip**

Learn some of the reasons why Buddhists and Christians either agree or disagree with animal experimentation.

Summary

You should now be able to explain Buddhist attitudes towards animals, including views on animal experimentation and vegetarianism.

■ Abortion in the UK

Abortion is the removal of a foetus from the womb to end a pregnancy before the child is born. This happens naturally when a woman has a miscarriage, but abortion usually refers to the deliberate termination of a pregnancy through a medical procedure.

Before 1967 abortion was illegal in the UK. It is now allowed up to the twenty-fourth week of pregnancy in a licensed clinic if two doctors agree that one of the following conditions applies:

- The woman's life is in danger if the pregnancy continues.
- There is a risk to the woman's physical and mental health.
- There is a significant risk that the baby will be born with severe physical or mental disabilities.
- An additional child may affect the physical or mental health of existing children in the family.

There is no time limit if the mother's life is in danger or if the foetus is severely deformed.

■ Buddhist views about abortion

The first moral precept teaches that Buddhists should try to avoid killing, because it causes suffering to oneself and others. Buddhists vary in their thinking about when conscious life begins. Some believe it begins at the moment of conception, and others believe that consciousness is an unbroken flow from life to life. Either way, most Buddhists see abortion as a form of killing and therefore unskilful. The Buddha taught that unskilful behaviour is behaviour which does not lead towards the happiness, wisdom and compassion of enlightenment.

However, the five moral precepts are considered to be guidelines rather than commandments or rules that one either gets wrong or right. The Buddha wanted people to apply the five moral precepts thoughtfully, with sensitivity and flexibility depending on the situation.

Abortion throws up a variety of complex ethical issues and no two cases are the same. Some Buddhists may feel that abortion is always unskilful. However, they may also feel that in a particular situation, having an abortion would be the best thing to do. An example might be if the baby is likely to be born with a serious disability, or if the mother already has several children she can hardly afford to care for, so the new child will have a poor quality of life as a result.

Many Buddhists want to judge each situation on its own merits, and act in a way to minimise the suffering of those involved. They consider the potential emotional and physical suffering of both the

> **Objectives**
>
> - Examine Buddhist attitudes towards abortion.
> - Consider arguments for and against abortion.

> **Key term**
>
> - **abortion:** the removal of a foetus from the womb to end a pregnancy, usually before the foetus is 24 weeks old

> **Discussion activity**
>
> Buddhism teaches that the motivation or intention behind an action is very important. Discuss how you think this relates to abortion.

▲ *A computer-generated model of a 24-week-old foetus. In most cases, abortion is legal in England up to 24 weeks.*

parents and the child. This sometimes means balancing two kinds of harm and choosing which one seems lesser.

We have also seen how personal choice is important in Buddhism. This means that while holding strong values about kindness and care, many Buddhists believe that deciding whether or not to have an abortion is a personal choice. Buddhist views on abortion also vary from country to country depending on social norms and traditions.

▲ *Most Buddhists see abortion as breaking the first moral precept*

■ Arguments for and against abortion

Pro-choice groups, such as Abortion Rights, believe that human life does not truly start until birth, or at the moment when the foetus becomes able to survive outside the womb. They argue that this means the mother's life is more valuable and should come first. They might say that since the mother carries the baby, goes through childbirth and looks after the child, she should have the right to choose whether she continues the pregnancy. These groups also believe it is cruel to bring a severely disabled child into the world if they will have a poor quality of life as a result.

Pro-life groups, such as the Society for the Protection of the Unborn Child (SPUC), argue that life begins at the moment of conception and abortion is therefore a form of murder. They believe that disabled people can enjoy a good quality of life with the right support, and that unwanted children could be adopted by those who are unable to have children of their own.

Research activity

The Japanese have a ceremony called mizuko kuyo, which is for mothers who have had a stillbirth, miscarriage or abortion. Research this ceremony and make some brief notes about it. What does it tell you about Buddhist attitudes towards abortion in Japan?

Activities

1 Explain why Buddhists may take a variety of views on abortion.

2 The Japanese Buddhist Nichiren once said that 'life is the most precious of all treasures'. Do you agree with this statement? Explain how it relates to abortion.

3 'Buddhists who have abortions contradict themselves. They cannot claim to follow the first moral precept, that people should not harm other living beings, and then tolerate abortion.' Evaluate this statement. Include more than one point of view, and refer to Buddhist beliefs and teachings in your answer.

Contrasting beliefs

Research Christian beliefs about abortion. Do they agree or contrast with Buddhist beliefs?

★ Study tip

When thinking about Buddhist attitudes towards abortion, consider the difference that a belief in kamma might make.

Summary

You should now be able to discuss arguments for and against abortion, and be able to identify Buddhist views on both sides.

4.7 Euthanasia

What is euthanasia?

Euthanasia is a term that means 'good death'. It describes a situation in which someone helps another person to die by deliberately administering life-ending medication. For example, if a doctor deliberately gives a patient a lethal injection because the patient is suffering, and their condition has no cure or hope of improvement, this is euthanasia.

There are three main types of euthanasia:

- **Voluntary euthanasia** is when a person asks a doctor to end their life because they do not wish to live anymore. This is their own choice.

- **Non-voluntary euthanasia** is when the person is too ill to request to die, but a doctor ends their life for them because this is thought to be in their best interests.

- **Involuntary euthanasia** is when the person is able to provide consent but does not, either because they do not want to or because they are not asked, but their life is ended anyway.

Euthanasia is sometimes described as 'active euthanasia' because it involves active, deliberate steps to end a person's life. Active euthanasia is illegal in the UK and treated as murder or manslaughter. Doctors can also decide to withhold or withdraw medical treatment or life support that is keeping the person alive because they are not going to get better, or because the person asks them to. Medical professionals call this a non-treatment decision. Controversially it is also sometimes called passive euthanasia.

Buddhist attitudes towards euthanasia

Many Buddhists are against euthanasia because it breaks the first moral precept. However, views towards euthanasia vary between Buddhists and may depend on the circumstances in which euthanasia is carried out. Buddhists would be guided by the following considerations when deciding what they think about euthanasia.

The first moral precept

The first moral precept states that Buddhists should not kill or harm any living being. Many Buddhists are against euthanasia for this reason.

Personal choice

Buddhism emphasises personal choice and responsibility. Some Buddhists argue that if a person has a clear mind and is not affected by any outside pressure, they should be allowed to choose what to do with their own life, including whether to end it or not.

Discussion activity

The Human Rights Act means that everyone in the UK has a right to live. Discuss with a partner whether or not you think that people should also have a right to die.

Kamma, rebirth and suffering

Buddhism teaches that when a person dies, their consciousness passes on into a new life. According to the teaching of kamma, in this new life a person will experience the consequences of the skilful or unskilful actions in their previous lives. This could mean that the person being reborn would suffer as a consequence of the forced ending of their previous life.

Compassion

Compassion is an important quality for Buddhists. Some Buddhists would argue that it is compassionate to help someone to die, to end their suffering. Others might argue, also out of compassion, that ending a person's life may relieve their suffering in the short term, but lead to more suffering in the future.

State of mind

Buddhism teaches that it is important to have a calm and positive state of mind at the moment of death, as this is something that influences a person's rebirth. If a person is helped to die quickly and peacefully, it could be argued that this is beneficial for their future consciousness. Equally, there may be other times when euthanasia is chosen for the wrong reasons, because a person's suffering is negatively influencing their state of mind. In such instances it might be better to use meditation, combined with strong painkillers, for example, to manage pain while gradually approaching a natural death.

▲ Hospices provide valuable care for the dying

All of these factors and more influence a Buddhist's approach to euthanasia. Many Buddhists' attitudes towards this issue can be summed up by the Dalai Lama's thoughts. In 1993 he said that it was best to avoid euthanasia except in exceptional circumstances (such as when a person is in a coma with no hope of recovery), and that it should be considered on a case-by-case basis.

Contrasting beliefs

Like Buddhists, Christians differ in their views on euthanasia. Some believe that God has given people the free will to choose when to end their lives, and that euthanasia is sometimes the most compassionate option. Many others believe that only God has the right to take life away, and that quickening a person's death interferes with God's plan.

Find out more about Christian teachings on euthanasia. Do Christian beliefs agree or contrast with Buddhist beliefs on this issue?

Activities

1   Explain the difference between euthanasia and a non-treatment decision.

2   Give two reasons why Buddhists might find euthanasia unacceptable, and two reasons why they might consider it the best course of action in some circumstances.

★ Study tip

Remember that Buddhist ethics are never just about 'wrong' or 'right'. They are about what is most 'skilful' or 'unskilful' in a life committed to developing wisdom and compassion.

Summary

You should now be able to explain Buddhist attitudes towards euthanasia, including arguments for and against euthanasia.

4.8 Death and the afterlife

Celebrating a human life

Just like anyone else, Buddhists experience grief and loss at the death of people they love or admire. It may take them a long time to get over their loss, even if they are used to thinking about life as change and impermanence, and death as another example of this. Even for someone who is very at home with the idea of death, it will be important to celebrate the qualities and achievements of the person who has died and express gratitude for their life. This is a very important part of saying goodbye and reminding people of the meaning of a human life.

Buddhist teachings about death

Buddhist traditions differ on what exactly happens when a person dies. However, most teach that death is not a single final moment but a process of transition in which consciousness passes on from the physical body over a period of hours or days.

This means it is important to most Buddhists that a person dies as peacefully as possible, and that the body is left in peace for many hours after the point at which medical opinion would regard the person as dead. The question is, what happens next?

Rebirth

Some Buddhists today doubt the possibility of rebirth. However, most traditions teach that for those who are not yet perfect in wisdom and compassion, there are more lives to live in which to keep making progress towards enlightenment. So, in some mysterious way, days, weeks or months after death, the dead person's consciousness enters another life at the point of its conception.

> **Objective**
> - Understand Buddhist teachings about death and an afterlife.

> **Links**
>
> To read more about rebirth and the cycle of samsara see pages 18–19.

▲ Buddhism teaches that after a person dies, their consciousness enters a new life

What then happens is said to depend partly on the skilful or unskilful habits cultivated in this lifetime and previous lives. Traditionally, skilful behaviour is said to help Buddhists to build up a store of 'merit'. This merit will lead to good fortune in future lives.

> **❝** At the hour of death, the king and the beggar are exactly equal in that no amount of relatives or possessions can affect or prevent death. But who is the richer at the time of death? If the beggar has created more merits, then although he looks materially poor he is really the rich man. **❞**
>
> Thubten Zopa Rinpoche (Nepalese Buddhist monk)

Many Buddhists believe that what happens after death depends strongly on their state of mind when they die. Particularly in Tibetan Buddhism it is believed that, as consciousness leaves the body, there is an opportunity to choose the freedom of enlightenment instead of another human life. For both these reasons, and also because death can occur at any time, it is believed to be important to do one's best to live kindly and with awareness in every moment.

Enlightenment

The Buddha said he had lived many lives before he reached the life in which he became the Buddha. Life after life, becoming more and more kind, more fearless, more generous and more subtly conscious, he progressed towards Buddhahood. Following his enlightenment, there were no more physical lives to live. The Buddha broke the cycle of samsara – once he achieved enlightenment and then died, he was not reborn in a physical body. Nothing more can be said about what happens to an enlightened Buddhist after death, since nobody knows what happens; the Buddha himself refused to say what happens after death to someone who has been enlightened.

▲ A statue of the Buddha in the final days before his death

The origins and value of the universe – summary

You should now be able to:

✔ explain Buddhist teachings about the origins of the universe, and how these relate to religious and scientific views (such as the Big Bang theory)

✔ explain Buddhist teachings about the value of the world and the duty of humans to protect it, including the ideas of stewardship, dominion, responsibility, awe and wonder

✔ explain Buddhist attitudes towards the use and abuse of the environment, including pollution and the use of natural resources

✔ explain Buddhist attitudes towards the use and abuse of animals, including animal experimentation and the use of animals for food.

The origins and value of human life – summary

You should now be able to:

✔ explain Buddhist teachings about the origins of life, and how these relate to religious and scientific views (such as evolution)

✔ explain the concepts of sanctity of life and the quality of life

✔ explain Buddhist attitudes towards abortion

✔ explain Buddhist attitudes towards euthanasia

✔ explain Buddhist teachings about death and an afterlife, and their impact on beliefs about the value of human life

✔ explain similar and contrasting perspectives in contemporary British society to all the above issues

✔ explain similar and contrasting beliefs in contemporary British society to the three issues of abortion, euthanasia and animal experimentation, with reference to the main religious tradition in Britain (Christianity) and one or more religious traditions.

Sample student answer – the 12-mark question

1. Write an answer to the following practice question:

   'There must be life after death.'

   Evaluate this statement. In your answer you:
   - should give reasoned arguments to support this statement
   - should give reasoned arguments to support a different point of view
   - should refer to religious arguments
   - may refer to non-religious arguments
   - should reach a justified conclusion.

   [12 marks]
   [+ 3 SPaG marks]

2. Read the following sample student answer:

   "People who are religious might say what would be the purpose of life if there isn't something after it? If there isn't then we can be totally selfish and do exactly what we want, as long as we don't break the law. We don't have to worry about any consequences in an afterlife. People could just think about themselves and their own happiness without worrying about anyone else.

   Buddhists don't believe there's a God who judges you when you die, but they do believe in kamma and rebirth. Buddhists think that when you die your consciousness gets reborn in another body. This could be human or animal or something else. What sort of body it is and the quality of the new life depends on how well they behaved in their old life. Then when a Buddhist becomes enlightened they aren't reborn anymore and go to nibbana, which is like heaven but without God. Buddhists think this is true because it's what happened to the Buddha.

Christians believe that there must be life after death because Jesus died on a cross and came back to life three days later. This proves that life after death exists. Jesus also taught that people will go to heaven or hell, depending on how well they've lived their lives.

Atheists don't think there is life after death. They think you just die and that's it. They would say that you can't prove there's life after death because no one's died and then communicated with living people.

Lots of religious people would say there must be life after death, because that's what their religions teach, like heaven in Christianity and rebirth in Buddhism. But this doesn't mean there definitely is life after death."

3. With a partner, discuss the sample answer. Is the focus of the answer correct? Is anything missing from the answer? How do you think it could be improved?

4. What mark (out of 12) would you give this answer? Look at the mark scheme in the Introduction (AO2). What are the reasons for the mark you have given?

5. Swap your answer with your partner's and mark each other's responses. What mark (out of 12) would you give? Refer to the mark scheme and give reasons for the mark you award.

Practice questions

1. Which **one** of the following refers to the belief that there is a duty to look after the world on behalf of God?

   A) Euthanasia   **B)** Dominion   **C)** Stewardship   **D)** Awe   [1 mark]

2. Give **two** reasons why religious believers might oppose animal experimentation.   [2 marks]

3. Explain **two** contrasting beliefs in contemporary British society about euthanasia.

   In your answer you must refer to one or more religious traditions.   [4 marks]

4. Explain **two** religious beliefs about what happens when a person dies.

   Refer to sacred writings or another source of religious belief and teaching in your answer.   [5 marks]

5. 'Religious believers should not eat meat.'

   Evaluate this statement. In your answer you:
   • should give reasoned arguments in support of this statement
   • should give reasoned arguments to support a different point of view
   • should refer to religious arguments
   • may refer to non-religious arguments
   • should reach a justified conclusion.   [12 marks]
   [+ 3 SPaG marks]

Buddhism and God

Buddhism is generally regarded as a non-theistic religion, which means that it does not include worship of a creator God. Instead, Buddhists aim to liberate themselves from suffering by moving towards enlightenment. However, this does not mean that there are no divine beings. Buddhist traditions do acknowledge the presence of many kinds of spirits and even gods, but not a creator God who is responsible for everything.

Arguments for the existence of God

▲ Buddhists do not believe in a creator God, but some believe there are divine beings who can help them to achieve enlightenment

Over the centuries, Christian thinkers and other people have presented various arguments that aim to prove the existence of God. Two of these are the First Cause argument and the Design argument.

The First Cause argument

The First Cause argument is also called the cosmological argument because it aims to explain the origins of the universe. It argues that at some point in time, the universe began to exist, and also that one day it will come to an end. In other words, the universe is finite. The medieval thinker Thomas Aquinas explained the First Cause argument like this: everything must have a beginning and this beginning must have a cause. So what was the cause that began the universe? It was God. God does not have a cause because he is eternal. Therefore, God was the First Cause of everything else that came into being. If God had needed a cause to begin his existence, he would not be all powerful and so would not be God. Since God is all powerful, he cannot have a cause.

The First Cause argument attempts to use reason to prove the existence of God. However, some people argue that there are a number of difficulties with this approach. They might disagree with the First Cause argument for the following reasons:

Objectives

- Understand the First Cause and Design arguments, examining their strengths and weaknesses.
- Understand a Buddhist response to these arguments.

Key terms

- **First Cause argument:** also called the cosmological argument; the argument that there has to be an uncaused cause that made everything else happen, otherwise there would be nothing now
- **eternal:** without beginning or end
- **Design argument:** the argument that God designed the universe, because everything is so intricately made in its detail that it could not have happened by chance
- **samsara:** the repeating cycle of birth, life, death and rebirth

Activities

1 In two sentences, explain the Design argument for the existence of God.

2 How might a Buddhist criticise the First Cause argument?

- The First Cause argument rests on the idea that everything must have a cause, yet resorts to the claim that there is an uncaused cause (God). If everything has a cause, surely the first cause too must have a cause?
- Although we generally think everything must have a cause, perhaps there are some things we don't know about that don't have causes.
- Even if there were such a thing as an uncaused cause, this does not prove that the cause was God.

The Design argument

The Design argument states that because nature is so complex and intricate, God must have designed it. It could not have come about by accident or random chance. Most Christians believe that the account of creation in Genesis 1 in the Bible supports the Design argument, because it shows that God planned the development of the universe.

Different philosophers have come up with their own examples to support the Design argument. For example, Thomas Aquinas said that only an intelligent being could keep things in regular order. The planets, sun, moon, and stars rotate in the solar system in a set pattern because God holds them in place. In the 1930s, the theologian F. R. Tennant said that God must have designed the world because everything was just right for human life to develop.

Some of the objections to the Design Argument include the following:

- Since the process of natural selection happens by chance, species must have designed themselves over time. Complex life forms are the result of evolution, not a designer God.
- If God designed the universe, why is there so much suffering in the world? Why would God have designed the universe with evil in it?
- The order of the universe is necessary to support life, so it merely gives the appearance of design. Humans impose order on nature to try to explain it.

■ A Buddhist response to these arguments

The idea of causation and the First Cause argument is based on the idea that the universe is linear: it began and it will end. However, Buddhism presents a vision of the universe that is more like an endless cycle. Samsara is the endless process of birth, death and rebirth. There is no absolute beginning and no absolute end. After all, where does a circle begin? So the Buddhist response to the question of how the universe began is: it didn't. There was no beginning of time and there will be no end of time. Instead, there is just endless change. So the idea of a first cause does not come into the discussion.

Similarly, Buddhism does not teach that there is a creator God who designed the universe. Instead, it teaches that all things come into existence when the necessary conditions are there. For example, life first came into existence when the necessary conditions were present for this to happen. This process of change happens by itself, without any help from an outside creator or god.

Discussion activity

Discuss with a partner the differences between gaining knowledge by learning something yourself, through your own personal experience, versus gaining knowledge by learning from someone or something else, such as a teacher or a book.

Which method do you think is better? Do you tend to learn different things through each method? Are there instances where it is only possible to learn something through one of the methods?

Links

Read more about the Buddha's approach to questions about the origins of the universe on page 93.

Links

Read more about Buddhist views on how life came into being on page 94.

⭐ Study tip

When analysing any argument, try to identify its strengths and weaknesses.

Summary

You should now be able to explain the First Cause and Design arguments. You should have considered the strengths and weaknesses of these arguments. You should also be able to compare them with Buddhist ideas of a cyclical universe that has no beginning and therefore no creator.

5.2 Further arguments against the existence of God

The problem of evil and suffering

For some people, the existence of **evil** in the world is an obstacle to belief in the existence of God. According to this line of reasoning, if God really is **benevolent** and created a good world, how can there be so much evil in it? Some people argue that God, being good, could not have created a world that allows so much evil. Therefore he did not create the world and so does not exist. Alternatively, if he did create a world that allows so much evil, then he is not really benevolent or **omnipotent** (with the power to destroy all evil). If God is able to see all and know all, he could not permit all of the evil that goes on in human life.

One counter-argument to this is that God has given humans **free will**. This is a good thing, but it also allows people to choose whether to act in a good or evil way. If God were to stop people acting in an evil way, he would be undermining their free will. However, this argument does not address evil situations that are not caused by human choice, such as natural disasters (like earthquakes or famines) that cause many people to die. Moreover, some people say that the free-will argument does not help to explain why animals suffer (because they do not have free will).

Some people try to explain that God and evil both exist because suffering and evil offer the chance for spiritual growth. Through confronting and overcoming evil, human beings develop spiritually. Suffering also enables people to recognise what is truly valuable.

In the Christian Bible, God sends all kinds of afflictions on Job, who thinks he is a righteous man. At first, he cannot understand why he is being afflicted if he serves God. However, he eventually sees that serving God has nothing to do with worldly benefits. Suffering then is a test of faith. The Bible teaches that one should love God independently of whether life is easy or difficult.

Buddhism and evil

The existence of evil does not go against the Buddhist vision of the world. From a Buddhist point of view, it is perfectly understandable that evil exists. According to Buddhism, people act in evil ways because they are in the grip of greed, hatred, and ignorance. Each person has the ability to act in a good or evil way, but much of the time they do not have enough awareness to be able to make good choices.

Objectives

- Examine arguments against the existence of God based on science and on the problem of suffering and evil.
- Understand Buddhist teachings about evil and how they compare with Christian ideas.

Key terms

- **evil:** the opposite of good, a force or personification of a negative power that is seen in many traditions as destructive and against God
- **benevolent:** all-loving, all-good; a quality of God
- **omnipotent:** almighty, having unlimited power; a quality of God
- **free will:** belief that God gives people the opportunity to make decisions for themselves

▲ *Why does God allow natural disasters to happen, such as earthquakes that kill many people?*

Buddhism teaches that people who do evil are not punished by God. Instead, they suffer the consequences of their actions because of kamma.

It is sometimes said that Buddhists believe in an 'ethical universe'. This does not necessarily mean that people are always punished by the law for their evil. It means that, because of kamma, evil actions always lead to suffering for the person who acts in an evil way. It usually means that others suffer too.

For Buddhists, natural disasters are not punishments for acting in an evil way. Instead, natural disasters are simply caused by biological and climatic conditions. For example, the fact that someone lives in a country that suffers a famine does not mean that they must be a bad person.

Sometimes, evil is understood as a force outside a person that tempts them to act in evil ways. Usually, Buddhism sees evil as coming from within a person. However, in early Buddhism, evil was sometimes personified as a figure called Mara. Mara represents the forces that want to undermine progress towards enlightenment: greed, hatred and ignorance.

Some people argue that Buddhism has the opposite problem to Christianity: not how to explain the existence of evil, but how to explain the existence of good. If all beings are driven by greed, hatred and ignorance, where does the impulse towards enlightenment come from? One answer to this has been to say that within each person there is the essence of a Buddha that, given the right conditions, can grow into enlightenment.

■ Science and belief in God

Some atheists and humanists use developments in scientific knowledge to challenge belief in God. For example, in the past, the origins of life on Earth could not be explained, so people thought that life was created and controlled by God. Today, some people use the theory of evolution to argue that God did not create life. Instead, it just happened by chance through the process of natural selection.

The question of whether science proves or disproves the existence of a creator God is not relevant to Buddhism, which does not teach that there is such a god. In general, Buddhists do not regard scientific explanations as presenting a challenge to Buddhist teachings.

> **❝** Not in the sky, not in the middle of the sea, not entering an opening in the mountains is there that place on earth where standing one might be freed from evil action. **❞**
>
> The Buddha in the *Dhammapada*, verse 127

Discussion activity

Think of three evil things happening in the world today. Discuss with a friend how you think:

a people who believe in God might explain these events

b people who don't believe in God might explain them.

Links

Read more about the idea that everyone has the essence of the Buddha inside them on page 39.

⭐ Study tip

The Buddha taught that everyone has the potential to change for the better and move towards enlightenment. This means that most Buddhists do not believe there are 'evil people'. Instead, they believe that everyone is suffering, to a greater or lesser extent, from the three poisons of greed, hatred and ignorance, from which they need to free themselves.

Summary

You should now understand how evil can be used to argue against the existence of God, and some of the arguments to counter this. You should also understand Buddhist attitudes to evil.

Activities

1 Why do some people think that the existence of evil means there cannot be a God?

2 Give two arguments that people use to explain why God allows evil to exist.

3 According to Buddhism, why do people act in evil ways?

5.3   The argument from miracles

■ What is a miracle?

The argument from miracles is usually regarded as one of the less convincing arguments for the existence of God. A **miracle** is an event outside the usual range of human experience that causes amazement and wonder. It is something that seems supernatural which cannot be explained. Some religious believers think that such events are caused by God and so prove his existence. For example, Christians believe that Jesus performed various miracles (including rising from the dead) and this is seen as evidence of his divine status.

Miracles are sometimes divided into different types. For example, a nature miracle is when something happens in the natural world which seems to contradict the laws of science. An example of this in the Bible is when Jesus and his disciple Peter walked on water. There are also healing miracles, which seem to cure people who are dying or in terrible pain, even when doctors have given up. A famous example from Christianity is when Jesus restored the dead Lazarus to life.

■ Objections to the argument from miracles

Many **atheists** might say that a miracle is simply a natural event that science has yet to explain. They would argue that the existence of God is not necessary to explain supposed miracles, especially where natural explanations can be found.

Some people argue that when miracles happened so long ago, it is difficult to prove that they really took place. Even where a miracle has happened in recent times, it is still difficult to prove, because it is usually based on personal testimony. In addition, with many supposed miracles it is difficult to show that they could not have happened by natural means.

David Hume's objection to miracles

According to the philosopher David Hume, even when there is good evidence in favour of a miracle, it is always more rational to reject this explanation. He noted that there are two ways to judge whether a miracle seems likely to have happened or not. First, how reliable the witness is, and second, how possible the miracle itself is. If someone claims to have seen a UFO, for example, it is more likely that their claim is false rather than true.

Hume argued that a miracle is very unlikely to occur because it involves breaking the laws of nature, which are well established. It is therefore more likely that a miracle claim will be false rather than true, and so it is more rational to reject a miracle claim than to accept it.

Hume did not reject the possibility of miracles. He simply said that it will always be more rational to believe that the supposed miracle can

---

Objectives

- Understand the concept of miracles and how, for some people, they offer proof of God's existence.
- Consider how Buddhists might understand the significance of miracles.

Key terms

- **miracle:** a seemingly impossible event, usually good, that cannot be explained by natural or scientific laws, and is thought to be the action of God
- **atheist:** a person who believes that there is no God

Contrasting beliefs

Use the internet or a library to research different beliefs about miracles. Note down different opinions between religious believers (including Christians) and non-religious believers.

Activities

1 Write your own definition of a miracle.

2 How do some people use miracles to justify the existence of God?

3 How might a Buddhist interpret a story about a miracle?

be explained in other ways. The cosmologist Carl Sagan once said that 'extraordinary claims require extraordinary evidence.'

The evidence from miracles is unlikely to convince someone who doubts that God is real, but for some religious believers it helps to confirm their faith.

■ Buddhism and miracles

According to Buddhist tradition, meditators are able to develop all kinds of extraordinary powers. However, these powers in themselves are not necessarily signs of spirituality, and are not seen as evidence of the existence of God. For example, the power to see beings in all worlds (as well as in the past and future), and the ability to read other people's minds, are just two of the powers which, according to tradition, are said to result from meditation practice.

The Buddhist scriptures are full of examples of the Buddha, and of other monks, doing things that seem outside the natural order. Many of these miracles serve to show how the Buddha has gone beyond the limitations of ordinary experience. For example, as the Buddha was meditating after his enlightenment, a heavy rainstorm occurred. Mucalinda, king of the serpents, emerged from his lair, encircled the Buddha and spread his great hood over him to give him protection from the rain. After seven days, the Buddha emerged from his deep meditation and Mucalinda, seeing that the storm had passed, uncoiled himself, assuming the appearance of a youth. He then bowed before the Buddha.

For many traditional Buddhists, some statues and scriptures are seen as sources of miracles. Through praying or making offerings to a special statue, or by reciting a scripture, they believe that they will be healed from illness or protected from danger. For example, there is a temple in Tokyo, Japan, that houses a statue of the Bodhisattva Jizo. It is a curious figure because it is bound by thousands of ropes. It is believed that this figure can help bring justice to people who have been robbed, as well as fulfil other wishes. In order to ask the statue for aid, you tie a rope around it. If your request is granted, you should return to the statue and 'release it' by untying one of the ropes.

The Buddhist scriptures make clear that supernormal powers should not be used to convince people to become Buddhists, because it is not really what the practice of Buddhism is about. They are likely to be convinced for the wrong reasons. It is clear that 'miracles' often serve a symbolic function in order to communicate a spiritual truth. They need not necessarily be taken literally. For example, according to legend, when the Buddha was born it is said that he took seven steps and with each step a lotus blossom miraculously appeared for him to step on. He then declared that he would become enlightened in this very lifetime. While some traditional Buddhists might take this story literally, many see it as symbolising how special and important the birth of the Buddha was.

▲ *The Buddha being protected by Mucalinda*

★ Study tip

Remember that you should be able to explain contrasting beliefs about miracles from Christian and non-religious perspectives.

Summary

You should now be able to discuss and evaluate the argument from miracles.

5.4 General revelation

What is revelation?

General revelation refers to knowledge of God, or the divine, that is discovered through natural means. For example, through seeing the beauty of nature, or through philosophy and reasoning. Christians use the term to describe knowledge of God that is available to all. Examples of general revelation might include experiencing or coming to know God through seeing a beautiful sunset, or attending worship and hearing the scriptures.

For Christians, the world itself is evidence of God. They believe that God is revealed to them through his creation. Just as a painting gives insight into an artist, so nature gives believers an insight into God.

▲ Coming to know God through seeing a beautiful landscape is one example of general revelation

In contrast, atheists might argue that nature only confirms the existence of God to those who already believe in God. Non-believers may see the world as confirming a process of evolution, not an all-powerful God. Atheists might say that it is possible to marvel at the beauty and mystery of the world without thinking that God is behind it all.

Many religious believers think that God reveals himself to some chosen followers. This is known as special revelation and usually has a dramatic, transformative effect. It sometimes inspires people to found new religions or movements.

Buddhism and revelation

Revelation is not a term that is generally used in Buddhism. However, the Buddha's enlightenment can be thought of as a type of revelation. According to Buddhism, everyone can reach the same insight into the nature of reality that the Buddha achieved. He is only special because

Objectives

- Understand the meaning of general revelation.
- Consider how Buddhists might think about the concept of revelation or enlightenment.

Key terms

- **general revelation:** God or the divine as revealed through ordinary, common human experiences
- **divine:** that which relates to God, gods or ultimate reality
- **special revelation:** the revelation of God, or the divine, through direct personal experience or an unusual specific event

Contrasting beliefs

Use the internet or the library to find out more about the idea of God being revealed through nature. How do Christians and non-religious believers differ in their opinions of nature as general revelation?

Activities

1 Explain what is meant by general revelation.
2 Explain how the following can be seen as examples of general revelation:
   a nature
   b the Bible
   c Buddhist enlightenment.
3 Give two differences between Buddhist and Christian ideas about revelation.

he accomplished this before others and so opened the way for them. For Buddhists, revelation does not provide evidence of God. Instead, the Buddha revealed the true nature of reality. This revelation inspires people to change, so they begin to live with less selfishness, and more generosity and compassion for others. Importantly, people can gain an understanding of the nature of reality through everyday experience.

For Buddhists, teachings about the three marks of existence can help to reveal the nature of reality. These teachings say that:

1. suffering is an unavoidable part of reality

2. everything is impermanent

3. nothing has a fixed, unchanging nature.

Through these teachings, Buddhists can deepen their awareness of the nature of reality, which inspires a way of living that is in harmony with how things are.

For Buddhists, images can also help to reveal the nature of reality. For example, through an image of the Buddha or other sacred figure, Buddhists may recognise that they too can become enlightened. Some Mahayana Buddhists believe they can also communicate directly with the sacred figure, who shows the nature of reality.

> **Links**
>
> To read more about the three marks of existence, see pages 20–25.

▲ *Buddhist scriptures can be thought of as revealing the true nature of reality*

■ Revelation and scripture

For Christians, scripture is perhaps the most important expression of general revelation. Christians believe that the Bible is a sacred book because it contains the words of God. However, they often disagree about how to interpret the Bible, and over which passages are most important. Consequently, they reach different conclusions about God and spiritual life based on the same general revelation.

Buddhists too give special importance to scripture. Generally, Buddhist scriptures are regarded as the 'enlightened word', which means they are seen as expressing the enlightened mind, and usually the mind of the Buddha. For this reason, they act as a form of general revelation about the nature of truth or reality. Some Buddhists think they contain a sacred power that affects people who hear the words. Certain scriptures are even believed to heal or protect people.

Nagarjuna and the revelation of perfect wisdom

According to legend, the Buddhist monk Nagarjuna received a whole body of sacred texts, known as the Perfection of Wisdom scriptures, from the serpent deities who had been guarding them at the bottom of the ocean. These scriptures were given to the serpent deities by the Buddha so they could keep them safe until humans were ready to understand them. The idea of buried or hidden revelations, which are later discovered and shared, has been important in some Mahayana traditions.

> ★ **Study tip**
>
> Make sure you can explain the differences between general and special revelation. Remember that anyone can experience general revelation through everyday experiences; special revelations are unique, rare, life-changing events.

Summary

You should now understand what general revelation is, and how it is seen as a way to know God. You should also understand what revelation means for Buddhists, and some of the ways through which the nature of reality is revealed to them.

5.5 Special revelation and visions

■ What is special revelation?

Special revelation describes a situation when a person, or even a group of people, experiences a vision or a miraculous event which they, and others, consider to be a communication from God. In many religious traditions, knowledge of the divine is believed to have been given to individuals or groups of people through special revelation. They were then inspired to start new religions, or to develop existing traditions with new ideas.

Scriptures can be understood as either special or general revelations, depending on the circumstances. For example, Jews and Christians believe that the Ten Commandments were revealed to Moses, and Muslims believe that the Qur'an was given to Muhammad. These are both examples of special revelation. Special revelation may be transmitted through the appearance of a vision or even through dreams.

An example of special revelation

In 1917, three Portuguese shepherd girls reportedly saw a series of visions of the Virgin Mary (Our Lady of Fátima) and received spiritual teachings from her. When word got around, thousands of people flocked to the site in Fátima, Portugal. The visions were later agreed to be authentic and believable by the Catholic Church. Following the reported visions, Fátima quickly became a Catholic pilgrimage site and now attracts hundreds of thousands of people each year.

Pope John Paul II credited Our Lady of Fátima with saving his life following an assassination attempt which occurred on the Feast of Our Lady of Fátima in 1981. The bullet that wounded him was later placed in the crown of the statue of the Virgin Mary in the sanctuary at Fátima.

■ Arguments against special revelation

One argument against special revelation is that it often depends on the word of just one person. First, how can the person who experiences the revelation know that it is a revelation from God and not simply their own imagination? Second, how can others trust that they are telling the truth? Maybe the person is making it all up to get attention or maybe they are mentally ill. Special revelation is really only a revelation to one person, and others must take the revelation on trust because they have not experienced it directly.

A special revelation seems unlikely to bring someone to believe in God, but is more likely to confirm the faith they already have. It may also help others, who did not experience the special revelation, to deepen their faith. Whether a believer interprets an experience as a special revelation (as opposed to simply a strange experience) will depend on their belief system.

Objectives

● Examine special revelation, including visions, as a source of knowledge about the divine.

● Be able to give examples of special revelation within Buddhism and Christianity.

Key term

● **special revelation:** the revelation of God, or the divine, through direct personal experience or an unusual specific event

Contrasting beliefs

Use the internet or the library to research visions. Note down different opinions between religious believers (including Christians) and non-religious believers.

Activities

1 How is special revelation different to general revelation?

2 How might the meaning of a special revelation be different for a Buddhist and a Christian?

3 Why do some people find it difficult to believe in the concept of special revelation?

Discussion activity

Discuss with a partner whether you think it is possible to experience visions if you are not a religious person.

■ Buddhism and revelation

Buddhists are unlikely to interpret an apparent revelation as the intervention of God, because they do not believe in the concept of an omnipotent, omniscient God. However, they generally accept the possibility that special wisdom may be transmitted through visionary experiences, and even by visionary figures. Many Buddhists practise teachings that were supposedly revealed to revered teachers. The content of these teachings is often more important than their supposed source. For instance, if a Buddhist claimed to have received a revelation that contradicted basic Buddhist teachings, it is unlikely that other Buddhists would want to follow such a teaching.

▲ *Buddhists may have visions when meditating*

Bahiya's vision

An example of a vision from the Buddhist scriptures is the story of Bahiya, who lived in the western part of India. Bahiya was revered and respected as a holy man, but a doubt entered his mind: was he really enlightened? When this doubt emerged, he had a vision of a deva (spiritual being) who confirmed that he wasn't as wise as he could be. Bahiya then asked the deva, 'So who is enlightened? Who can I learn from?' The deva advised him to go and seek out the Buddha. So Bahiya travelled hundreds of miles on foot to find the Buddha, asked for his teaching, and immediately became enlightened. Shortly afterwards, he died.

★ Study tip

It would be helpful to know one example of a vision that you could write about in detail.

Meditation and visionary experience

In Buddhism, people may have visions while meditating. They may see Buddhas or Bodhisattvas, who are seen as specific sources of knowledge, and who can influence the spiritual development of the meditator. In some cases, such visions may be seen as special revelation. In addition, in some Mahayana traditions, believers regularly meditate on Buddhas and Bodhisattvas, chant mantras, and perform various rituals, in the belief that this will bring them into direct contact with the Buddha or Bodhisattva. Through doing these things, they may believe that they have received a specific revelation, which they may then transmit to others.

▲ *In Japan, the Bodhisattva Jizo is particularly called on by mothers who have lost babies or children*

The Tibetan Book of the Dead

There is a famous Tibetan text widely known in English as *The Tibetan Book of the Dead*, which emerged through what could be understood as a special revelation. Tibet has a tradition of 'hidden treasures' and a tradition of treasure finders. Tibetan Buddhists believe that *The Tibetan Book of the Dead* was written by the great monk Padmasambhava in the eighth century. He decided to hide it until a later date when people would be ready to study it. It was then discovered several centuries later, and has become central in the Tibetan Buddhist approach to dying, death, and rebirth.

Summary

You should now be able to explain the meaning of special revelation, and understand how visions can be a source of knowledge about the divine.

What is enlightenment?

Enlightenment is a term that describes a profound spiritual insight which transforms the life of the individual. Some religions believe that through enlightenment, people come to know God. In contrast, Buddhism teaches that people can gain a deep understanding of themselves and of the nature of reality.

Enlightenment may be gained through spiritual discipline, such as prayer, silence and solitude. For example, the Anchorites were Christians who lived austere lives of solitude, with the intention of knowing God and releasing themselves from sin. Through separating themselves from the world, they believed that they could come to know God more intimately through personal experience.

In Buddhism, enlightenment is gained through practising the Dhamma (the teachings of the Buddha). The path to enlightenment is often presented as having three elements: ethics, meditation and wisdom. While each of these aspects can be developed at the same time, Buddhists believe that if a person improves their ethical behaviour, then they will be able to have deeper meditation experiences. Through the stability and concentration developed in meditation, Buddhists can gain an understanding of the nature of reality, which leads to enlightenment. Enlightenment results in a state of profound freedom, peace, wisdom and compassion.

▲ *Buddhists use meditation to gain a deeper understanding of the nature of reality*

The enlightenment of the Buddha

The most famous example of an enlightened person in Buddhism is, of course, the Buddha. He is said to have gained enlightenment after six years of strenuous spiritual practices. When sitting under a peepul tree, the Buddha saw how all things come into being because of certain conditions, and cease when those conditions cease. In particular, he came to understand how people create their own suffering, and how they can release themselves from that suffering through letting go of desire and hatred. The Buddha's enlightenment is said to be beyond words. It produced a profound transformation that inspired him to share his experience with others, and to begin what later turned out to become a major world religion.

Objectives

- Understand what enlightenment means for different religious believers.
- Understand terms that attempt to describe the nature of God or the divine.

Key terms

- **enlightenment:** the gaining of true knowledge about God, self or the nature of reality, usually through meditation and self-discipline; in Buddhist, Hindu and Sikh traditions, gaining freedom from the cycle of rebirth
- **omnipotent:** almighty, having unlimited power; a quality of God
- **omniscient:** knowing everything; a quality of God
- **omnibenevolent:** all good; a quality of God
- **impersonal:** the idea that God has no 'human' characteristics, is unknowable and mysterious, more like an idea or force
- **personal:** the idea that God is an individual or person with whom people are able to have a relationship or feel close to
- **transcendent:** the idea that God is beyond and outside life on Earth and the universe; a quality of God
- **immanent:** the idea that God is present in and involved with life on Earth and in the universe; a quality of God

While in English the term commonly used to refer to the Buddha's experience is 'enlightenment', it may be more accurate to talk about 'awakening'. Both of these terms are metaphors that point to something that is perhaps indescribable.

Different ideas about the nature of God

Different religions, and even different followers, sometimes have very different ideas about the nature of God or the divine. Some of these ideas are not easy to understand and may seem to involve contradictions.

For example, God is sometimes described as all powerful (**omnipotent**), all knowing (**omniscient**), and all loving (**omnibenevolent**). However, if God really does have these qualities, how can he permit evil and suffering to continue?

Sometimes God is seen as **impersonal**, beyond the world, and so detached from people.

▲ *The Buddha sitting under the peepul tree*

Other believers regard God as **personal**: someone with whom they can develop a relationship and who may answer their prayers.

Some religious believers think of God as **transcendent**, remote from day-to-day events, beyond the world. When understood in this way, the divine may be seen as beyond the grasp of human understanding, something unknowable, even mysterious. Others believe that God, or the divine, is constantly at work in the world and is therefore **immanent**, present in all things, accessible at each moment. The ideas that God or the divine is transcendent or immanent do not necessarily exclude one another. The divine may be accessible through the world but still be somehow beyond it.

Ideas about the nature of the Buddha

Different Buddhists think of the Buddha in many different ways:

- Some see him as a person; a teacher and example to be followed.
- Others see him as a symbol of their own potential.
- Some see him as a transcendent figure to be worshipped.
- Others believe that the Buddha is immanent: an ever-present reality with which they can enter into a relationship through meditation and devotional practices.
- The Buddha is sometimes seen as a supremely compassionate force that is actively reaching out to help human beings in order to relieve their suffering. If people become more receptive then they can experience this influence, and it will direct their lives in a more fulfilling way.

Philosophical arguments for and against the existence of God – summary

You should now be able to:

✔ explain and evaluate the Design argument, including its strengths and weaknesses

✔ explain and evaluate the First Cause argument, including its strengths and weaknesses

✔ explain and evaluate the argument from miracles, including its strengths and weaknesses

✔ describe one example of a miracle

✔ explain and evaluate the arguments against the existence of God posed by science and by the problem of evil and suffering.

The nature of the divine and revelation – summary

You should now be able to:

✔ explain what is meant by special revelation and enlightenment as sources of knowledge about the divine (God, gods or ultimate reality)

✔ describe one example of a vision

✔ explain what is meant by general revelation, including nature and scripture as a way of understanding the divine

✔ explain the different ideas about the divine that come from revelation

✔ explain the meaning of qualities of God such as omnipotent, omniscient, benevolent, personal, impersonal, immanent and transcendent

✔ explain the value of revelation and enlightenment as sources of knowledge about the divine

✔ explain and evaluate the difficulties in accepting the reality of some examples of revelation

✔ explain and evaluate the problem of different ideas about the divine arising from these experiences

✔ explain and evaluate alternative explanations for the experiences and the possibility that the people who claimed to have them were lying or mistaken

✔ explain similar and contrasting perspectives in contemporary British society to all the above issues

✔ explain similar and contrasting beliefs in contemporary British society to the three issues of miracles, visions, and nature as a source of revelation, with reference to the main religious tradition in Britain (Christianity) and non-religious beliefs such as atheism or humanism.

Sample student answer – the 12-mark question

1. Write an answer to the following practice question:

    'The enlightenment of the Buddha has little value for Buddhists today.'

    Evaluate this statement. In your answer you:

    • should give reasoned arguments to support this statement
    • should give reasoned arguments to support a different point of view
    • should refer to religious arguments
    • may refer to non-religious arguments
    • should reach a justified conclusion.

    [12 marks]
    [+ 3 SPaG marks]

2. Read the following sample student answer:

"Most Buddhists think that even describing or explaining what it means to be enlightened, to someone who has not had the experience, is a difficult thing to do. That makes it really hard to become enlightened if no one can really explain what it means. There are descriptions of what it's like to overcome problems that might stop someone from achieving enlightenment, so this might have value for Buddhists today. Though they were written so long ago, maybe they're not helpful for Buddhists today. The Buddha described nibbana or enlightenment in different ways, like supreme happiness, peace and immortality, but these are hard concepts to understand and not so useful today.

But it could be argued that the Buddhist aim in life is complete freedom from conflict and selfishness, and to end craving, hatred and ignorance. The Buddha was just a man who achieved this very thing, so why not others too? The Buddha was a great example of how nibbana can be achieved in a person's lifetime. Every religion has a goal for its followers to achieve and for Buddhists it is becoming enlightened, so if this state was not achievable, what would be the point in following the religion at all?"

3. With a partner, discuss the sample answer. Is the focus of the answer correct? Is anything missing from the answer? How do you think it could be improved?

4. What mark (out of 12) would you give this answer? Look at the mark scheme in the Introduction (AO2). What are the reasons for the mark you have given?

5. Swap your answer with your partner's and mark each other's responses. What mark (out of 12) would you give? Refer to the mark scheme and give reasons for the mark you award.

Practice questions

1 Which **one** of the following best expresses the idea that the divine (God, gods or ultimate reality) is all-powerful?

A) Omnipotent   **B)** Immanent   **C)** Transcendent   **D)** Impersonal   **[1 mark]**

2 Give **two** descriptions of nibbana.   **[2 marks]**

3 Explain **two** contrasting beliefs about miracles as an argument for the existence of God.

In your answer you must refer to one or more religious traditions.   **[4 marks]**

4 Explain **two** religious beliefs about visions.

Refer to sacred writings or another source of religious belief and teaching in your answer.   **[5 marks]**

5 'The First Cause argument is the strongest argument for the existence of God.'

Evaluate this statement.

In your answer you:
- should give reasoned arguments to support this statement
- should give reasoned arguments to support a different point of view
- should refer to religious arguments
- may refer to non-religious arguments
- should reach a justified conclusion.   **[12 marks]**
      [+ 3 SPaG marks]

6.1 Peace, justice, forgiveness and reconciliation

Right from the beginnings of humanity, people have attempted to gain territory or settle disputes through fighting. Even today, somewhere in the world, it is likely that people will be injured, killed or displaced as a result of **war**. While all countries have laws against murder, the rules of war are different – in war, killing is generally considered to be acceptable.

Buddhism is very much a religion that promotes peace. Buddhist teachings say there are no justifiable reasons for war. War is wrong because it expresses and encourages hateful and greedy attitudes and behaviour, which result in suffering. Buddhism teaches that people cannot relieve their own suffering through making others suffer.

■ Peace

One definition of **peace** is the absence of war. The intention of those fighting in a war is to create peace once the war is over. But this is often difficult to achieve, because the instability and resentment left after a war often leads to fighting breaking out again.

The Buddha also taught that peace comes from within, and that it is important for Buddhists to try to develop a sense of peace. The Buddha said that violence comes from people's minds, so to stop violence people must begin by developing a sense of peace within themselves. This idea is echoed in the constitution of the United Nations Educational, Scientific and Cultural Organisation (UNESCO), which states that:

▲ *Buddhist monks leading a peace rally in Katmandu, Nepal*

> **❝** Since wars begin in the minds of men, it is in the minds of men that the defences of peace must be constructed. **❞**

Objectives

- Understand war as a way of resolving differences.
- Explain the concepts of peace, justice, forgiveness and reconciliation.

Key terms

- **war:** fighting between nations to resolve issues between them
- **peace:** an absence of conflict, which leads to happiness and harmony
- **justice:** bringing about what is right and fair, according to the law, or making up for a wrong that has been committed
- **forgiveness:** showing compassion, and pardoning someone for what they have done wrong
- **reconciliation:** when individuals or groups restore friendly relations after conflict or disagreement; also a sacrament in the Catholic Church

Discussion activity

Is the best way to achieve peace to encourage everyone to develop a peaceful state of mind? Discuss with a partner.

★ Study tip

Remember that the four concepts of peace, justice, forgiveness and reconciliation are linked. When writing about one of them, it is likely that you will need to refer to at least one other.

Buddhist teachings agree with this statement. The Buddha taught that if people have peaceful minds, this will lead to peaceful speech and peaceful actions. If people's minds are at peace then the world will be at peace. Many Buddhists therefore focus on developing this sense of peace within themselves. Some Buddhists also take part in campaigns that further global peace, because creating peace through non-violent means is an important goal in Buddhism.

■ Justice

Justice is often linked with equality. If people are not given the same opportunities, this may be seen as unfair and could create resentment. This could lead to conflict, especially if more privileged parts of the world are seen to be the cause of inequality. Many wars are fought to try to create justice.

Buddhism teaches that inflicting suffering on people through war is not the way to create a just world, because it simply causes more suffering. Most Buddhists think it is better to use non-violent means to accomplish this goal, while practising generosity and letting go (non-attachment).

■ Forgiveness

Buddhism teaches that forgiveness is important, both to prevent war in the first place and to establish peace after a war has ended. Forgiveness is also important in reducing suffering, because it allows people to let go of the hatred and anger that they feel.

Buddhists believe that forgiveness can be developed through meditation. It is often a part of loving-kindness meditation, where a Buddhist might think forgiving thoughts towards themselves as well as other people. For Buddhists, people who have wronged them provide them with the opportunity to develop patience and forgiveness. Buddhism teaches that all beings want to be happy, but if someone has done something wrong, they will suffer as a consequence. It is therefore better to develop compassion for them rather than hatred or resentment.

■ Reconciliation

Reconciliation follows conflict. It is when two people or groups who have disagreed or fought with each other make up. This requires more than just words. It involves a conscious effort to rebuild a relationship, and to work to ensure there is no more conflict. Both sides have to play an active part in this.

In order to bring about reconciliation, Buddhist teachings stress the importance of letting go of blame and resentment, because these attitudes prevent a person from developing a more harmonious relationship with others. They also contribute to the person's own suffering.

Once forgiveness and reconciliation have taken place, a relationship is much stronger, because the two parties have learned to appreciate and accept each other for what they are. Forgiveness and reconciliation do not mean denying the difficulties of the past, but learning from the past to build a better, more peaceful future.

Activities

1 Explain how the four concepts of peace, justice, forgiveness and reconciliation link together in the context of a war and what happens after a war.

2 Imagine that you have been ordered by your government to take part in a war. Write a letter to the government explaining why you do not want to take part, referring to Buddhist teachings and beliefs.

> ❝ 'He abused me, he struck me, he overcame me, he robbed me.' Of those who wrap themselves up in it hatred is not quenched. ❞
>
> The Buddha in the *Dhammapada*, verse 3

Links

Read more about loving-kindness meditation on pages 68–69, and more about forgiveness on pages 150–151.

Summary

You should now understand how the concepts of peace, justice, forgiveness and reconciliation are linked to each other, particularly in the context of war. You should also be able to explain Buddhist attitudes towards these concepts.

6.2 Violence, violent protest and terrorism

■ Buddhism and violence

Buddhist teachings are generally against **violence** because it contradicts the most basic ethical precept, which is not to cause harm. However, there may be circumstances where a Buddhist might view violence as justifiable, for example in the case of self-defence.

In contrast, Thich Nhat Hanh (a well-known Buddhist teacher) has maintained a firm commitment to non-violence. When asked what he would do if he were the last monk in the world and someone were about to kill him and thus wipe out Buddhism, he answered that it would be better to let himself be killed than betray his Buddhist principles.

Some Buddhists might justify a violent action if it could save a life, but others think that this would be to abandon Buddhism.

■ Violent protest

The right to **protest** is considered to be a fundamental democratic freedom. The law in the UK allows individuals and groups to protest in public to demonstrate their point of view. If the protest involves a procession or march, the law says that the police must be informed at least six days before it takes place. The police can request alterations to the route of a march, and can also apply to a court for an order banning the march. They may do this if they feel that the march may intimidate other people or if they predict that violence will be involved.

▲ *An anti-austerity protest in London becomes violent as protesters clash with the police*

Objective

● Examine Buddhist attitudes towards violence, violent protest and terrorism.

Key terms

● **violence:** using actions that threaten or harm others
● **protest:** an expression of disapproval, often in a public group
● **terrorism:** the unlawful use of violence, usually against innocent civilians, to achieve a political goal

❝ Whoever injures with violence creatures desiring happiness, seeking his own happiness he does not gain happiness when he has passed away. ❞

The Buddha in the *Dhammapada*, verse 131

Extension activity

Find out more about the Cambodian monk Ghosananda, and his work for peace.

Activities

1 Do you think violent protest is ever justified? Explain why.

2 'Buddhists should never act violently.' Evaluate this statement. Include more than one point of view, and refer to Buddhist teachings and beliefs in your answer.

Generally, Buddhism advocates non-violent forms of protest. The Cambodian monk Ghosananda provides a good example of this. In the 1990s, he led a series of non-violent marches through his country in order to encourage reconciliation and peace after decades of civil conflict, even defying the army of the Khmer Rouge (a cruel and repressive government in Cambodia). He once said, 'If I am good to someone, he or she will learn goodness and, in turn, will be good to others.' He believed that violent acts should be condemned, but that hatred should not be shown towards the person who commits them.

Some Buddhist monks have committed suicide to draw attention to the repression of Buddhist teachings. For instance, in 1963 a Vietnamese monk, Thich Quang Duc, set himself alight on a busy street in protest against repressive government policies. Some Buddhists see this as a breach of the first moral precept, while others think it is heroic.

Despite the general Buddhist commitment to non-violence, in recent decades some monks in Myanmar have supported violent protests against Muslims whom they believe to be the source of their problems. This has resulted in many deaths. In contrast, the Buddhist politician Aung San Suu Kyi, who is also from Myanmar, is famous for her non-violent opposition to a repressive government, which resulted in her imprisonment for many years.

▲ *A peace march in Cambodia led by Ghosananda*

■ Terrorism

A much more serious form of violent protest is terrorism. This is where an individual, or a group who share certain beliefs, use terror as part of their campaign to further their cause. Their violence usually deliberately targets civilians and takes place in public. Suicide bombers, car bombs, and gunmen shooting into crowds of people are all tactics of terrorism. Terrorists believe that by killing people in this way, the rest of society will become more aware of their cause, will be scared of them, and will push the authorities into giving way to their demands.

While a terrorist may associate their cause with a religion, no religion promotes terrorism.

Terrorism is a violent expression of hatred, and often leads to the harm of many people. Many Buddhists believe it is important to condemn terrorism and imprison terrorists (so that they do not harm more people), but it is also important to try to understand the root causes that provoke someone to act in such a violent way. The underlying causes are often complex and not easily understood, but a Buddhist response to terrorism involves recognising that terrorists sometimes act in extremely violent ways because they are suffering. Buddhism teaches that acts of terrorism should be countered with acts of love and compassion, rather than retaliation and more violence. Revenge solves nothing.

Research activity 🔍

Use the internet to find out more about the violence between Buddhists and Muslims in Myanmar, and the reasons behind it. Why are some Buddhists in Myanmar encouraging violence towards Muslims?

★ Study tip

When writing about a topic you feel strongly about, try to stick to the facts and do not let your emotions affect what you write or the language that you use.

Summary

You should now understand Buddhist attitudes towards violence, violent protest and terrorism.

6.3 Reasons for war

There is rarely a single, clear cause for any war. Most wars are fought for a number of reasons, some more obvious than others, which are linked together in complex ways. However, it is fair to say that most if not all wars are caused to some extent by greed, self-defence or retaliation.

Greed

Throughout history, war has been used as a way to gain more land or territory, or to regain land lost in a previous war. Greed can also lead countries to invade others in order to control important resources, such as oil. Buddhism teaches that greed is one of the three poisons, and one of the main causes of suffering. There are always unhealthy consequences from actions based on greed.

Self-defence

Whenever one country attacks another, it expects to meet some resistance from the invaded country. Most people consider fighting in self-defence to be morally acceptable, and believe they have a right to defend the values, beliefs and ways of life that their country lives by.

The most fundamental ethical principle in Buddhism is not to take life. While it might be acceptable to resist violence with some force, the Vietnamese monk Thich Nhat Hanh, himself a refugee of war, has emphasised that killing is never justified, and that people should instead develop compassion for those who wish to harm them. Not all Buddhists agree, and some might even feel justified in taking a life if this would save the life of a loved one.

Retaliation

Wars are sometimes fought against a country that is seen to have done something very wrong. From a Buddhist point of view, retaliation is just another word for vengeance, and is an expression of hatred (one of the three poisons). Actions based on hatred are not ethical, and so do not lead to healthy consequences. Responding to hatred with hatred only increases suffering; it does not relieve it. To break the cycle of violence, a different kind of response is needed, based on compassion.

■ The just war theory

St Augustine was one of the first Christians to write about the morality of war, in the fourth century. His thoughts were developed into a distinct set of criteria by Thomas Aquinas in the thirteenth century. Further adaptations have been made to the just war theory up until the present day. It aims to lay out the conditions under which fighting a war is justifiable. The war must have a just cause, it must be lawfully declared by the correct authority, its intention must be to promote good, and it should be a last resort. There must be a reasonable chance of success, and the methods used should be proportional. Civilians must not be harmed.

Objectives

- Understand why wars are fought.
- Examine Buddhist attitudes towards the reasons for war.
- Consider Buddhist attitudes towards the just war theory.

Key terms

- **greed:** selfish desire for something
- **the three poisons:** greed, hatred and ignorance; the main causes of suffering
- **self-defence:** acting to prevent harm to yourself or others
- **retaliation:** deliberately harming someone as a response to them harming you
- **just war theory:** a set of criteria that a war needs to meet before it can be justified

Activities

1 Can you think of any reasons that justify fighting a war?

2 Why do you think the Dalai Lama does not want Tibetans to retaliate against the Chinese?

Discussion activity

The Dhammapada, a Buddhist scripture, contains the following quote: 'For not by hatred are hatreds ever quenched here, but they are quenched by non-hatred. This is the ancient rule.' Discuss with a partner what you think this means, and how it reflects Buddhist teachings.

China and Tibet

In 1950, the Chinese army entered Tibet. At the time, Tibet considered itself to be an independent state, while China argued that it was simply consolidating its rule over a region that was already a part of China. Either way, the Communist Party of China wished to incorporate Tibet into the new People's Republic of China.

Tibetan forces were greatly outnumbered and they could put up little resistance. The Dalai Lama, the spiritual leader of Tibet, tried to negotiate peace with the Chinese. Fears for his safety grew, and in March 1959, rumours that he was going to be arrested by Chinese forces prompted thousands of Tibetans to surround his palace to prevent him from being removed. This led to a violent uprising during which it is estimated that 10,000 to 15,000 Tibetans were killed. The Dalai Lama fled the palace and has been living in exile since. Many Tibetans have been persecuted as a result of the Chinese invasion, and many monasteries and temples have been looted or destroyed.

The Dalai Lama has only ever encouraged a peaceful response to the Chinese occupation,

▲ *Buddhist prayer flags in Tibet are hung up outside as a symbol of peace, compassion and wisdom. They have been strongly discouraged by the Chinese.*

reflecting Buddhist teachings that retaliation is not the answer. Tibetans themselves have mostly shown resistance through non-violent means, following the teachings of the Dalai Lama. Such means include protesting peacefully, trying to alert the rest of the world to the situation in Tibet, and openly expressing Tibetan identity despite Chinese oppression.

According to Buddhist ethics, all violence should be abandoned, and people should instead cultivate compassion for all beings. Consequently, there can be no such thing as a just war, even in self-defence. The general Buddhist view is that to respond to violence with more violence only adds to the problem. Buddhism teaches that people should conquer the violent tendencies within themselves, and have confidence that this will have a positive impact on the world. Most Buddhists question whether it would really be possible to fight in a war and maintain a compassionate attitude.

Some Japanese Buddhist priests justified Japanese military aggression in World War II on the grounds that it was defending the nation and enabling Buddhism to survive, but many Buddhists disagree with this attitude.

⭐ Study tip

Remember that Buddhists do not all necessarily think the same. While there is a general principle of non-violence in Buddhism, this may be interpreted in different ways.

Contrasting beliefs

Christianity also strongly promotes peace. However, Christians hold different views about whether war can be justified.

Find out more about Christian teachings on violence. Do Christian beliefs agree or contrast with Buddhist beliefs on this issue?

Summary

You should now understand three different causes of war and Buddhist attitudes towards them. You should be able to explain what Buddhists think about the just war theory.

6.4 Religion and belief as causes of war

Holy war

In the past, some wars have been fought on behalf of a religious belief. The purpose of a **holy war** is usually to defend the faith from attack. It has to be declared by a religious leader, and those who take part in it believe they will gain spiritual rewards by fighting for God. The Crusades are the best-known examples of a holy war. These were fought between Christians and Muslims in the eleventh to fifteenth centuries. Various popes (heads of the Christian Church) called on Christians to try to regain control of the Holy Land and Jerusalem.

The idea of a holy war does not make much sense for Buddhists because there is a basic commitment to non-violence in Buddhism. As we saw on the previous page, Buddhism teaches that no war can be justified, even in self-defence. This includes holy war to defend or spread the faith.

Japanese Buddhism and war

While most Buddhists are against war and violence, there are also examples of some Buddhists who have supported war. For example, in the twentieth century, Japanese Buddhist monks supported aggression towards China and Korea. This included providing army chaplains and conducting rituals in the belief that they would help to ensure victory. Moreover, after Japan had taken control of parts of mainland Asia, Japanese priests were sent to spread Buddhist teachings there. They acted in the belief that Japanese culture was superior, and so would benefit the occupied territories and people. In supporting the war, some monks believed that they were helping to ensure the survival and spread of the Buddha's teachings.

One Zen master, Soen Shaku, went to the battlefield during the Russo–Japanese War because he 'wished to inspire our valiant soldiers with the ennobling thoughts of the Buddha, so as to enable them to die on the battlefield with confidence that the task in which they are engaged is great and noble'.

Religion and belief as a reason for war and violence

Buddhism teaches that all things come into being because they are dependent on certain conditions, and often those conditions are complex. To reduce the reasons for starting a war to just 'religion' is probably simplifying what is a complicated matter. Most wars are caused by a number of interrelated factors – politics, economics, self-defence, retaliation, even the desire to gain territory or resources, may all play a part. While religion may divide the two sides, it is rarely the sole or main reason for the conflict.

▲ *Religion is rarely the main or sole reason for a war*

However, there are examples in the contemporary world of religious believers who have acted violently to defend what they perceive to be attacks on their faith, or to advance a specific vision of the world. Buddhism is no exception here.

Anti-Muslim violence in Myanmar

Buddhists and Muslims have largely lived in peace for centuries in Myanmar, but attacks against the Muslim community have increased in recent years. For example, in 2013, there were riots and clashes in several cities that led to a number of deaths. Muslim-owned businesses and mosques were destroyed or set alight. In July 2016, two mosques were burnt and there were mass protests. Muslims are frequently discriminated against.

Muslims in Myanmar form a small and mainly peaceful minority – about 90 per cent of the country is Buddhist. However, some Buddhists in Myanmar feel threatened by their presence. They see Muslims (particularly Rohingya Muslims living in Rakhine State) as being foreigners who have no right to exist in their country, and worry that Islam will spread in Myanmar. Their hatred for Muslims is fuelled primarily by nationalism rather than Buddhist teachings.

Many Buddhists around the world, including many in Myanmar, have condemned the violence. A number of monks in Myanmar have helped to shelter Muslims during riots. Those who have spoken out against the violence include nearly 300 Buddhist teachers and leaders who signed 'An open letter from the Buddhist community on Islamophobia', which included the following plea:

▲ *Buddhist monks and nuns in Indonesia campaigning for the rights of Rohingya Muslims*

'In the wider Buddhist community, we ask our fellow Buddhists to refrain from using the Dharma to support nationalism, ethnic conflict, and Islamophobia. We believe that these values are antithetical to the Buddha's teachings on loving-kindness, compassion, sympathetic joy, and equanimity.

The vast majority of Muslims the world over are peaceful, law-abiding people who share much the same dreams, hopes, and aspirations as their non-Muslim neighbours … they are our fellow sentient beings, all of whom, the Buddha taught, have loved and cared for us in the past.'

Discussion activity

With a partner, think of some of the ways that Buddhists could defend their faith without resorting to violence.

Activities

1 'People should never use violence to defend their religion.' Evaluate this statement. Include more than one point of view, and refer to Buddhist teachings and beliefs in your answer.

2 Why do you think some people try to impose their religious beliefs on others by using force?

★ Study tip

Remember that even 'religious' wars might be fought for a number of complex reasons that are not all to do with religion.

Summary

You should now be able to give examples of religion and belief being used as a cause of violence and war. You should also be able to explain Buddhist attitudes towards this issue.

Nuclear war and weapons of mass destruction

■ The use of nuclear weapons

The first nuclear bomb to be used in warfare was dropped on the Japanese city of Hiroshima by American forces during the Second World War. Around 80,000 people in Hiroshima died as a result of the explosion. The death toll rose to around 140,000 as many more people died from radiation poisoning. Three days later the Japanese city of Nagasaki was destroyed by a second

▲ *The city of Hiroshima shortly after the bomb was dropped*

nuclear bomb. Five days after that, Japan surrendered and stopped fighting against the Allied forces. This marked the end of the Second World War which, for some people, justified the use of such weapons.

Since the end of the Second World War, many of the wealthier countries in the world, including the UK, have researched and developed considerably more powerful **nuclear weapons**. Despite some countries agreeing to reduce the number of nuclear weapons they possess, there are now sufficient weapons to completely destroy the world we live in several times over.

The countries that possess nuclear weapons argue that they are an important deterrent. This means that the threat that a country could retaliate with nuclear weapons prevents countries from attacking it in the first place. So far, the threat of full-scale nuclear war – which could potentially lead to human extinction – has deterred any countries from using nuclear weapons in warfare since the Second World War ended.

Most Buddhists believe that nuclear weapons should be abolished. They believe that as long as nuclear weapons exist, there is the risk that they will be used – perhaps through mechanical failure, human error, or because someone in power chooses to ignore the potential consequences. This means there is always the risk of full-scale nuclear war.

But the situation is really more complicated than this. Thich Nhat Hanh once said:

> ❝ For peace, the basic thing to do is not to remove nuclear weapons but to remove the fear, anger and suspicion in us. If we reduce them, reconciliation is easy. ❞

This indicates that the real problem is not the weapons themselves but rather human attitudes, including the belief that we might solve our

---

Objectives

- Know about different weapons of mass destruction, including nuclear weapons.
- Examine Buddhist attitudes towards the use of weapons of mass destruction.

Key terms

- **nuclear weapons:** weapons that work by a nuclear reaction, devastate huge areas, and kill large numbers of people
- **weapons of mass destruction:** weapons that can kill large numbers of people and/or cause great damage
- **chemical weapons:** weapons that use chemicals to harm humans and destroy the natural environment
- **biological weapons:** weapons that use living organisms to cause disease or death

Contrasting beliefs

Christianity is another religion that does not promote the use of weapons of mass destruction. Reasons for this include the fact that their use would go against the teachings of Jesus, and the Christian belief that only God has the authority to end life.

Find out more about Christian teachings on weapons of mass destruction. Do Christian beliefs agree or contrast with Buddhist beliefs on this issue?

problems by using a weapon that would kill huge numbers of people. In a similar way, Daisaku Ikeda, a Japanese Buddhist and anti-nuclear activist, has said:

> 66 The real enemy that we must confront is the ways of thinking that justify nuclear weapons; the readiness to annihilate others when they are seen as a threat or as a hindrance to the realisation of our objectives. 99

■ Weapons of mass destruction

In addition to nuclear weapons, there are other **weapons of mass destruction**:

Chemical weapons contain lethal chemicals that, when released, can damage the environment and cause many deaths. In 1993, the Chemical Weapons Convention made the production, stockpiling and use of these chemicals illegal worldwide. However, since then they are believed to have been used in countries such as Iraq and Syria.

Biological weapons introduce harmful bacteria and viruses into the atmosphere. When they enter the food chain or water supplies, they can cause illness and death on a massive scale. As with chemical weapons, they are illegal but there have been instances of their use, and many countries still possess them.

Weapons of mass destruction make it easy to kill large numbers of people based on a single decision. This is why they are particularly dangerous from a Buddhist point of view, because just a single moment of rage could lead to harming many beings. Many Buddhists think that better safeguards are needed against the power of people's aggressive, even hateful impulses, and the availability of weapons of mass destruction offers a potentially catastrophic outlet for them. Moreover, the people who suffer as a consequence of such weapons are not usually the ones responsible for conflict. Weapons of mass destruction kill indiscriminately and so their use cannot be defended.

▲ *Buddhists taking part in an anti-nuclear weapons march in New York*

Discussion activity

Should the UK keep its nuclear weapons or get rid of all its nuclear weapons? Consider this question with a partner. Try to think of arguments both for and against stockpiling nuclear weapons.

Research activity

Daisaku Ikeda is one Buddhist who has been very vocal in his support for nuclear disarmament. Find out what some of his arguments are for the abolition of nuclear weapons.

Activities

1 Do you think the use of weapons of mass destruction can ever be justified? Give reasons for your answer.

2 'Countries with nuclear weapons are no safer than countries without them.' Do you agree? Give reasons for your answer.

★ Study tip

Learn some of the arguments for and against the stockpiling of nuclear weapons.

Summary

You should now be able to describe the effects of nuclear weapons and other weapons of mass destruction. You should understand some of the arguments for and against the stockpiling of nuclear weapons, including Buddhist views on this issue.

6.6 Pacifism and peacemaking

■ What is pacifism?

Pacifism is the belief that violence and war can never be justified, and that peaceful means should always be used to resolve disputes. Pacifists strongly believe that it is best to work at preventing war from becoming a possibility. Promoting justice and human rights is an important part of this. If people are not denied basic freedoms and rights, they are less likely to engage in conflict.

Pacifists usually refuse to fight in wars, but sometimes help in wars by tending to the sick and wounded. In the past, pacifists have been punished for their beliefs. For example, the boxer Muhammad Ali, a Muslim, was fined and sentenced to five years in prison for refusing to join the US army when it was fighting in Vietnam in the 1960s.

■ Buddhism and pacifism

Buddhist teachings strongly promote pacifism. The first moral precept teaches that Buddhists should not harm or kill any living beings. The Buddha taught that Buddhists should try instead to develop compassion for all beings and that violence should be avoided. However, this does not mean that Buddhists cannot show non-violent resistance. For Buddhists, it is important to resist oppression and intolerance, since such behaviour causes suffering for many beings. A compassionate response to the world is active but not violent.

For Buddhists, non-violence is something that emerges from inner practice and transformation; it comes from inside each person. In principle, someone could be committed to the theory of pacifism but act in a violent way, especially in their speech and their thoughts. Buddhism recognises that true peace starts from within each person.

At the same time, structures of power and institutions can breed and support violence, so in order to become peaceful and to live in peace with others, it is also necessary to create conditions that encourage skilful attitudes and behaviour. This involves active involvement in social issues to create a world that favours more peaceful states of mind.

■ The Parable of the Saw

In one Buddhist scripture, the Buddha recommends that people should respond to violence not with violence but with patience and love. He uses a rather gruesome example to illustrate his point. 'Suppose,' says the Buddha, 'that bandits were to tear you limb from limb with a monstrous saw.' Even if in a circumstance such as this, people give way to hatred, then they cannot say they are Buddhists. Instead the Buddha talked of how someone should ideally react in this type of situation. He said that, 'Our minds will remain unaffected, and we shall utter no evil

Objectives

- Examine Buddhist teachings and attitudes to pacifism.
- Know about the work of a Buddhist peacemaker.

Key terms

- **pacifism:** the belief of people who refuse to take part in war and any other form of violence
- **peacemaker:** a person who works to establish peace in the world or in a certain part of it
- **Engaged Buddhism:** a movement in Buddhism that is particularly concerned with applying the Buddha's teachings to matters of social and environmental injustice
- **peacemaking:** the action of trying to establish peace

Links

Read more about skilful attitudes and behaviour on pages 140–141.

words; we shall abide compassionate for their welfare, with a mind of loving-kindness, without inner hate.'

The parable emphasises the importance of having the right attitude, since people's attitudes guide their behaviour. It does not necessarily mean that people should not act, but that they should not act from hatred.

■ A Buddhist peacemaker

Born in Vietnam in 1926, Thich Nhat Hanh has been a **peacemaker** since his ordination as a Buddhist monk at the age of 16. During the Vietnam War, he helped villagers who were suffering as a result of bombing. He opposed his government's policies and as a consequence was exiled from his country. He later settled in France. He is a pioneer of **Engaged Buddhism**, which argues that if Buddhists are to achieve true inner peace, they must work on changing the structures of society that influence people's mental states and behaviour. Inner and outer change go hand in hand.

▲ *Thich Nhat Hanh leading a peace walk in Los Angeles*

Thich Nhat Hanh has combined traditional meditative practices with non-violent protest, emphasising how meditation can help to dissolve anger, which is a primary cause of conflict. On one occasion, he was organising the rescue of hundreds of Vietnamese refugees using boats from Singapore. When the police found out his plan they ordered him out of the country and did not permit the boats to leave. He wrote, 'What could we do in such a situation? We had to breathe deeply and consciously. Otherwise we might panic, or fight with the police, or do something to express our anger at their lack of humanity.'

Extension activity

Research the life of Nichidatsu Fujii, a Japanese Buddhist who helped to build peace pagodas around the world. Make notes on how he campaigned for peace.

Links

Read more about Engaged Buddhism on page 155.

Research activity

Find out more about the work that Thich Nhat Hanh has done to promote peace.

★ Study tip

While the general principle of non-violence in Buddhism is very clear, Buddhists have varying views on pacifism. For example, there are hundreds of Buddhists in the British Army.

Summary

You should now be able to discuss Buddhist attitudes towards pacifism. You should also be able to describe the work of a Buddhist peacemaker.

Activities

1   What is a pacifist?
2   How does the Parable of the Saw imply that Buddhism supports pacifism?
3   What does Buddhism say about how to create peace?

Contrasting beliefs

Christian pacifists take inspiration from the teachings of Jesus, who strongly encouraged **peacemaking**. However, not all Christians are pacifists. Many Christians believe there are circumstances when war may be justified (see the just war theory on pages 128–129).

Find out more about Christian teachings on pacifism. Do Christian beliefs agree or contrast with Buddhist beliefs on this issue?

■ Providing help to victims of war

Casualties are an unavoidable part of war. In addition to the harm that is caused to those directly involved in the fighting, harm is also caused to their families and friends. For example, if the main wage earner dies in a war, their family may struggle financially without them. If a place of work is destroyed in a war, nobody can earn a wage there. If crops are destroyed or water supplies polluted, starvation could follow for those who live in the surrounding area.

In the UK if a member of the military is killed or injured, financial systems are in place to look after those left behind. Injured military personnel receive free health care, with some specialised care being provided by charities such as Help for Heroes. However, injury or death still has devastating effects on friends and families and can cause long-term emotional wounds.

There are many organisations that offer help and care for victims of war, wherever they live and whichever side of the conflict they fought on. These organisations believe that the life and welfare of human beings is what matters.

Buddhists believe that all suffering should be stopped, whatever its origin. This means that Buddhists want to help victims of war, as well as victims of natural disasters, or victims of poverty or violence. In addition to this, Buddhists believe that the perpetrators of war and violence also need people's compassion because they too suffer.

▲ *Victims of war whose homes have been destroyed may have to live in refugee camps, where conditions are often very poor*

⭐ **Study tip**

Remember that someone who has experienced the trauma of war is not only likely to have material needs, like food and shelter, but also psychological and perhaps spiritual needs.

Research activity 🔍

Use the internet to find out about other religious organisations that offer help to victims of war. Write down some examples of the work that they do.

Activities

1 'People who fight in wars don't deserve our compassion.' Evaluate this statement. Include more than one point of view, and refer to Buddhist teachings and beliefs in your answer.

2 If you were in charge of an organisation to help victims of war, what would your organisation do? What sort of help do you think it would be most important to provide?

Tzu Chi Foundation

One example of the many Buddhist organisations that help victims of war is the Tzu Chi Foundation, founded in Taiwan by the Buddhist nun Cheng Yen. Tzu Chi has projects in many countries with the aim of alleviating suffering in all its forms. Its work is inspired by the Bodhisattva goal to help all beings become free of suffering and ultimately to reach enlightenment. Its mission is 'expressing great kindness to all sentient beings, and taking their suffering as our own'.

Tzu Chi runs projects to address many kinds of suffering: educational projects, welfare projects, health projects and cultural projects. Among these, the organisation has opened a clinic in Istanbul, Turkey, to respond to the needs of the many Syrian refugees who have fled their country because of civil war. The clinic responds to all kinds of medical and health needs, and received more than 10,000 patients in its first three months. The Istanbul clinic has incorporated refugee Syrian doctors into its work to reduce language barriers, and to enable those doctors to make meaningful use of their skills. All treatment is free and the clinic is funded by charitable donations.

Tzu Chi also has a programme to distribute food and other basic necessities to refugees in several Turkish

▲ *A Tzu Chi Foundation volunteer helping to give out rice to Syrian refugees in Jordan*

cities. In addition, it has been providing food to Syrian refugees stranded in Serbia.

Cheng Yen believes that suffering is caused not by material deprivation alone but also by spiritual poverty. She maintains that a lack of compassion for others is at the root of many of the world´s problems. Consequently, a motto of Tzu Chi is to 'help the poor and educate the rich'.

Many Buddhists believe that victims of war need psychological and spiritual help, in addition to the basic necessities required for survival. Refugees have often witnessed horrible events, been displaced from their homes, and lost most or all of their possessions. They must live with the memories of what they have passed through, and this may mean that they need psychological support to adjust to all of the changes they have experienced. One aspect of this is their attitude towards their oppressors. A refugee can be left not only with psychological trauma but with anger, bitterness and even hatred towards the aggressors. Buddhism teaches that these attitudes are self-destructive and victims of war are likely to need help to let go of them. Cultivating compassion towards the aggressors not only helps the victims but also enables the aggressors to change. The aggressors too want to be happy but are going about it in the wrong way.

Thich Nhat Hanh confirms that it is not only the victims that need help but also the aggressors. He argues, 'When another person makes you suffer, it is because he suffers deeply within himself, and his suffering is spilling over. He does not need punishment; he needs help. That's the message he is sending.'

Extension activity

Search online to find out more about the life and work of Cheng Yen, the founder of the Tzu Chi Foundation. Explain how her work has been influenced by Buddhist beliefs.

Summary

You should now know about and understand support given to victims of war, including the work of the Tzu Chi Foundation.

Religion, violence, terrorism and war – summary

You should now be able to:

✔ explain beliefs and teachings about the meaning and significance of peace, justice, forgiveness and reconciliation

✔ explain beliefs and teachings about violence, including violent protest

✔ explain beliefs and teachings about holy war and terrorism

✔ explain beliefs and teachings about reasons for war, including greed, self-defence and retaliation

✔ explain beliefs and teachings about the just war theory, including the criteria for a just war

✔ explain beliefs and teachings about pacifism.

Religion and belief in twenty-first century conflict – summary

You should now be able to:

✔ explain attitudes to the use of nuclear weapons and weapons of mass destruction, including Buddhist beliefs

✔ consider religion and belief as a cause of war and violence in the contemporary world

✔ explain beliefs and teachings about pacifism and peacemaking

✔ explain Buddhist responses to the victims of war

✔ explain similar and contrasting perspectives in contemporary British society to all of the above issues

✔ explain similar and contrasting beliefs in contemporary British society to the three issues of violence, weapons of mass destruction and pacifism, with reference to the main religious tradition in Britain (Christianity) and one or more other religious traditions.

Sample student answer – the 12-mark question

1. Write an answer to the following practice question:

   'The best way to bring about world peace is for more individuals to become pacifists.'

   Evaluate this statement. In your answer you:

   • should give reasoned arguments to support this statement
   • should give reasoned arguments to support a different point of view
   • should refer to religious arguments
   • may refer to non-religious arguments
   • should reach a justified conclusion.

   [12 marks]
   [+ 3 SPaG marks]

2. Read the following sample student answer:

   "I disagree with this statement because if people become pacifists, they will make themselves easy targets for their enemies. If you are fighting for a cause or for your country, it is safest to attack the easiest targets. This will achieve nothing. The best way to bring about world peace is to take on those who threaten peace and defeat them. Peace will follow once those who threaten war are removed from the scene. Some Buddhists might support this view, particularly from the past when some monks have stood against a government who is oppressing them and their right to follow Buddhism.

   Having said this, being violent or showing some sort of violent protest could work in some situations, but in some others it could end badly. Most Buddhists are actually pacifists and they would tend to trust that if you do not pose a threat to people, they will leave you alone. This may work but people like Hitler would probably just see it as a sign of weakness and take advantage.

Real pacifism is more than refusing to fight though. True pacifists love their neighbour and work hard at making sure they live in peace and don't upset people or make them feel the need to retaliate. They actually work at establishing peace by getting on with everybody. If this is what a pacifist really does then maybe the statement could be true, although it will have to be worked at.

Some Buddhists are involved in what is called 'engaged Buddhism' and they work actively to ensure that people do not retaliate. Buddhists would always be first at the negotiating table and the Buddha would favour dialogue as opposed to fighting, which he would have argued only brings about more dukkha. The whole emphasis in the Buddhist faith is to get rid of dukkha or suffering. The first precept asks Buddhists not to harm any living thing, so if Buddhists were not pacifists they would end up harming living beings and breaking the first precept. Certainly the more pacifists there are, the fewer people there are left to fight, so maybe it is true."

3. With a partner, discuss the sample answer. Is the focus of the answer correct? Is anything missing from the answer? How do you think it could be improved?

4. What mark (out of 12) would you give this answer? Look at the mark scheme in the Introduction (AO2). What are the reasons for the mark you have given?

5. Swap your answer with your partner's and mark each other's responses. What mark (out of 12) would you give? Refer to the mark scheme and give reasons for the mark you award.

Practice questions

1. Which **one** of the following most accurately means a violent protest?

   A) Demonstration   **B)** Riot   **C)** Campaign   **D)** March   [1 mark]

2. Give **two** reasons for war.   [2 marks]

3. Explain **two** contrasting beliefs in contemporary British society about whether countries should possess nuclear weapons.

   In your answer you should refer to the main religious tradition of Great Britain and one or more other religious traditions.   [4 marks]

4. Explain **two** reasons why religious believers should help victims of war.

   Refer to sacred writings or another source of religious belief and teaching in your answer.   [5 marks]

5. 'Pacifism is the approach that religious believers should take when discussing whether it is right to fight.'

   Evaluate this statement. In your answer you:
   • should give reasoned arguments to support this statement
   • should give reasoned arguments to support a different point of view
   • should refer to religious arguments
   • may refer to non-religious arguments
   • should reach a justified conclusion.   [12 marks]
   [+ 3 SPaG marks]

Religion, crime and punishment

7.1 Crime and punishment

■ What are crime and punishment?

A **crime** is any action which is against the laws that have been put in place by the rulers of a state. In the UK, the police arrest people who are suspected of having broken the law by committing crimes. If after questioning the police are confident they have got the right person, they charge the person with having committed the crime.

Once someone is charged of a crime, they usually appear before a court where a judge or a jury will determine what their **punishment** should be. The most serious crimes such as murder and rape result in a life sentence in prison, although this rarely means that offenders spend the rest of their lives in prison. Less serious offences might result in a shorter time in prison, community service or a fine. There are no circumstances in the UK where a court can impose a punishment that causes physical harm (corporal punishment) or death (capital punishment).

▲ *In the UK, punishments are usually determined by a judge or jury in a court*

■ Good and evil intentions and actions

Buddhism tends not to speak in terms of 'good' and 'evil' but rather in terms of '**skilful**' and '**unskilful**' actions. A skilful action is rooted in generosity, kindness and understanding, whereas an unskilful action is rooted in selfishness, hatred and ignorance.

The principle of kamma teaches that what is most important for Buddhists is the intention that drives an action. However, sometimes it is difficult for a person to know what their motives really are, and so a further way to understand if their actions are skilful or not is to work out whether their actions cause harm to themselves and/or others. The five moral precepts can also be used to help identify unskilful and skilful actions.

What counts as a crime is defined by the government of each country. There are many unskilful actions that are not crimes, and there may even be crimes that are not unskilful from a Buddhist perspective. For instance, it would be unskilful to lie but most lies are not considered crimes. Yet a lie could potentially cause much more suffering than a minor crime (such as trespassing).

Generally, Buddhists believe that it is correct to follow the law, but that it is even more important to cultivate skilful actions and abandon unskilful ones. There might be some circumstances where Buddhists feel compelled to disregard or disobey a law that they consider to be unjust, but probably not in a violent way. For instance, if a law were made that said it was illegal to meditate, many Buddhists would feel justified in ignoring that law, even if it meant that they might be punished for doing so. They would consider it a matter of principle to resist a law that restricted spiritual development.

■ Buddhist views on punishment

The idea of punishment, in any form, goes against Buddhist ethics, since punishment involves causing suffering to someone who has made others suffer. To some degree it is rooted in the idea of vengeance, and the idea that someone must 'pay' for their crimes. Buddhism seeks to relieve suffering rather than to increase it.

However, Buddhists do believe that there are consequences for a person who acts in an unskilful way. First, there will be consequences for themselves. The principle of kamma teaches that unskilful actions lead to suffering both now and even in future lives. Equally, people who act in unskilful ways usually have few friends.

According to Buddhists, everyone can change, and so even if someone has committed a crime there is always the possibility of rehabilitation. No one should ever be beyond hope or redemption, even if they have done terrible things. Without excusing or ignoring seriously unskilful actions, Buddhists aim to avoid feeling hatred towards criminals. Instead they try to show compassion towards the victims of crime, to understand the causes of crime, and to develop a constructive response to criminals. How can the criminal be rehabilitated so that they do not continue to commit further crimes? How can the suffering of the victims be healed?

Buddhism considers the practice of confession to be very important. If someone has acted unskilfully, it is important for them to recognise this and to try to make amends.

A famous example from the Buddhist scriptures is Angulimala ('Finger garland'), whose name derived from the fact that he had killed many people and took a finger from each of them, which he hung around his neck. When he met the Buddha, the Buddha did not seek to punish him for his crimes, but instead encouraged him to live a better life. Angulimala renounced violence and became a follower of the Buddha.

Links

Read more about the relationship between intentions, actions and kamma on page 71.

Activities

1 What happens to someone when they are caught committing a crime in the UK?

2 Explain how a Buddhist can determine whether an action is 'good' ('skilful') or 'evil' ('unskilful').

3 How might Buddhists deal with criminals?

▲ *Buddhism teaches that all criminals have the potential to redeem themselves*

★ Study tip

It helps to remember Buddhist teachings about kamma when thinking about crime and punishment.

Summary

You should now know more about the meanings of crime and punishment. You should also be able to explain Buddhist attitudes towards good and evil intentions and actions, and Buddhist views on punishment.

■ Reasons why people commit crimes

There are many reasons why people commit crimes. These range from specific, immediate reasons – such a stealing someone's wallet to pay for a drug addiction – to more complex reasons to do with the way that society is structured, which affect, for example, people's upbringing and education.

For Buddhists, while some actions that are considered crimes may arise from a skilful motive, such as defying a law that causes harm, crimes usually involve a lack of kindness or awareness of others. However, Buddhism recognises that

▲ *Education and upbringing can affect whether children later turn to crime*

various factors influence criminal activity, and that it is not simply a question of people being 'bad'. While Buddhism might condemn a crime, it would not condemn the criminal. Instead it would recognise that there were complex reasons and various outside influences that led the person to commit a crime. However, this does not mean that criminals are free of responsibility for their actions.

Poverty

There are many people living in **poverty** around the world who cannot afford basic necessities. This can sometimes lead people to steal food and other essentials that they do not have the money to buy. While poverty in itself is not a motive for crime, Buddhist scriptures make it clear that poverty is one of the underlying drivers of crime.

The quotation to the right from the Digha Nikaya indicates that if people do not have basic necessities, crime is likely to follow. While breaking the law for such reasons is understandable, it is still likely to cause harm to others. For Buddhists, stealing contradicts the second moral precept (to abstain from taking what is not freely given).

Upbringing

If a child has a troubled upbringing – for example, because of violence, addiction or neglect within the family – this could affect them negatively in a number of different ways, and they might turn to crime as a result. Buddhism recognises that various conditions influence people's

Objectives

● Understand some of the reasons why people commit crimes.

● Examine Buddhist attitudes to the reasons why people commit crimes.

Key terms

● **poverty:** being without money, food or other basic needs of life (being poor)

● **mental illness:** a medical condition that affects a person's feelings, emotions or moods and perhaps their ability to relate to others

● **addiction:** a physical or mental dependency on a substance or activity that is very difficult to overcome

● **greed:** selfish desire for something

> " … from goods not being bestowed on the destitute poverty grew rife; from poverty growing rife stealing increased, from the spread of stealing violence grew apace, from the growth of violence the destruction of life became common, from the frequency of murder both the span of life in those beings and their comeliness also wasted away … "
>
> The Buddha in the *Digha Nikaya*, p. 67

behaviour and values, and that in order to live an ethical life, people need supportive conditions that encourage sensitivity to others.

Mental illness

Mental illness, such as anxiety and depression, does not often lead to crime. Even more serious mental health problems are responsible for only a fraction of violent crimes. Treatments such as therapy and medication can usually bring control, if not a cure, for mental illness.

According to Buddhism, everyone sees reality in a distorted way, which leads people to inflict suffering on themselves and others.

 Places where wealth is seen as a sign of status may help to fuel crime committed because of greed

Addiction

Addiction to drugs means that the human body becomes dependent on them and cannot cope without them. Addicts face the choice of not taking drugs – an action they know will make their life physically and mentally very hard – or spending money to acquire more drugs. They may commit crimes to be able to fuel their addiction.

The drug that causes more crime than any other is alcohol. People who have drunk too much alcohol lose control of their thoughts and actions to such an extent that they may commit acts of violence or other crimes.

The fifth moral precept teaches that Buddhists should abstain from taking drugs (including alcohol). People who are under the influence of drugs lose their awareness. This means they are less sensitive to others and so are more likely to cause them harm.

Greed

If the material rewards to be gained by committing crime are much greater than any possible punishment, then people may be tempted to break the law. In places where personal possessions and wealth are seen as signs of status, this can help to fuel crime that is committed because of **greed**. Buddhism teaches that acting out of greed is unskilful and leads to suffering.

Hate

Hatred is a negative feeling or reaction that can lead to prejudice and violence against whoever or whatever the offender hates. According to Buddhism, hatred is one of the three poisons and one of the main causes of suffering. Buddhists believe it is important not to feel hatred towards others, even when provoked.

Opposition to an unjust law

According to lawmakers, breaking the law is always wrong. However, throughout history people have broken laws that they believed to be unjust. Buddhists might want to disobey a law that expresses prejudice and hatred, such as a law that supports racial discrimination.

Activities

1 Pick three of the reasons for crime mentioned on this page, and explain some of the ways you think these reasons could be solved. For example, how might society solve the problems of drug addiction or poverty?

2 Which of the reasons for crime do you think Buddhists would be most accepting and understanding of, and which do you think they would be least accepting of? Give reasons for your answers.

Discussion activity

With a partner, try to think of any other reasons why people might commit crime that are not already mentioned here.

⭐ Study tip

Check that you can list and explain the main causes of crime.

Summary

You should now understand some of the main reasons why people commit crimes. You should also have considered Buddhist attitudes towards these reasons.

■ Buddhist views about different types of crime

For Buddhists, one way in which the seriousness of a crime might be evaluated is through the degree of harm that it causes: the more harm, the worse the action. However, motivation would also be a significant factor. Committing a crime unintentionally is different to deciding to commit a crime. In addition, it might be possible to commit a crime with a skilful motivation, in which case Buddhism would not consider the action wrong, even if the law did.

■ Hate crimes

A **hate crime** expresses hostility or prejudice towards someone, or even a group of people. It might be because of their disability, ethnicity, religion or belief, or sexual orientation. Hatred is one of the three poisons, and the direct opposite of the emotions that Buddhists want to cultivate: loving-kindness and compassion. In Buddhism, there is therefore no justification for acting on the basis of hatred or intolerance.

▲ People gather in London to remember victims who were killed at a gay nightclub in Orlando, USA, in 2016

Hate crimes are often rooted in fear, insecurity and even envy. For Buddhists, the idea that causing harm to others will make someone happier is wrong. A person who acts from hatred causes suffering both for others and for themselves, so nobody wins.

The Buddha encouraged his followers to avoid falling into conflict with others based on differences of religious belief, because he recognised that this led to unskilful speech and even violent behaviour.

Objective

● Examine Buddhist attitudes towards different types of crime, including hate crimes, theft and murder.

Key terms

● **hate crimes:** crimes, often including violence, that are usually targeted at a person because of their race, religion, sexuality, disability or gender

● **theft:** stealing the property of another person

● **murder:** the taking of a life by deliberate intention

❝ Whoever is not hostile among the hostile, at rest among those who are violent, not clinging among those who are clinging, him I call a [holy man]. ❞

The Buddha in the *Dhammapada*, verse 406

Discussion activity

Can killing someone in order to prevent that person from harming others ever be justified? With a partner, discuss whether you think there are any situations where killing might be the best course of action.

■ Theft

Theft can cause great upset to the person whose property is stolen, but the crime is usually more about the property and not about the victim, who is often unknown to the offender. Greed and poverty are two of the main causes of theft.

Theft breaks the second moral precept, which is to abstain from taking what has not been freely given. It strengthens the habit of greed, and weakens any tendency towards generosity. It leads people to place their needs and interests above those of others.

▲ *Poverty is one of the main causes of theft*

For Buddhists, theft expresses the delusion that people will be happier simply through acquiring something they do not have. Buddhism says that this is not the case. In fact, if a person steals something then they will suffer, because this undermines the trust that exists between people. Stealing expresses a lack of respect and empathy for others. If the criminal does not know the person they are stealing from, it may seem as if there is no real victim, but this point of view expresses a lack of awareness, and often disguises a person's own selfishness.

For Buddhists, stealing from a monk or other revered person may be seen as even more unskilful, because it expresses a lack of reverence for the spiritual order of things.

■ Murder

In many people's eyes, the most serious crime is **murder**. Murder means the unlawful and deliberate killing of another person, and clearly contradicts the most basic Buddhist precept, which is not to take life. Traditionally, killing another human being is one of the causes for expulsion from a Buddhist monastery.

While it might seem obvious that murder is wrong, some people argue that murdering an 'evil' person can be justified in certain situations, particularly if this prevents them from harming or even killing others. There is a story in the Buddhist scriptures that tells of an incident during a previous life of the Buddha, in which he was a captain of a ship carrying 500 merchants. One of those passengers was a bandit who was planning to kill all the other passengers. The Buddha concluded that the most skilful thing to do in this circumstance was to kill the bandit to prevent all of the other people from being harmed.

Murdering someone involves not only inflicting suffering on the victim, but also on their family and friends. Perhaps the person has a spouse and children who depend on them. The consequences of a murder can impact on a whole community.

Activities

1 Why do Buddhists think that hate crimes are wrong?
2 Do you think there are ever circumstances where theft is acceptable? Give reasons for your answer.

★ Study tip

Make sure you can explain what Buddhists think about different types of crime.

Summary

You should now understand what Buddhism teaches about different types of crime, including hate crimes, theft and murder.

7.4 The aims of punishment

Whenever a punishment is imposed by a court, the judge has to consider what purpose the punishment will serve. In the UK, no matter how severe the punishment, it is usually intended as a positive action – to protect society, to assist the offender, to stop others from making the same mistakes, or a combination of these. Three of the main aims of punishment are retribution, deterrence and reformation.

■ Retribution

Retribution is one of the least positive aims of punishment. In simple terms, it means wanting to make a criminal pay for what they have done wrong. People who believe that retribution is important tend to think that criminals should be made to suffer in proportion to how serious their crimes are. This means that more serious crimes should have more serious punishments. For example, some people argue that murderers should be put to death because they need to be severely punished for what they have done.

According to Buddhism, retribution is a form of violence that contradicts basic ethics. Committing violence against the offender does not wipe away the suffering caused by a crime, nor does it encourage the criminal to accept responsibility for their actions in order to act better in the future. Instead, it usually creates bitterness and breeds further violence and crime.

The Buddhist thinker David Loy once said, 'We are not punished for our sins but by them.' According to the principle of kamma, a person's unskilful deeds will cause them to suffer. Consequently, there is no need to inflict further suffering on those who have acted badly.

On the other hand, it might be argued that without lawful retribution, people would want to punish the criminals themselves, possibly more seriously than the criminals deserve. Lawful retribution helps to reduce the urge towards vengeance on the part of the victims.

■ Deterrence

One of the aims of punishment is to prevent other people from committing crimes. If someone knows they will be punished as a result of committing a crime, they might be less likely to commit it. For example, the threat of being banned from driving might prevent people from driving while drunk. This is called deterrence.

While deterrence may be effective in controlling some people's behaviour, many doubt whether people have been persuaded not to commit murder because they don't want to spend many years in prison. The United States, for instance, has a huge prison population but still has a high crime rate. Reasons why people commit serious crimes are more complex than a simple fear of punishment. However, people considering committing less serious offences may be influenced by possible punishment.

Traditionally, the belief that a person might be reborn in a realm of suffering if they act badly in this life has functioned as a deterrent in Buddhism. But this seems to only go so far. If criminals are in the grip of greed, hatred and delusion, they can lose sight of what may happen afterwards. People need to train their minds to imagine the consequences of their actions, and criminals often seem unable to imagine the damage they may cause.

Buddhists might agree that it is important to protect society from certain criminals. For this reason they may support putting criminals in prison. However, the motive would not be to punish or even to deter, but to ensure the welfare of society.

▲ *Buddhism teaches that people who act badly may be reborn in a realm of suffering*

■ Reformation

The UK punishment system emphasises the importance of **reformation**. It is hoped that punishment will encourage offenders to change their attitude and become responsible, law-abiding members of the community. In order for this to work, the offender needs to realise that their behaviour is wrong before they can hope to be reformed. This may involve group therapy sessions, individual counselling and treatment (if required), meeting their victims so they realise the harm they have caused, or working in the community (community service).

According to Buddhism, a criminal should be encouraged to recognise the suffering they have caused and to apologise to the victims, perhaps even face-to-face. It might also be appropriate to do some corrective action, for instance, to repair damage caused by vandalism. The overall aim of a Buddhist approach to justice is to encourage the transformation of the criminal so that they begin to act in a more sensitive and responsible way. This will rehabilitate the criminal in their own eyes, and in the eyes of society and of the victim. In addition, the victim may need help to recover from the suffering caused by the crime, and to let go of any anger or resentment towards the criminal.

Activities

1 Three main aims of punishment are retribution, deterrence and reformation. Put these in order of which you think is most important to Buddhists and which is least important. Give reasons for your answer.

2 How important do you think retribution is as an aim of punishment? Explain your answer.

Discussion activities

1 Discuss with a partner whether you think the main aim of prison should be retribution, deterrence or reformation. If you were in charge of a prison, what changes would you make to try to make sure you were successful in your main aim?

2 With a partner, design a plan to help reform a criminal who has stolen a car. What would you do to help the criminal not to commit the same crime in the future?

★ Study tip

Learn some of the reasons why Buddhists might support some forms of punishment more than others.

Summary

You should now understand Buddhist attitudes towards the different aims of punishment.

In UK law, there are many ways that criminals can be legally punished, and several ways that they cannot. How severe the punishment is depends on the seriousness of the crime. Punishment can range from a long-term stay in prison for a serious crime, to a fine or community service for a less serious one. In the UK, all people who are tried in a court are treated equally, have the same rights, and face the same range of punishments. This is one of the principles that underpins the UK legal system.

■ Prison

Prison is reserved for people who have committed serious crimes. The main punishment of imprisonment is a loss of liberty. Prisoners are locked in cells for some of the day, are fed at set times, and have to do manual work for little money.

For Buddhists, the primary purpose for putting someone in prison is to protect society from them. If someone is a serial killer, for instance, it would be irresponsible to allow them to live freely in society. A further reason for using prison might be to give the criminal time and space to reflect on their actions and so rehabilitate themselves.

■ Corporal punishment

Corporal punishment involves punishing an offender by causing them physical pain, for example by whipping them or striking them with a cane. Corporal punishment was allowed in all schools in the UK until 1987, and using a cane was a common method of disciplining children until it was banned. Today many people believe corporal punishment is a breach of human rights. It is illegal in the UK, but exists in some other parts of the world.

For Buddhists, corporal punishment expresses violence, and is likely to encourage resentment rather than reformation. It does not solve the underlying motives for crime.

■ Community service

Criminals who have committed less severe crimes, such as vandalism or benefit fraud, might be punished with **community service**. Community service offers the offender a chance to make up for what they have done, and to receive help in reforming their behaviour. In the UK, it might involve anywhere from 40 to 300 hours of unpaid work in the local area, doing tasks such as removing graffiti, clearing wasteland or decorating public buildings.

Most Buddhists approve of community service that helps to rehabilitate the criminal. For this to work, the community service needs to address their crime directly, and help them to recognise its negative impacts.

Objectives

- Examine Buddhist attitudes towards different types of punishment.
- Understand arguments for and against the death penalty.

Key terms

- **prison:** a secure building where offenders are kept for a period of time set by a judge
- **corporal punishment:** punishment of an offender by causing them physical pain
- **community service:** a way of punishing offenders by making them do unpaid work in the community
- **death penalty:** capital punishment – a form of punishment in which a prisoner is put to death for crimes committed
- **principle of utility:** philosophical idea that an action is right if it promotes maximum happiness for the maximum number of people affected by it

---

Discussion activity

Discuss with a partner which forms of punishment you think are the most effective and why. Does it depend on the particular crime?

Community service that directly addresses the needs of the victim might be more effective.

▲ *Painting and decorating public buildings or areas may form a part of community service*

■ The death penalty

Some people and countries feel very strongly that someone who has taken a life must pay by having their own life taken away, and that this is the only real deterrent to murder. Others think that no one has the right to take the life of another person. In the UK, the **death penalty** was abolished in 1965 as a temporary experiment, and then permanently banned in 1969.

Most Buddhists are against the death penalty for a number of reasons. It breaks the first moral precept, and does not allow the possibility of rehabilitation. In addition, it makes revenge part of the system, which is unskilful. It should also be remembered that people are sometimes wrongly convicted.

Some people argue for the death penalty because of the philosophical **principle of utility**. This states that the best action is the one that creates the greatest amount of happiness for the greatest number of people. This could be applied to the death penalty by arguing that only the criminal suffers (and to some extent the criminal's family and friends), while the victim's family and friends, and any future victims (and their family and friends) are happier.

Most Buddhists disagree with this approach, because Buddhism teaches that it is not possible to create happiness by making other people suffer. This encourages vengeance and cruelty, which express hatred (one of the three poisons). Thailand, which is a Buddhist country, legally allows capital punishment for more than 30 crimes, including drug trafficking. This shows that Buddhist ethics don't necessarily impact on government policy.

Activities

1   What does Buddhism teach is the most important purpose of prisons?

2   Give three reasons why most Buddhists are against the death penalty.

Contrasting beliefs

Most Christians are against corporal punishment and the death penalty. This might be because they believe it is unacceptable to cause physical pain to someone, or because only God has the right to take away life, or because Jesus taught that forgiveness is important.

Find out more about Christian teachings on corporal punishment and the death penalty. Do Christian beliefs agree or contrast with Buddhist beliefs on these issues?

Links

To connect the idea of the sanctity of life with arguments about the death penalty, see page 95.

★ Study tip

When thinking about Buddhist attitudes to different types of punishment, remember that reformation is very important in Buddhism.

Summary

You should now be able to explain Buddhist attitudes towards prison, corporal punishment, community service and the death penalty.

■ What is forgiveness?

Buddhism teaches that it is important for someone to show **forgiveness** when they are holding on to a sense of being wronged, which leads them to feel angry or resentful. Forgiving involves letting go of these feelings, and also letting go of the desire to see the other person being punished or suffering for what they have done. Forgiveness does not imply that a person's actions are acceptable. Instead, it shows a willingness to move on, and recognises that the other person can change.

Buddhism teaches that if people do not forgive then they will suffer, because they will continue to be angry and resentful. As the Dhammapada says:

> ❝ 'He abused me, he struck me, he overcame me, he robbed me.' Of those who wrap themselves up in it hatred is not quenched. ❞
>
> The Buddha in the *Dhammapada,* verse 3

This means that people should forgive for the sake of their own health and welfare.

If someone is close to a person who has suffered from a serious crime, they may think that forgiveness involves betraying the victim. However, forgiving a criminal does not mean that their actions will not have consequences. It may still be the case that the person is punished by the law or by someone else for what they have done. In addition, Buddhism says that unskilful actions lead to suffering, so whether or not criminals are punished, they will face the consequences of their behaviour.

It is easier to forgive if the other person confesses their wrongdoing and apologises. If the offender is not sorry for what they have done, or even thinks that they have done nothing wrong, it is much more difficult to forgive. Sometimes, offenders may find it difficult to forgive themselves for what they have done. This results in more guilt and suffering. It can even result in further criminal behaviour.

Apology and forgiveness can sometimes bring about reconciliation. Reconciliation helps the offender and the victim learn to trust one another. However, unless the offender recognises that they have done wrong, there can be no reconciliation, even if the victim forgives the offender.

▶ *The Buddha taught that anyone should be forgiven if they are genuinely sorry for what they have done*

> **Objective**
>
> ● Examine Buddhist teachings and attitudes about forgiveness.

> **Key term**
>
> ● **forgiveness:** showing compassion, and pardoning someone for what they have done wrong

⭐ **Study tip**

Remember that many Buddhists may practise confession and seek forgiveness for things they have done wrong. By doing this, they free their minds from the burden of secrecy and guilt, but they still experience the consequences of their actions.

One Buddhist scripture says:

> " Bhikkhus [monks], there are these two kinds of fools. What two? One who does not see his transgression as a transgression and one who does not, in accordance with the Dhamma, accept the transgression of one who is confessing. These are the two kinds of fools.
>
> Bhikkhus [monks], there are these two kinds of wise people. What two? One who sees his transgression as a transgression and one who, in accordance with the Dhamma, accepts the transgression of one who is confessing. These are the two kinds of wise people. "
>
> The Buddha in the *Anguttara Nikaya*, vol. 1, p. 59

Anh-Huong Nguyen on forgiveness

Anh-Huong Nguyen is a Zen Buddhist from Vietnam. She spent ten months in a refugee camp in Malaysia before going to the USA. In the refugee camp, she came across many girls and women who had been raped by pirates – men who had boarded their boats while they were in the waters near Malaysia.

To begin with, Anh-Huong was very angry with the pirates, but through meditation she came to understand that the pirates were themselves victims of their own upbringings and local environments. She realised that if she had been born as a male into a family where piracy was accepted and expected, she might well have become a pirate herself.

Anh-Huong recognises that suffering can sometimes make it very hard to forgive someone. But she thinks that understanding and compassion can help lead to forgiveness. She believes that a helpful question to ask is, 'How can I better understand myself and the other person?'

By trying to understand the pirates, Ann-Huong learnt to forgive them.

■ Are some crimes unforgiveable?

Some crimes are so bad that it might seem impossible to forgive them. How can we forgive mass murder, for instance? Elie Wiesel, a Jewish survivor of the Nazi holocaust, once said, 'I cannot and I do not want to forgive the killers of children; I ask God not to forgive.' He believed that he would dishonour all the murdered Jews if he forgave the Nazis, and he would find it hard to live with himself. Buddhism teaches that even in these circumstances it is best to learn to forgive, but this does not mean to excuse or forget what has happened.

Summary

You should now understand Buddhist teachings about forgiveness.

Discussion activity

There is a Tibetan Buddhist story about two monks who were tortured by their captors in prison. They met each other again a number of years after they were released. The first monk asked the second monk, 'Have you forgiven them?' The second monk replied, 'I will never forgive them!' The first monk then said, 'Well, I guess they still have you in prison, don't they?'

Discuss with a partner what you think the first monk meant.

Activities

1 'If you forgive someone, it means you approve of their behaviour.' Evaluate this statement. Include more than one point of view, and refer to Buddhist teachings and beliefs in your answer.

2 Using Buddhist teachings, suggest some ways that people can learn to forgive others.

Contrasting beliefs

Forgiveness is a core belief in Christianity, and one that Jesus emphasised in his teachings. For example, even while he was dying on the cross, Jesus asked God to forgive the people who had crucified him. Christians believe they should follow the example of Jesus and forgive those who do wrong things.

Find out more about Christian teachings on forgiveness. Do Christian beliefs agree or contrast with Buddhist beliefs on this issue?

Religion, crime and the causes of crime – summary

You should now be able to:

✔ explain beliefs and teachings about good and evil intentions and actions, including whether it can ever be good to cause suffering

✔ explain different reasons for crime, including poverty and upbringing, mental illness and addiction, greed and hate, and opposition to an unjust law

✔ explain views about people who break the law for these reasons

✔ explain views about different types of crime, including hate crimes, theft and murder.

Religion and punishment – summary

You should now be able to:

✔ explain beliefs and teachings about the aims of punishment, including retribution, deterrence and reformation

✔ explain beliefs and teachings about the treatment of criminals, including prison, corporal punishment and community service

✔ explain beliefs and teachings about forgiveness

✔ explain beliefs and teachings about the death penalty

✔ explain ethical arguments related to the death penalty, including those based on the principle of utility and sanctity of life

✔ explain similar and contrasting perspectives in contemporary British society to all of the above issues

✔ explain similar and contrasting beliefs in contemporary British society to the three issues of corporal punishment, the death penalty and forgiveness, with reference to the main religious tradition in Britain (Christianity) and one or more other religious traditions.

Sample student answer – the 4-mark question

1. Write an answer to the following practice question:

   Explain two contrasting beliefs in contemporary British society about corporal punishment.

   In your answer you should refer to the main religious tradition of Great Britain and one or more other religious traditions. **[4 marks]**

2. Read the following student sample answer:

   "Most people in Britain disagree with corporal punishment. It is not a loving action because it harms people, some of whom may be innocent, and doesn't reform them. Buddhists follow the first precept, which is to not harm any living being, so do not agree with corporal punishment. Some Christians might quote from the Bible where it says, 'He who spares the rod hates his son.'"

3. With a partner, discuss the sample answer. Can you identify two contrasting beliefs? Is there reference to the main religious tradition in Great Britain (Christianity) and at least one other religious tradition? Can it be improved? If so, how?

4. What mark (out of 4) would you give this answer? Look at the mark scheme in the introduction (AO1). What are the reasons for the mark you have given?

5. Now swap your answer with your partner's and mark each other's responses. What mark (out of 4) would you give the response? Refer to the mark scheme and give reasons for the mark you award.

Sample student answer – the 5-mark question

1. Write an answer to the following practice question:

   Explain **two** religious beliefs about the reasons why some people commit crimes.

   Refer to sacred writings or another source of religious belief and teaching in your answer.

   [5 marks]

2. Read the following student sample answer:

   "If a person has a mental illness, such as difficulty controlling anger, minor assaults on people who upset them can be excused even though they are still wrong. Offering them help to control their anger is a loving action that Christians favour. Buddhists would say that metta, which means loving kindness, can be offered to a criminal. If a person steals because they are greedy, greed is wrong and one of the three poisons in Buddhism and should be avoided. Buddhists would be against punishment for the person who committed the crime, but would rather want to reform the person."

3. With a partner, discuss the sample answer. Can you identify two religious beliefs about the reasons why people commit crimes? Are the beliefs detailed, and is the teaching relevant and accurate? Can it be improved? If so, how?

4. What mark (out of 5) would you give this answer? Look at the mark scheme in the introduction (AO1). What are the reasons for the mark you have given?

5. Now swap your answer with your partner's and mark each other's responses. What mark (out of 5) would you give the response? Refer to the mark scheme and give reasons for the mark you award.

Practice questions

1. Which **one** of the following is not a cause of crime?

   A) Hate   **B)** Forgiveness   **C)** Addiction   **D)** Poverty   **[1 mark]**

2. Give **two** different aims of punishment.   **[2 marks]**

3. Explain **two** contrasting beliefs in contemporary British society about whether a person can commit a crime to oppose an unjust law.

   In your answer you must refer to one or more religious traditions.   **[4 marks]**

4. Explain **two** reasons why religious believers believe forgiveness is important for criminals.

   Refer to sacred writings or another source of religious belief and teaching in your answer.

   [5 marks]

> 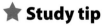 **Study tip**
>
> You are asked to write reasons why religious believers believe forgiveness is important for criminals. If you give reasons why some people think criminals should not be forgiven, you will not be given credit.

5. 'It is never right to punish a murderer by killing them.'

   Evaluate this statement. In your answer you:

   - should give reasoned arguments to support this statement
   - should give reasoned arguments to support a different point of view
   - should refer to religious arguments
   - may refer to non-religious arguments
   - should reach a justified conclusion.   **[12 marks]**
   [+ 3 SPaG marks]

■ What is social justice?

Social justice exists when people in a society are treated equally under the law, and have equal rights and opportunities. It means that no one is exploited, resources and wealth are shared fairly, and care is taken of the least advantaged members of society.

Many people around the world campaign for greater social justice in their countries. In some countries, people are denied the freedom to follow the religion of their choice or express opinions about the actions of government. Other societies suffer because of a breakdown of law and order, or from violent attacks from terrorists. Some people live in societies where the rich are very rich and the poor struggle to survive. Those who campaign for social justice wish to see a world where people are treated more fairly and given equal opportunities, whatever their gender, sexual orientation, religion, politics, ethnicity, disability or age.

■ Buddhism and social justice

The common image of Buddhists is of quiet, meditative, peaceful people who have withdrawn from the world's problems. It is true that the Buddha encouraged monks and nuns to withdraw from society in order to have more time and space for meditation and study. However, he also criticised monks who failed to look after the sick and he talked to kings seeking advice. It has always been the case that most of his followers have been lay people active in society, not monks or nuns.

The Buddha taught that suffering is an inevitable part of life, and that on a fundamental level the world is unsatisfactory – it cannot be made perfect. People will suffer if they keep expecting life to be completely satisfying. Buddhists try to improve their understanding of suffering to help them to accept life's disappointments.

However, this does not mean that Buddhists think it is pointless to try to relieve suffering or make the world a better place. The Buddha taught again and again the importance of kindness, compassion, generosity and unselfishness as a way of bringing communities together. As always in Buddhism, the middle way is best, accepting imperfection while doing what one can to make a better world.

> **Objective**
> - Understand Buddhist teachings about social justice.

> **Key terms**
> - **social justice:** ensuring that society treats people fairly whether they are poor or wealthy; protecting people's human rights
> - **Engaged Buddhism:** a movement in Buddhism that is particularly concerned with applying the Buddha's teachings to matters of social and environmental injustice

▲ *Taking part in peaceful protest is one way that people can try to create a more just world*

■ Engaged Buddhism

Engaged Buddhism is a term that was first used in the 1990s by Vietnamese Zen Buddhist teacher Thich Nhat Hanh. It is used by Buddhists who want to tackle social issues, including injustice, through the application of Buddhist teachings.

Engaged Buddhists can be found within all Buddhist traditions and countries, among lay people, monks and nuns. They might be helping people to recover from drug and alcohol addiction, or caring for people with AIDS. There are Buddhist projects working with the homeless in New York City, teaching mindfulness meditation in prisons, and helping those living with chronic pain and illness.

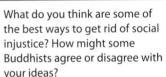
▲ *Thich Nhat Hanh, a Zen Buddhist monk from Vietnam*

Projects dealing directly with social injustice include the Sarvodaya movement in Asia, which has focused on the fair distribution of land among the poor. However, perhaps the world's largest and least-known Buddhist social justice movement has taken place in India. Since the 1950s, millions of Dalit people, at the bottom of India's caste system, have converted to Buddhism, following their leader, Dr Ambedkar. These 'new Buddhists', having transformed their own lives, do a great deal of social work helping India's poorest people (not just Buddhists) to escape from poverty. Much of the money for this is raised by the Karuna Trust, a British Buddhist charity. Karuna's Buddhist fundraisers walk around British cities, knocking on doors and inviting people to give money to help the poor in India.

The term Engaged Buddhism seems to be used less frequently now, perhaps because the message of Engaged Buddhism has been so successfully communicated that many people now assume that being a Buddhist automatically means caring about social issues. For example, the UK's Network of Engaged Buddhists closed down in 2014, saying that this was probably a sign not of failure but of success. People didn't need it anymore because so many British Buddhist groups were now more socially engaged anyway.

Discussion activity

What do you think are some of the best ways to get rid of social injustice? How might some Buddhists agree or disagree with your ideas?

Research activity

Use the internet to find out about the International Network of Engaged Buddhists and some of the work that they do.

★ Study tip

Remember that even though Buddhism teaches that the world will always contain suffering, many Buddhists still think it is important to try to make the world a better place.

Summary

You should now be able to explain Buddhist attitudes towards social justice, and give specific examples of how Buddhists are working to overcome social injustice.

Activities

1   The Buddha taught that suffering is inevitable and the world will always be unsatisfactory. Does this mean that Buddhists do not care about trying to make the world a better place? Give reasons for your answer.

2   Give some examples of how Engaged Buddhists try to improve social justice.

3   'Improving society begins with improving oneself.' Evaluate this statement. Include more than one point of view, and refer to Buddhist teachings and beliefs in your answer.

8.2 Human rights and responsibilities

What are human rights?

In 1948 the United Nations General Assembly adopted the *Universal Declaration of Human Rights,* a document setting out the basic **human rights** everyone in the world should be entitled to. These include rights such as the right to an education, the right to be treated fairly by the law, the right to follow a religion of your choice, and the right to free speech. This declaration has helped to shape the law in most countries around the world. In the UK, it helped lead to the creation of the Human Rights Act, which sets out the basic rights that everyone in the UK is entitled to.

Rights and responsibilities

It is easy to see that not everyone in the UK has access to basic human rights. For example, celebrities are often denied the 'right to respect for private and family life', and victims of human trafficking have been denied the right that 'no one shall be held in slavery or servitude'.

Why are human rights denied? One of many reasons is that it is not possible to have basic human rights for everyone without acknowledging the **responsibility** that people have to help make those rights available. This includes the responsibility to respect other people's rights, and the responsibility to help create access to those rights.

Nobody can insist on their own rights without also acknowledging that other people have the same rights. This means there are sometimes limits to what any one person can do. For example, if someone uses their right of free speech to encourage violence, this threatens other people's right to live without fear.

People also have a responsibility to help make sure everyone has access to human rights. For example, a right to education involves many people being willing to pay taxes to pay for schools, as well as the responsibility of pupils and students to be willing to learn.

Buddhism and human rights

Being committed to reducing suffering, most Buddhists recognise the great importance of human rights in society. Some Buddhists work very actively for human rights, for example supporting the work of charities such as Amnesty International. British Buddhists are part of the European Buddhist Union, which sends a representative to the Council of Europe's Human Rights Commission. In 2014 the Commission elected this representative, a French Buddhist, as its president for three years.

However, Buddhists would probably say that rights are of relatively limited use unless everyone takes personal responsibility for cultivating

Objectives

- Consider basic human rights and the need to act responsibly to protect them.
- Understand Buddhist teachings and attitudes about human rights and responsibilities.

Key terms

- **human rights:** the basic rights and freedoms to which all human beings should be entitled
- **responsibility:** a duty to care for, or having control over, something or someone

> ❝ All human beings are born free and equal in dignity and rights. They are endowed with reason and conscience and should act towards one another in a spirit of brotherhood. ❞
>
> *The Universal Declaration of Human Rights*

Activities

1 Give three examples of ways in which individuals and governments would have to behave in order to ensure everyone could exercise their right to free speech.

2 The Buddha said that people should be aware of their duties towards each other. Why is this important for ensuring that everyone has access to basic human rights?

wisdom and compassion. The Buddha spoke on different occasions about the duties that people have towards each other. For example, he advised rulers to put other people first, and to be honest, kind, free from anger and patient. He also said a ruler should respect differing points of view, and rule for the benefit of their people and according to the will of the people. The Buddha understood that everyone needs to take responsibility for helping people to have access to human rights.

A Buddhist approach to freedom of speech

Human rights include the right to freedom of speech. This means the right to speak or write publicly about what one thinks, even if it includes criticising those in government. But what if someone is criticising your religion, or your culture, or you personally?

▲ *A march in London against the Chinese occupation of Tibet*

The Buddha talked a great deal about the importance of speaking kindly and truthfully, even if the truth is sometimes painful to hear. He said some of the greatest harm is committed in communication, and each person has a responsibility for what they say and how they say it.

Yet he also said that ethical communication involves responsibility on the part of the person listening. They need to accept that if they are offended by what is said, that is their responsibility. If they get angry, blame the speaker and hit back, all that is also their responsibility. With training in awareness, it is quite possible to hear difficult things without reacting, so reaction is a choice.

■ Tibet and human rights

Many British people, including Buddhists, have campaigned for the human rights of the people of Tibet. Tibet is a largely Buddhist region that was invaded by the Communist Party of China in 1959. China sees Tibet as being part of China, but the people of Tibet would prefer it to be an independent country.

Since 1959, thousands of Tibetans have been killed or put in prison. Many monasteries and temples have been destroyed. Tibetans are required to speak Chinese instead of Tibetan, there are limits on their right to practise Buddhism, and they are not free to disagree with the actions of the government.

When Tibet was invaded, its government moved to northern India, along with its leader, the Dalai Lama. Although he had to leave his home and his people have suffered greatly, he continues to teach the importance of non-violence. Not all Tibetans agree with him, and some have tried to fight back against the Chinese government.

Discussion activities

1 Thinking about the way you and your friends communicate online, what do you think about the Buddha's claim that some of the greatest suffering is caused by what we say (or write)?

2 What would your school be like if everybody demanded their own rights but refused to do anything to support the rights of other people?

★ Study tip

You should aim to understand why it is not possible for people to have access to basic human rights if people do not also take responsibility for providing them.

Summary

You should now be able to explain what human rights are, and understand how people have to take responsibility for providing them. You should also be able to explain Buddhist attitudes towards rights and responsibilities.

8.3 Religious freedom

Religious freedom in the UK

The Universal Declaration of Human Rights states that everyone should have the right to **freedom of religion** or belief. In the UK, the Human Rights Act guarantees the protection of this right. Each person has the freedom to choose to belong to any religion they wish, or to have no religious belief at all. They also have **freedom of religious expression** – the right to practise and express their faith however they want to. For example, Buddhists, Christians, Hindus, Jews, Muslims and Sikhs in the UK are allowed to worship as they choose. Organisations like the Inter Faith Network for the UK work to promote good relations, understanding and cooperation between people of different faiths.

Buddhist attitudes towards religious freedom

The Buddha often talked to people who had met other religious teachers with different ideas. Sometimes these people asked the Buddha how they should decide whose teachings to follow. He encouraged them to listen to him and others with respect, and then decide which teachings did, in their own experience, lead to greater happiness and wellbeing.

▲ *In Tibet, Buddhists may be persecuted and even jailed for expressing their religious beliefs*

Very few Buddhist traditions try to persuade others that they should become Buddhists.

The Buddha's teachings are his description of reality as he saw it, and a series of suggestions for the kind of life which leads to greater happiness and a profound understanding of reality. It is entirely up to the individual whether they wish to follow this. Buddhism teaches that if a Buddhist breaks one of the precepts then nobody will punish them, but they will

Objectives

- Understand freedom of religion as a basic human right.
- Examine Buddhist teachings and attitudes about freedom of religion.

Key terms

- **freedom of religion:** the right to believe or practise whatever religion one chooses
- **freedom of religious expression:** the right to worship, preach and practise one's faith in whatever way one chooses

Discussion activity

Discuss the following statement with a partner or in a small group: 'People should have the freedom to say whatever they want about religion.'

❝ I always say that every person on this earth has the freedom to practise or not practise religion. It is all right to do either. **❞**

Tenzin Gyatso
(the Dalai Lama)

experience the consequences of their actions, just like anyone else. In Buddhism there is no God to be held accountable to. This means there is quite a lot of freedom within Buddhism to decide how to practise the faith.

■ Religious freedom in Buddhist countries

In traditionally Buddhist countries in Asia, the culture and law may be strongly influenced by Buddhism, but individuals are free to practise Buddhism with as much or as little commitment as they like. Buddhism is a path of personal transformation, rooted in the wish to end suffering by developing wisdom and compassion, so it is not possible to force someone to be Buddhist.

▲ A Buddhist and a Muslim walk together through the city of Yangon in Myanmar, to show their disapproval of the violence between the two religions

However, there are places in some Buddhist countries where it is not easy to be Hindu or Muslim. In recent years many Buddhists around the world have been shocked by the violence and hatred shown by a small number of Buddhists towards religious or ethnic minorities in countries including Thailand, Myanmar, Sri Lanka and Bhutan. For example, in Myanmar in 2013, there were a series of violent riots and clashes where both Muslims and Buddhists were killed. The reasons for such violence are complex, but are usually rooted in disputes over land, as well as a fear of foreigners.

Concerned by the violence, a number of respected Buddhist leaders (including Thich Nhat Hanh) wrote an open letter to their 'brother and sister Buddhists in Myanmar', asking them to remember Buddhist teachings, and to act compassionately towards everyone in Myanmar:

> ❝ Buddhist teaching is based on the precepts of refraining from killing and causing harm. Buddhist teaching is based on compassion and mutual care. Buddhist teaching offers respect to all, regardless of class, caste, race or creed.
>
> It is only through mutual respect, harmony and tolerance that Myanmar can become a modern great nation benefiting all her people and a shining example to the world. ❞

Contrasting beliefs

Like Buddhism, Christianity teaches that freedom of religious expression is a fundamental human right. Most Christians believe that Jesus taught about the importance of tolerance and freedom of religion. They also believe that God gave people the free will to choose whether to follow Christianity, another religion or no religion.

Find out more about Christian teachings on freedom of religious expression. Do Christian beliefs agree or contrast with Buddhist beliefs on this issue?

★ Study tip

Learn about the difficulties for religious minorities in Myanmar or another country, so you can use it as an example when discussing religious freedom.

Summary

You should now be able to explain Buddhist attitudes towards freedom of religion and religious expression.

■ Equality

Many people consider **equality** to be hugely important for creating a fair and just world, and for overcoming social injustice. Many Buddhists care deeply about this too, as an expression of their commitment to kindness and relieving suffering. As we have seen, they also believe that people need to accept that life, by its very nature, is ultimately unfair and unsatisfactory. Still, it is important that they do what they can to avoid adding unnecessarily to life's difficulties through their own actions.

Not treating people equally can lead to **prejudice** and **discrimination**. Prejudice means thinking less of someone because of their ethnicity, religion, gender, sexual orientation and so on. It is an opinion which has been formed without good reason, knowledge or experience. Prejudice can lead to discrimination, which means treating someone or a group of people differently. Usually this is unfair, and can lead to people feeling worthless, hated and very vulnerable.

■ Gender prejudice and discrimination

While gender discrimination has been illegal in the UK since the Sex Discrimination Act of 1975, it still occurs in a number of different situations. For example, on average women are still paid less than men, and while women make up roughly half the workforce, men hold a higher proportion of senior positions.

There are examples of gender discrimination within religion in the UK as well. For example, the Catholic Church does not allow women to become priests, and only men can lead the worship in Orthodox Jewish services. But there are also examples where religions are changing to promote greater equality. For example, the Church of England decided to allow ordination for women in 1993, and in 2014, Libby Lane became the first female bishop in the Church of England.

As we saw on pages 88–89, there is gender discrimination in Buddhism. There are also traditions where women and men are ordained equally. Two examples in Britain are the Triratna Buddhist Order and the Order of Buddhist Contemplatives. Many leading Buddhist teachers in America are women.

■ Homosexuality

Buddhist scriptures say very little about **homosexuality**. Though some Asian Buddhist teachers, such as the Dalai Lama, have said it is inappropriate for Buddhists to have same-sex relationships, most Buddhists in the West simply think that the moral precepts apply to any couple, whether heterosexual or homosexual.

There are no Buddhist teachings that say same-sex relationships are simply wrong, because there is no God who could decide such a thing.

Objectives

- Explore attitudes towards prejudice and discrimination, including the treatment of women and homosexuals.
- Understand views on racial prejudice and discrimination.

Key terms

- **equality:** the state of being equal, especially in status, rights, and opportunities
- **prejudice:** unfairly judging someone before the facts are known; holding biased opinions about an individual or group
- **discrimination:** actions or behaviour that result from prejudice
- **homosexuality:** being sexually attracted to members of the same sex
- **positive discrimination:** treating people more favourably because they have been discriminated against in the past or have disabilities

★ Study tip

Make sure you understand the difference between prejudice and discrimination.

Contrasting beliefs

Find out more about Christian beliefs and teachings about the status of women. Do Christian beliefs agree or contrast with Buddhist beliefs on this issue?

Buddhist ethics are about noticing and deciding for oneself what actually causes harm. This contrasts for example with the teaching of the Catholic Church, which states that homosexual people should remain celibate.

In general, Western Buddhists tend to see same-sex relationships as a normal part of everyday life. There are lots of homosexual British Buddhists, including ordained teachers. Views vary, however. Some Asian Buddhists are less likely to accept same-sex relationships, but this is more a reflection of local culture than Buddhist teaching.

▲ *The Triratna Buddhist Community has ordained men and women equally since its foundation*

■ Racial discrimination

If someone shows racial prejudice, this means they have a negative attitude towards another person based on the ethnic group to which they belong. This is often linked to the colour of a person's skin, which is one of the more obvious indicators that a person belongs to a different race. Various Acts have been passed that make racism illegal in the UK. Despite this, it still occurs regularly. For example, some football supporters shout abuse during matches, particularly at black players. 'Show Racism the Red Card' is a campaign in England that uses top footballers to combat this, and aims to educate people about the negative effects of racism.

Racial discrimination can be 'positive' as well as 'negative'. Positive discrimination happens when, in an attempt to counteract negative discrimination, people who have previously been discriminated against are given preferential treatment. An example might be employing someone from an ethnic minority partly in order to help make the workplace more racially diverse. Some people think positive discrimination is important to help rectify centuries of negative discrimination. Others think that despite the good intentions behind the idea, it is still a form of discrimination, and it would be better to try to treat all people equally.

As a form of unkindness which causes suffering, racism is not in keeping with the Buddha's teaching. Most Buddhists are completely against it and would say they are not racist themselves.

However, Buddhists are imperfect human beings like everyone else. Black and Asian Britons who become Buddhists often feel they don't quite fit in at the Asian temples, where perhaps everything is in Chinese or Sinhala, or follows Thai or Tibetan tradition. They may prefer to attend centres and temples run mostly by white Buddhists, even though they may feel invisible there. The white teachers may unconsciously behave as if everyone is white, always referring to white culture in their teaching, never using readings from black authors, and so on. While there are rarely if ever instances of overt racism in Buddhist centres in the UK, some might argue that more could be done to help minorities feel welcomed.

Research activity

Soka Gakkai International (SGI-UK) is probably the most ethnically diverse Buddhist movement in Britain today. Use the internet to find out about SGI-UK.

Discussion activity

Black and Asian Britons may say they don't feel they fit in at traditional Asian British or mostly white-run Buddhist temples. Are these feelings indications of racism? What do you think is the problem, and how do you think people need to behave in order to overcome it?

Summary

You should now be able to explain the terms prejudice and discrimination, and discuss Buddhist attitudes towards equality, prejudice and discrimination with reference to gender and sexuality.

■ How much wealth should a Buddhist have?

Many Buddhists think it is important to earn enough for a simple but dignified life that leaves time to concentrate on spiritual practice.

However, there are no restrictions on how much wealth a Buddhist should have, unless, perhaps, they are a monk or nun. There are some rich Buddhists around the world, and some of them use their money to do a great deal of good. For Buddhists, what matters is how people get their money, how they relate to it, and what they do with it.

For example, even without committing crime, it is possible to get rich while not paying your workers properly or looking after their health, or from an industry that harms the environment. It is also common for people to rely on being rich for a sense of self-worth, and to use money to gain power over others. Buddhists tend to see such uses of wealth as being unhelpful in developing wisdom and compassion.

According to legend, the Buddha grew up in a palace with everything he could possibly want, but abandoned this life of luxury to search for enlightenment. He then tried living as an extreme ascetic. While he eventually gave this up, realising that hunger made it impossible to develop wisdom and compassion, he continued to live very simply all his life.

For the Buddha, true happiness did not come from having everything he wanted. Being desperately poor and hungry didn't bring happiness either. The Buddha realised that the important thing was to have enough for one's needs, and if one had more than that, to use every opportunity for generosity.

Traditionally, when a man became a monk in the Theravada tradition, he chose to live with just a handful of possessions including a bowl, a robe, a needle and thread (to mend the robe) and a razor (to shave his head and face). Though other monastic Buddhist traditions may not require quite such simplicity, all encourage a letting go of attachment to material possessions.

Buddhists who are not monks or nuns need to be able to earn a livelihood and provide for their family if they have one. Everyone needs clothing, food and shelter. Without them, spiritual life is a luxury.

■ Valuing wealth

Buddhism teaches that a person's worth does not depend on how much

Objective

- Understand Buddhist teachings about wealth and its uses.

Discussion activities

1. How do you feel about yourself when you have money? How do you feel about yourself when you don't?

2. In the Triratna Buddhist Community in Britain there are ethical businesses where people are paid according to what each person needs. This means people get different amounts of money for the same job. How do you think you would feel about working in a place like that?

▲ For Buddhists, a person's worth does not depend on how much money they have, but on how it is used

wealth they have, and that money in itself is not good or bad. Used well, money can do a great deal of good in this world.

Craving or greed is one of the three poisons, which the Buddha saw as the main cause of suffering. He advised that true happiness does not come from an accumulation of wealth fuelled by greed and an attachment to material possessions.

> ❝ By action, knowledge and Dhamma, by virtue and noble way of life – By these are mortals purified, not by lineage or wealth. ❞
>
> The Buddha in the *Majjhima Nikaya*, vol. 3, p. 262

■ Using wealth

The Adiya Sutta lists three main benefits of wealth. It suggests that a person can use their wealth to:

1. provide pleasure and satisfaction for themselves, their family and their friends
2. keep themselves safe
3. make offerings to monks, nuns or the poor.

▲ *Buddhist monks usually live a simple lifestyle, and rely upon offerings from the local community*

Buddhism does not condemn using wealth for one's own entertainment and enjoyment, as long as it does not also create suffering through attachment and craving.

However, Buddhism also places much value on using wealth generously for the benefit of others. Giving to monasteries and to charity is important for many Buddhists. Giving without expecting to receive anything in return is a central part of Buddhist ethics.

In Buddhist tradition, someone who put his wealth to good use was Anathapindika, a lay disciple of the Buddha. An extremely wealthy banker, he used his wealth to purchase a park and then build a monastery in it for the Buddha and his followers. He provided daily meals for the monks and their visitors, including the sick and other local people. When he had almost nothing left, he still continued to give what he could to others.

Contrasting beliefs

Christians also believe it is important to use wealth to help others, as Jesus taught them. Many believe that wealth is a gift from God, to be used in his service and to help carry out his work on Earth.

Find out more about Christian teachings on the uses of wealth. Do Christian beliefs agree or contrast with Buddhist beliefs on this issue?

★ Study tip

Remember that most Buddhists are not monks or nuns, so you should be able to explain how lay Buddhists might think about their relationship with money, and the way they earn it and spend it.

Activities

1 'Money is important for Buddhists.' Evaluate this statement. Include more than one point of view, and refer to Buddhist teachings and beliefs in your answer.
2 If you were rich, how would you use your money to make the world a better place? Give three examples.
3 Give some examples of how a person might accumulate wealth in a way that Buddhists would disapprove of.

Summary

You should now understand Buddhist attitudes towards wealth, including how to use it.

Fair pay

An important way to stop **exploitation** of the poor is to make sure they are paid fairly for the work they do. There are many poor people in the world today who are not paid fair wages. This is often because large international companies pay their workers in developing countries tiny wages in order to make large profits for their shareholders. This practice helps to prevent the poor from escaping **poverty**, because working long hours for tiny wages means they do not have the time or money to gain an education, and acquire the skills they need to find better-paid work.

One example of this type of exploitation in Thailand (a primarily Buddhist country) is in the shrimp-processing industry. Hundreds of thousands of workers are forced to work almost like slaves in the shrimp-processing factories, being paid very little while working long hours in poor conditions. Sometimes workers' passports or identity cards are confiscated so they cannot find work elsewhere.

In the UK, the introduction of the National Minimum Wage Act in 1998 made an important difference to fair pay. This set the lowest amount of money an employer can legally pay a worker per hour in the UK. This law was designed to protect workers at the lowest end of the pay structure from exploitation. Another important initiative has been the Fair Trade movement. This aims to improve working conditions and wages for farmers and workers in developing countries.

Many Buddhists consider it very important to balance profit with ethics. Taking workers' time and energy without paying them a reasonable wage goes against the second Buddhist precept, to avoid taking what has not been freely given. Many Western Buddhists try to avoid buying their clothes from Western companies believed to treat their Asian factory workers very badly.

A number of British Buddhist places of worship promote Fair Trade. For example, Taraloka Buddhist Retreat Centre for Women in Shropshire is an official 'Fairtrade Temple'. This means that the centre uses Fair Trade products in its meals as much as possible.

Excessive interest on loans

People with poor credit ratings or bad financial histories are often not allowed to borrow money from mainstream banks or money lenders. Instead they have to borrow money from organisations that charge very high rates of interest on their loans. Interest rate figures are usually given as percentages that show how much extra money a person will owe over the

▲ *In Thailand, many workers in the shrimp-processing industry are exploited*

course of a year. For example, an interest rate of 100 per cent means that if a person initially borrows £500, at the end of the year they will owe twice that amount – the original £500 and the interest on the loan, which in this case is 100 per cent, so another £500.

Some money lenders in the UK charge interest rates around 3000 or 4000 per cent. They often target low-income families who need short-term loans to help them out until the next payday. If people cannot repay the loans fast enough, the huge interest rates mean they can quickly end up in debt.

Like underpaying workers, charging excessive interest is also against the Buddha's second precept, to avoid taking what has not been freely given. Making money by exploiting the poor is a clear example of greed. It is a form of deliberate harm, which means it also goes against the first precept. It causes suffering to the person doing it as well as to the person being exploited.

On the other hand, many Buddhists feel it is a person's responsibility not to get into debt if they can help it. Sometimes there is no alternative, but sometimes people borrow just to indulge their craving. One example is compulsive overspending on credit cards. Is someone hungry or in danger of being evicted from their home, or do they just want to buy a more fashionable television? Are they becoming addicted to spending? Debt tends to make people feel bad about themselves. This makes it harder to live the kind and honest life which can lead to enlightenment.

■ People-trafficking

People-trafficking is a worldwide problem, and a multi-billion pound industry. It is often referred to as modern-day slavery, because people are bought, sold and smuggled from one place to another like slaves. Sometimes people are kidnapped and forced to work as prostitutes. At other times, people who are desperate for a better way of life pay smugglers to get them out of their own poverty-stricken country and into a more prosperous country. Once in the new country, the migrants have few rights and the smugglers may force them to work in poor conditions for little pay.

Some of the world's most serious people-trafficking takes place in countries that are extremely poor, and that also happen to be traditionally Buddhist. It's unclear whether trafficking or slavery in the modern Western sense existed in northern India in the Buddha's time. However, he certainly spoke out against India's caste system, in which some groups of people were considered so inferior that they were forced to live outside their villages, doing only the worst jobs such as cleaning toilets, and were paid almost nothing to do it.

> **66** In five ways does [a] master minister to his servants and employees … by assigning them work according to their strength; by supplying them with food and wages; by tending them in sickness; by sharing with them unusual delicacies; by granting leave at times. **99**
>
> The Buddha in the *Digha Nikaya*, vol. 3, pp. 190–191

Research activity

Use the internet to find out about the Dharma Moli project in Nepal, where Buddhist nuns are helping to protect girls from trafficking.

★ Study tip

Buddhism is not against lending and borrowing money as long as it does good rather than harm. For example, there are Buddhists running micro-credit schemes in Asia, where groups of poor people (often women) save money together, which they agree to lend to each other in turn at very low interest rates, for example to buy a sewing machine to start a small business.

Summary

You should now be able to discuss issues surrounding the exploitation of workers, excessive interest on loans, and the problem of people-trafficking. You should have some idea of Buddhist attitudes towards these topics.

Activities

1 Why is it important to pay people fairly for their work?
2 Why do Buddhists think it is bad to charge excessive interest on loans?
3 Explain how human-trafficking exploits people.

■ The problem of poverty

Someone is defined as living in poverty if they do not have enough money to be able to meet basic daily needs. Poverty exists in all countries, but particularly in the developing world. The United Nations estimates that around 800 million people still live in extreme poverty. Each year this leads to millions of deaths, often from diseases caused by poor sanitation or unsafe drinking water, or from malnutrition due to a lack of food.

Poverty is a complex global problem that has many causes, from how society is structured to environmental issues such as drought. Often developing countries have huge debts that mean they cannot afford to provide adequate healthcare, education and similar necessities for their people. War and conflict can ruin a country's infrastructure and cause widespread poverty. Environmental disasters can destroy people's homes, livelihoods and crops. In the UK, one of the main causes of poverty is unemployment.

■ Helping those in poverty

There are two main ways to help the poor. The first is to give emergency aid to help provide basic necessities such as shelter and food. This type of aid is particularly important after a disaster or crisis such as an earthquake or civil war. It is also important for those who need help to survive in the short term, such as those living on the streets in the UK.

Some people argue that this type of help is important for people's immediate survival, and that providing it shows compassion and kindness. Others argue that while this type of short-term aid is important, it does not help to get people out of poverty, and it also makes them reliant upon whoever is giving out the aid.

Some people therefore feel it is more important to direct their energies towards solving the root causes of poverty. For example, they might campaign against multinational companies that exploit the poor, or they might donate to charities that provide education for those in poverty.

Several lists of Buddhist virtues start with dana, or generosity, indicating that this is viewed as a most basic Buddhist virtue. The Buddha talked of various possible motivations for giving, some less generous than others. For example, giving because you want something back from the person goes against Buddhist ethics. The Buddha taught that the best way to give is freely, out of desire for the wellbeing of others.

Objectives

- Understand Buddhist attitudes towards charity and giving money to the poor.
- Examine the responsibilities of those living in poverty.

Discussion activity

With a partner discuss the following questions:

1 What do you think might be the best ways to eliminate world poverty? If you were the prime minister of the UK, what actions would you take first to try to eliminate poverty?

2 Who do you think should take the most responsibility for helping people to get out of poverty? How much responsibility do you think should be placed on the people in poverty to get themselves out of it?

▲ Is it better to give money directly to the poor or to a charity that tries to solve the root causes of poverty?

However, for Buddhists it is important to give what is likely to be of genuine help. It could be argued that giving money to a homeless person who appears to be drunk is not ethical if there is a strong probability that they will spend it on more drink, which could harm their health. It could be more generous to buy them food, or give the money to a homeless charity instead.

There are a huge number of Buddhist charities working with the world's poor in various ways, but they tend to be little known. Many of them are very small, helping particular local groups of people, for example sponsoring girls in Cambodia to go to school. Probably the largest British Buddhist charity is the Karuna Trust, which raises money for projects working with the poor in Nepal and India.

▲ *The Karuna Trust helps to provide care and education for children living in poverty*

> ❝ Bhikkhus [monks], a donor who gives food gives the recipients five things. What five? One gives life, beauty, happiness, strength, and discernment. ❞
> The Buddha in the *Anguttara Nikaya,* vol. 3, p. 42

> ❝ Learn to live in this world with self-respect. You should always cherish some ambition of doing something in this world. ❞
> Dr Ambedkar

■ Responsibilities of the poor

Who is responsible for poverty: the people who are in poverty, or the social systems that have caused their poverty? Some argue that most people are in poverty through unfortunate circumstances that are a result of how society works, therefore it is society's responsibility to help them. Others think that more responsibility should be placed on the individuals in poverty, either not to get into poverty in the first place, or to make more of an effort to improve their situation.

There are many types and causes of poverty. Some poverty is the result of personal irresponsibility (such as gambling and drinking one's money away). Some poverty just happens for reasons completely out of a person's control (such as an earthquake destroying someone's village and livelihood). However, Buddhism teaches that all poverty deserves profound compassion. Relieving poverty requires responsibility on the part of poor people, governments, businesses and the wealthy.

Here is one example of the poor liberating themselves. Page 155 mentioned India's Dalit people, formerly known as 'untouchables', who are at the bottom of India's caste system. Since the 1950s, millions of them have freed themselves from extreme poverty. It is significant that many of them did this partly by changing religion. They converted to various religions but many became Buddhists, following their leader, Dr Ambedkar. He told them to 'educate, agitate and organise' to resist the people and laws keeping them in poverty. However, he also said that one of the most important things they could do to free themselves from poverty was to change their self view, to stop seeing themselves as poor and insignificant, to develop more self-respect, and to take themselves and each other seriously.

Activities

1 What are some of the causes of poverty?

2 Do you think it is a good idea to give money to homeless people on the streets? Explain your views.

3 What are Buddhist attitudes towards giving money to the poor and helping those in poverty?

★ Study tip

Buddhism sees nothing noble in poverty. Poverty should not be confused with choosing to live very simply, as many Buddhists do, especially some monks and nuns. There can be a great sense of freedom and joy in living simply, but poverty usually results in a struggle to survive.

Summary

You should now be able to explain something about the causes of poverty, and some views on how to relieve poverty, including Buddhist perspectives.

Human rights – summary

You should now be able to:

✔ explain prejudice and discrimination in religion and belief, including the status and treatment within Buddhism of women and homosexuals

✔ explain issues of equality, freedom of religion and belief, including freedom of religious expression

✔ explain what is meant by human rights and the responsibilities that come with rights, including the responsibility to respect the rights of others

✔ explain Buddhist views about social justice

✔ explain Buddhist attitudes to racial prejudice and discrimination.

Wealth and poverty – summary

You should now be able to:

✔ explain Buddhist teachings about wealth, including the right attitude to wealth

✔ explain religious teachings about the uses of wealth

✔ explain the responsibilities of having wealth, including the duty to tackle poverty and its causes

✔ describe and explain the problem of exploitation of the poor, including issues relating to fair pay, excessive interest on loans and people-trafficking

✔ explain the responsibilities of those living in poverty to help themselves overcome the difficulties they face

✔ explain what Buddhism teaches about charity, including issues related to giving money to the poor

✔ explain similar and contrasting perspectives in contemporary British society to all the above issues

✔ explain similar and contrasting beliefs in contemporary British society about the three issues of the status of women in religion, the uses of wealth, and freedom of religious expression, with reference to the main religious tradition in Britain (Christianity) and non-religious beliefs such as atheism or humanism.

Sample student answer – the 12-mark question

1. Write an answer to the following practice question:

    'Racism is the worst form of prejudice.'

    Evaluate this statement. In your answer you:
    • should give reasoned arguments to support this statement
    • should give reasoned arguments to support a different point of view
    • should refer to religious arguments
    • may refer to non-religious arguments
    • should reach a justified conclusion.

    [12 marks]
    [+ 3 SPaG marks]

2. Read the following sample student answer:

    "Some people have believed in the past that some races are inferior to others. Hitler believed this and picked on the Jews and had millions of them sent to concentration camps and then to the gas chambers. He wanted to wipe out the Jewish race and the holocaust resulted. So racism can be a horrible thing. It can cause genocide where one race kills people of another race simply because they are different. Some people would say that because racism can cause so much suffering, like the holocaust, it is the worst form of prejudice.

There are other types of prejudice, like thinking badly about people because of their gender or their religion or their sexuality. Some people might say that sexism is the worst type of prejudice because it affects about 50% of the world's population. Other people might say that religious prejudice is worse because it can lead to more extreme suffering for the people affected. Like in Myanmar, where Buddhists have destroyed Muslim mosques and businesses, and some Muslims have even died.

Maybe it depends what the prejudice leads to. For example, if someone is killed because of their race, this is much worse than if someone isn't given a job because of their gender. But at other times the racism might not lead to such bad things happening. So maybe it depends on the situation. For example, there are some Buddhist temples in the UK where black Buddhists don't feel like they fit in because the people running the temples are white. That might be a type of racism but it's not as bad as lots of other things that sometimes happen because of other types of prejudice."

3. With a partner, discuss the sample answer. Is the focus of the answer correct? Is anything missing from the answer? How do you think it could be improved?

4. What mark (out of 12) would you give this answer? Look at the mark scheme in the Introduction (AO2). What are the reasons for the mark you have given?

5. Swap your answer with your partner's and mark each other's responses. What mark (out of 12) would you give? Refer to the mark scheme and give reasons for the mark you award.

Practice questions

1. Which **one** of the following is the main religious tradition in Britain?

   A) Buddhism   **B)** Christianity   **C)** Islam   **D)** Hinduism   **[1 mark]**

2. Give **two** ways in which wealth can be used responsibly.   **[2 marks]**

3. Explain **two** contrasting beliefs in contemporary British society about the equality of men and women in religion.

   In your answer you must refer to or more religious traditions.   **[4 marks]**

4. Explain **two** religious beliefs about social justice.

   Refer to sacred writings or another source of religious belief and teaching in your answer.   **[5 marks]**

5. 'People who are poor need to help themselves to overcome their poverty.'

   Evaluate this statement. In your answer you:

   • should give reasoned arguments to support this statement
   • should give reasoned arguments to support a different point of view
   • should refer to religious arguments
   • may refer to non-religious arguments
   • should reach a justified conclusion.   **[12 marks]**
       [+ 3 SPaG marks]

Glossary

A

abortion: the removal of a foetus from the womb to end a pregnancy, usually before the foetus is 24 weeks old

adaptation: a process of change, in which an organism or species becomes better suited to its environment

addiction: a physical or mental dependency on a substance or activity that is very difficult to overcome

adultery: voluntary sexual intercourse between a married person and someone who is not their spouse (husband or wife)

Amitabha Buddha: the Buddha worshipped by Pure Land Buddhists

anatta: the idea that people do not have a permanent, fixed self or soul

anicca: impermanence; the idea that everything changes

Arhat: for Theravada Buddhists, someone who has become enlightened

ascetic: living a simple and strict lifestyle with few pleasures or possessions; someone who follows ascetic practices

atheist: a person who believes that there is no God

B

benevolent: all-loving, all-good; a quality of God

Big Bang: a massive expansion of space which set in motion the creation of the universe

biological weapons: weapons that use living organisms to cause disease or death

Bodhisattva: for Mahayana Buddhists, someone who has become enlightened but chooses to remain in the cycle of samsara to help others achieve enlightenment as well

Buddha: a title given to someone who has achieved enlightenment; usually used to refer to Siddhartha Gautama

Buddhism: a religion founded around 2500 years ago by Siddhartha Gautama

Buddha rupa: a statue of the Buddha, often sitting cross-legged in a meditation pose

Buddhahood: when someone achieves enlightenment and becomes a Buddha

Buddha-nature: the idea that everyone has the essence of a Buddha inside them

C

chanting: in Buddhism, reciting from the Buddhist scriptures

chemical weapons: weapons that use chemicals to harm humans and destroy the natural environment

civil partnership: a legal union of a same-sex couple

cohabitation: a couple living together and having a sexual relationship without being married to one another

community service: a way of punishing offenders by making them do unpaid work in the community

contraception: the artificial and chemical methods used to prevent a pregnancy from taking place

corporal punishment: punishment of an offender by causing them physical pain

crime: an offence which is punishable by law, for example stealing or murder

D

death penalty: capital punishment – a form of punishment in which a prisoner is put to death for crimes committed

dependent arising: the idea that all things arise in dependence upon conditions

Design argument: the argument that God designed the universe, because everything is so intricately made in its detail that it could not have happened by chance

deterrence: an aim of punishment – to put people off committing crimes

Dhamma (Dharma): the Buddha's teachings

discrimination: actions or behaviour that result from prejudice

divine: that which relates to God, gods or ultimate reality

divorce: legal ending of a marriage

dominion: dominance or power over something; having charge of something or ruling over it

dukkha: the first noble truth: there is suffering

E

Engaged Buddhism: a movement in Buddhism that is particularly concerned with applying the Buddha's teachings to matters of social and environmental injustice

enlightenment: the gaining of true knowledge about God, self or the nature of reality, usually through meditation and self-discipline; in Buddhist, Hindu and Sikh traditions, gaining freedom from the cycle of rebirth

environment: the natural world; the surroundings in which someone lives

equality: the state of being equal, especially in status, rights, and opportunities

eternal: without beginning or end

ethics (sila): a section of the threefold way that emphasises the importance of skilful action as the basis for spiritual progress

euthanasia: killing someone painlessly and with compassion, to end their suffering

evil: the opposite of good, a force or personification of a negative power that is seen in many traditions as destructive and against God

exploitation: misuse of power or money to get others to do things for little or unfair reward

extended family: a family which extends beyond the nuclear family to include grandparents and other relatives

F

family: a group of people who are related by blood, marriage or adoption

family planning: using contraception to control how many children couples have and when they have them

festival: a day or period of celebration for religious reasons

First Cause argument: also called the cosmological argument; the argument that there has to be an uncaused cause that made everything else happen, otherwise there would be nothing now

forgiveness: showing compassion and pardoning someone for what they have done wrong

free will: belief that God gives people the opportunity to make decisions for themselves

freedom of religion: the right to believe or practise whatever religion one chooses

freedom of religious expression: the right to worship, preach and practise one's faith in whatever way one chooses

G

gender discrimination: acting against someone on the basis of their gender; discrimination is usually seen as wrong and may be against the law

gender equality: the idea that people should be given the same rights and opportunities regardless of whether they are male or female

gender prejudice: unfairly judging someone before the facts are known; holding biased opinions about an individual or group based on their gender

general revelation: God or the divine as revealed through ordinary, common human experiences

gompa: a hall or building where Tibetan Buddhists meditate

greed: selfish desire for something

H

hate crimes: crimes, often including violence, that are usually targeted at a person because of their race, religion, sexuality, disability or gender

heterosexual: sexually attracted to members of the opposite sex

holy war: fighting for a religious cause or God, often inspired by a religious leader

homosexual: sexually attracted to members of the same sex

homosexuality: being sexually attracted to members of the same sex

human rights: the basic rights and freedoms to which all human beings should be entitled

human sexuality: how people express themselves as sexual beings

I

immanent: the idea that God is present in and involved with life on Earth and in the universe; a quality of God

impersonal: the idea that God has no 'human' characteristics, is unknowable and mysterious, more like an idea or force

J

Jataka: the Jataka tales are popular stories about the lives of the Buddha

just war theory: a set of criteria that a war needs to meet before it can be justified

justice: bringing about what is right and fair, according to the law, or making up for a wrong that has been committed

K

kamma (karma): a person's actions; the idea that skilful actions result in happiness and unskilful ones in suffering

karuna: compassion; feeling concerned for the suffering of other people and wanting to relieve their suffering

M

magga: the fourth noble truth: the way to stop suffering; the Eightfold Path

Mahayana Buddhism: an umbrella term to describe some later Buddhist traditions, including Pure Land Buddhism, Tibetan Buddhism and Zen Buddhism

mala: prayer beads that are used to count the number of recitations in a mantra

mandala: an intricate, circle-shaped pattern that is used for meditation

mantra: a short sequence of sacred syllables

Mara: a demon that represents spiritual obstacles, especially temptation

marriage: a legal union between a man and a woman (or in some countries, including the UK, two people of the same sex) as partners in a relationship

meditation: a practice of calming and focusing the mind, and reflecting deeply on specific teachings to penetrate their true meaning

meditation (samadhi): a section of the Threefold Way that emphasises the role of meditation in the process of spiritual development

mental illness: a medical condition that affects a person's feelings, emotions or moods and perhaps their ability to relate to others

metta: loving-kindness; showing a benevolent, kind, friendly attitude towards other people

mindfulness of breathing: a meditation practice focusing on the experience of breathing

miracle: a seemingly impossible event, usually good, that cannot be explained by natural or scientific laws, and is thought to be the action of God

monastery (vihara): a place where Buddhist monks and nuns live

murder: the taking of a life by deliberate intention

N

natural resources: materials found in nature – such as oil and trees – that can be used by people

nibbana (nirvana): a state of complete enlightenment, happiness and peace

nidanas: 12 factors that illustrate the process of birth, death and rebirth

nirodha: the third noble truth: suffering can be stopped

nuclear family: a couple and their dependent children regarded as a basic social unit

nuclear weapons: weapons that work by a nuclear reaction, devastate huge areas, and kill large numbers of people

O

omnibenevolent: all good; a quality of God

omnipotent: almighty, having unlimited power; a quality of God

omniscient: knowing everything; a quality of God

P

pacifism: the belief of people who refuse to take part in war and any other form of violence

Pali: the language of the earliest Buddhist scriptures

Parinirvana Day: a Mahayana festival that commemorates the Buddha's passing away

peace: an absence of conflict, which leads to happiness and harmony

peacemaker: a person who works to establish peace in the world or in a certain part of it

peacemaking: the action of trying to establish peace

people-trafficking: the illegal movement of people, typically for the purposes of forced labour or commercial sexual exploitation

personal: the idea that God is an individual or person with whom people are able to have a relationship or feel close to

pollution: making something dirty and contaminated, especially the environment

polygamy: the practice or custom of having more than one wife or husband at the same time

positive discrimination: treating people more favourably because they have been discriminated against in the past or have disabilities

poverty: being without money, food or other basic needs of life (being poor)

prejudice: unfairly judging someone before the facts are known; holding biased opinions about an individual or group

principle of utility: philosophical idea that an action is right if it promotes maximum happiness for the maximum number of people affected by it

prison: a secure building where offenders are kept for a period of time set by a judge

procreate: produce children

protest: an expression of disapproval, often in a public group

puja: an act of worship

punishment: something legally done to somebody as a result of being found guilty of breaking the law

Pure Land Buddhism: a Mahayana form of Buddhism based on belief in Amitabha Buddha

Q

quality of life : the general wellbeing of a person, in relation to their health and happiness; also, the theory that the value of life depends upon how good or how satisfying it is

R

reconciliation: when individuals or groups restore friendly relations after conflict or disagreement; also a sacrament in the Catholic Church

reformation: an aim of punishment – to change someone's behaviour for the better

remarriage: when someone marries again, after a previous marriage or marriages have come to an end

responsibility: a duty to care for, or having control over, something or someone

retaliation: deliberately harming someone as a response to them harming you

retreat: a period of time spent away from everyday life in order to focus on meditation practice

retribution: an aim of punishment – to get your own back

S

samatha meditation: calming meditation'; a type of meditation that involves calming the mind and developing deeper concentration

same-sex marriage: marriage between partners of the same sex

same-sex parents: people of the same sex who are raising children together

samsara: the repeating cycle of birth, life, death and rebirth

samudaya: the second noble truth: there are causes of suffering

sanctity of life: the belief that all life is holy or deeply valuable, and should not be misused or abused

Sanskrit: the language used in later Indian Buddhist texts

self-defence: acting to prevent harm to yourself or others

sex before marriage: sex between two single unmarried people

shrine: an area with a statue of a Buddha or Bodhisattva, which provides Buddhists with a focal point for meditation and devotion

skilful: good, ethical actions or behaviour

social justice: ensuring that society treats people fairly whether they are poor or wealthy; protecting people's human rights

special revelation: the revelation of God, or the divine, through direct personal experience or an unusual specific event

stewardship: the idea that believers have a duty to look after the environment on behalf of God

stupa: a small building in a monastery that sometimes contains holy relics

Sukhavati: the paradise where Amitabha Buddha lives, and where Pure Land Buddhists aim to be reborn

sunyata: emptiness; the concept that nothing has a separate, independent 'self' or 'soul'

T

tanha: craving (desiring or wanting something)

temple: a place where Buddhists come together to practise

terrorism: the unlawful use of violence, usually against innocent civilians, to achieve a political goal

thangka: a detailed painting of a Buddha or Bodhisattva

the Eightfold Path: eight aspects that Buddhists practise and live by in order to achieve enlightenment

the five aggregates: the five aspects that make up a person

the five asectics: the Buddha's first five students; five monks who followed ascetic practices

the five moral precepts: five principles that Buddhists try to follow to live ethically and morally

the Four Noble Truths: the four truths that the Buddha taught about suffering

the four sights: old age, illness, death, and a holy man; these Four Sights led the Buddha to leave his life of luxury in the palace

the four sublime states: the four qualities of love, compassion, sympathetic joy and equanimity which the Buddha taught that Buddhists should develop

the six perfections: the six qualities or virtues that Mahayana Buddhists try to develop in order to live as Bodhisattvas

the theory of evolution: the theory that higher forms of life have gradually developed from lower ones

the three poisons: greed, hatred and ignorance; the main causes of suffering

the three watches of the night: the three realisations that the Buddha made in order to achieve enlightenment

the threefold way: the Eightfold Path grouped into the three sections of ethics, meditation and wisdom

the Tibetan Wheel of Life: an image that symbolises samsara, often found in Tibetan Buddhist monasteries and temples

theft: stealing the property of another person

Theravada Buddhism: 'the school of the elders'; an ancient Buddhist tradition found in southern Asia

transcendent: the idea that God is beyond and outside life on Earth and the universe; a quality of God

U

unskilful: bad, unethical actions or behaviour

V

vegan: a person who does not eat animals or food produced by animals (such as eggs); a vegan tries not to use any products that have caused harm to animals (such as leather)

vegetarian: a person who does not eat meat or fish

violence: using actions that threaten or harm others

vipassana meditation: 'insight meditation'; a type of meditation that involves developing understanding of the nature of reality

visualisation: imagining or 'seeing' an object in one's mind

W

war: fighting between nations to resolve issues between them

weapons of mass destruction: weapons that can kill large numbers of people and/or cause great damage

Wesak: a Theravada festival that celebrates the Buddha's birth, enlightenment and passing away

wisdom (panna): a section of the threefold way that deals with Buddhist approaches to understanding the nature of reality

wonder: marvelling at the complexity and beauty of the universe

Z

zazen meditation: a type of meditation in Zen Buddhism that requires awareness of the present moment

Acknowledgements

The publisher would like to thank the following for permissions to use their photographs:

Cover: Peter Adams/Getty Images; **p9**: Titima Ongkantong/Shutterstock; **p10**: Godong/Alamy Stock Photo; **p11**: Visun Khankasem/Shutterstock; **p13**: Godong/Alamy Stock Photo; **p14(t)**: R.M. Nunes; **p14(b)**: mai111/Shutterstock; **p15**: steve estvanik/Shutterstock; **p17**: Nila Newsom/Shutterstock; **p19**: Godong/Alamy Stock Photo; **p30**: Godong/Alamy Stock Photo; **p31**: Janine Wiedel Photolibrary/Alamy Stock Photo; **p32**: George-Standen/iStockphoto; **p39**: Aurora Photos/Alamy Stock Photo; **p40**: Katoosha/Shutterstock; **p42**: NICK FIELDING/Alamy Stock Photo; **p43**: Thoai/Shutterstock; **p50**: blickwinkel/Alamy Stock Photo; **p51**: Harold Smith/Alamy Stock Photo; **p52**: Dietmar Temps/Shutterstock; **p53**: RichardBakerReligion/Alamy Stock Photo; **p55**: Maciej Wojtkowiak/Alamy Stock Photo; **p56**: Craig Lovell/Eagle Visions Photography/Alamy Stock Photo; **p57**: © Martin Jenkinson / pressphotos.co.uk; **p58**: Tim Gainey/Alamy Stock Photo; **p59**: Vladimir Melnik/Shutterstock; **p60**: pema/Shutterstock; **p61**: Lifebrary/Shutterstock; **p62(t)**: I love photo/Shutterstock; **p62(b)**: Calvin Chan/Shutterstock; **p63**: JTB MEDIA CREATION, Inc./Alamy Stock Photo; **p64**: Robert Preston Photography/Alamy Stock Photo **p65**: Agencja Fotograficzna Caro/Alamy Stock Photo; **p66**: Godong/Alamy Stock Photo; **p67**: Courtesy of ROKPA INTERNATIONAL/Lea Wyler; **p69**: Amos Chapple/Getty Images; **p71**: Hemis/Alamy Stock Photo; **p72**: Grant Rooney/Alamy Stock Photo; **p80**: Gina Smith/Shutterstock; **p81**: David Longstreath/Getty Images; **p84**: Peter Treanor/Alamy Stock Photo; **p86**: R.M. Nunes/Shutterstock; **p87**: Anders Ryman/Alamy Stock Photo; **p88**: simon kolton/Alamy Stock Photo; **p89(t)**: Darko Sikman/Shutterstock; **p89(b)**: Scott Stulberg/Getty Images; **p93**: REUTERS/Alamy Stock Photo; **p97**: Glasshouse Images/Alamy Stock Photo; **p98**: Sean Sprague/Alamy Stock Photo; **p100**: robertharding/Alamy Stock Photo; **p101**: Melvyn Longhurst/Alamy Stock Photo; **p104**: Karen Kasmauski/Superstock; **p112**: Simon_Watkinson/iStockphoto; **p117**: Jules2013/iStockphoto; **p119(b)**: coward_lion/123RF; **p124**: epa european pressphoto agency b.v./Alamy Stock Photo; **p126**: 1000 Words/Shutterstock; **p127**: Paolo VESCIA/Getty Images; **p131**: AMAN ROCHMAN/Getty Images; **p132**: Everett Historical/Shutterstock; **p133**: David Grossman/Alamy Stock Photo; **p135**: ZUMA Press, Inc./Alamy Stock Photo; **p137**: Copyright Owner, Buddhist Compassion Relief Tzu Chi Foundation of the Republic of China, a.k.a. Buddhist Compassion Relief Tzu Chi Foundation. All Rights Reserved; **p136**: Northfoto/Shutterstock; **p142**: SOMRERK KOSOLWITTHAYANANT/Shutterstock; **p144**: Paul Brown/Alamy Stock Photo; **p145**: tbradford/iStockphoto; **p147**: Godong/Alamy Stock Photo; **p149**: Roger Bamber/Alamy Stock Photo; **p154**: Michaelpuche/Shutterstock; **p155**: ZUMA Press, Inc./Alamy Stock Photo; **p157**: Janine Wiedel Photolibrary/Alamy Stock Photo; **p158**: Craig Lovell/Eagle Visions Photography/Alamy Stock Photo; **p159**: ROMEO GACAD/Getty Images; **p161**: Richard Baker/Getty Images; **p162**: Stratol/iStockphoto; **p163**: idmanjoe/iStockphoto; **p164**: ZUMA Press, Inc./Alamy Stock Photo; **p166**: Tatiana Morozova/iStockphoto; **p167**: Courtesy of The Karuna Trust.

iStockphoto: 12, 20, 22(b), 24, 28(b), 49(b), 68, 70, 79, 78, 83, 85, 94, 95, 96, 102, 106, 110, 115, 116, 119(t), 121, 130, 141, 140, 143, 150.

All other photos: Shutterstock

Artwork by Aptara

We are grateful to the authors and publishers for use of extracts from their titles and in particular for the following:

Scripture quotations [marked NIV] taken from the *Holy Bible, New International Version Anglicised*, Copyright © 1979, 1984, 2011 Biblica. Used by permission of Hodder & Stoughton Ltd, an Hachette UK company. All rights reserved. 'NIV' is a registered trademark of Biblica UK trademark number 1448790. Excerpts from *Collected Bodhi Leaves Publications (Numbers 122 to 157)*, (Buddhist Publication Society, 2012). Reproduced with permission from the Administrative Secretary, Buddhist Publication Society. Excerpts from *The Book of Gradual Sayings*, translated by F. L. Woodward, (Pali Text Society, 1995). Reproduced with permission from the Hon. Secretary, Pali Text Society. Excerpts from *The Connected Discourses of the Buddha: A New Translation of the Samyutta Nikaya*, translated by Bhikkhu Bodhi (Wisdom Publications, 2005). Copyright © 2000 byBhikkhu Bodhi. Reproduced with permission from The Permissions Company, Inc., on behalf of Wisdom Publications, www.wisdompubs.org. Excerpts from *Dialogues of the Buddha: Translated from the Pāli of the Dīgha-nikāya*, translated by T. W. and C. A. F. Rhys Davids (Pali Text Society, 2010). Reproduced with permission from the Hon. Secretary, Pali Text Society. Excerpts from *The Group of Discourses*, translated by K. R. Norman (Pali Text Society, 2015). Reproduced with permission from the Hon. Secretary, Pali Text Society. Excerpts from *The Middle Length Discourses of the Buddha: A New Translation of the Majjhima Nikaya*, translated by Bhikkhu Nanamoli and Bhikkhu Bodhi, (Wisdom publications, 2005). Copyright © 1995 by Bhikkhu Bodhi. Reproduced with permission from The Permissions Company, Inc., on behalf of Wisdom Publications, www.wisdompubs.org. Excerpts from *The Numerical Discourses of the Buddha: A Complete Translation of the Anguttara Nikaya*, translated by Bhikkhu Bodhi, (Wisdom Publications, 2012). Copyright © 2012 by Bhikkhu Bodhi. Reproduced with permission from The Permissions Company, Inc., on behalf of Wisdom Publications, www.wisdompubs.org. Excerpts from *Poems of Early Buddhist Nuns*, translated by C. A. F. Rhys Davids and K. R. Norman, (Pali Text Society, 1989). Reproduced with permission from the Hon. Secretary, Pali Text Society. Excerpts from *The Story of Gotama Buddha: The Nidāna-kathā of the Jātakatthakathā*, translated by N.A. Jayawickrama. (Pali Text Society, 1990). Reproduced with permission from the Hon. Secretary, Pali Text Society. Excerpts from *The Udāna and The Itivuttaka*, translated by Peter Masefield, (Pali Text Society, 2013). Reproduced with permission from the Hon. Secretary, Pali Text Society. Excerpts from *The Word of the Doctrine: Translation of Dhammapada*, translated by K.R. Norman, (Pali Text Society, 1997). Reproduced with permission from the Hon. Secretary, Pali Text Society. **R. Aitken**: *Mind of Clover: Essays in Zen Buddhist Ethics* (North Point Press, 1985). Copyright © 1984 by Diamond Sangha. Reproduced with permission from North Point Press, a division of Farrar, Straus and Giroux. **J. Chozen Bays**: quote, (Jan Chozen Bays). Reproduced with permission from JCB. **Bhadantacariya Buddhaghosa:** *The Path of Purification: Visuddhimagga*, translated by Bhikkhu Nanamoli (Buddhist Publication Society, 1991). Reproduced with permission from the Administrative Secretary, Buddhist Publication Society. **Lama Choedak**: *Understanding the Significance of a Buddhist Shrine*, Clear Mind Quarterly Newsletter No. 6, Nov 1990-Jan 1991 (Sakya Losal Choe Dzong, 1991). Copyright 1993 © by Lama Choedak Yuthok, Sakya Losal Choe Dzong, Canberra. **K. Crosby and A. Skilton**: *The Bodhicaryavatara: A Guide to the Buddhist Path of Awakening*, (Windhorse Publications, 2002). (c0 2002 Windhorse Publications. Reproduced with permission from Windhorse Publications. **V. Finlay and M. Palmer**: *Faith in Conservation: New Approaches to Religions and the Environment*, (World Bank Publications, 2003). Reproduced with permission from World Bank under the terms of the Creative Commons Attribution Licence CC-BY 3.0. **Maha Ghosananda:** *Step to*

Step: Meditations on Wisdom and Compassion, (Parallax Press, 1993). Reproduced with permission from Parallax Press. **B. H. Gunaratana:** *Meditation in Everyday Life* from *Mindfulness in Plain English: Updated and Expanded Edition*, (Wisdom Publications, 2011). Copyright © 2011 by Bhante Henepola Gunaratana. Reproduced with permission from The Permissions Company, Inc. on behalf of Wisdom Publications, www.wisdompubs.org. **Y. Hoffmann:** *Japanese Death Poems*, (Tuttle Publishing, 1998). Reproduced with permission from Tuttle Publishing. **His Holiness Tenzin Gyatso the Dalai Lama:** speech, New Delhi, India, February 4th 1992, (Dalai Lama, 1992). Reproduced with permission from His Holiness The Dalai Lama. **His Holiness Tenzin Gyatso the Dalai Lama:** *An Open Heart: Practising Compassion in Everyday Life*, (Hodder & Stoughton, 2002). Reproduced with permission from His Holiness The Dalai Lama. **His Holiness Tenzin Gyatso the Dalai Lama:** *My Land and My People*, (Srishti Publishers, 2002). Reproduced with permission from His Holiness The Dalai Lama. **His Holiness Tenzin Gyatso the Dalai Lama:** *The Compassionate Life*, (Wisdom Publications, 2003). Copyright © 2003 by Tenzin Gyatso, the Fourteenth Dalai Lama. Reproduced with permission from The Permissions Company, Inc. on behalf of Wisdom Publications, www.wisdompubs.org. **His Holiness Tenzin Gyatso the Dalai Lama:** speech, Inter-faith Seminar, Ladakh Group, August 25th 2005, (Dalai Lama, 2005). Reproduced with permission from His Holiness The Dalai Lama. **His Holiness Tenzin Gyatso the Dalai Lama:** *The Dalai Lama: What Can He Show You About Peace at Work?*, March 20, 2008 https://www.thedailymind.com/mindfulness/the-dalai-lama-what-can-he-show-you-about-peace-at-work/ (Dalai Lama, 2008). Reproduced with permission from His Holiness The Dalai Lama. **His Holiness Tenzin Gyatso the Dalai Lama:** *The Compassionate Life*, (Simon & Schuster, 2012). Reproduced with permission from His Holiness The Dalai Lama. **His Holiness Tenzin Gyatso the Dalai Lama:** *Living the Compassionate Life*, October 23, 2016 http://www.lionsroar.com/living-the-compassionate-life/?utm_content=buffer4c3d0&utm_medium=social&utm_source=facebook.com&utm_campaign=buffer (Lion's Roar, 2016). Reproduced with permission from His Holiness The Dalai Lama. **His Holiness Tenzin Gyatso the Dalai Lama:** Compassion and the Individual, https://www.dalailama.com/messages/compassion-and-human-values/compassion (The Office of His Holiness the Dalai Lama, 2016). Reproduced with permission from His Holiness The Dalai Lama. **D. Ikeda:** *Building Global Solidarity Toward Nuclear Abolition*, September 8th 2009, (Soka Gakkai International, 2009). Reproduced with permission from Soka Gakkai, International Office of Public Information, Josei Toda International Center. **D. Khyentse Rinpoche and P. Sangye:** *The Hundred Verses of Advice: Tibetan Buddhist Teachings on What Matters Most*, translated by Padmakara Translation Group (Shambhala Publications, 2006). Reproduced with permission from Shambhala Publications. **D. Loy:** *Loving the World as Our Own Body*, Worldviews: Global Religions, Culture, and Ecology, Vol. 1, Issue 3 (Brill, 1997). Reproduced with permission from Koninklijke Brill NV. **D. Morgan:** quote, (D. Morgan). Reproduced with permission from Rev. Daishin Morgan, courtesy of the Prior at Throssel Hole Buddhist Abbey. **Osho:** *Blessed are the Ignorant*, (Osho Foundation, 1979). Reproduced with permission from Osho International Foundation. **U. Sangharakshita:** *Who is the Buddha?* from *The Essential Sangharakshita:A Half-Century of Writings from the Founder of the Friends of the Western Buddhist Order*, edited by Vidyadevi Karen Stout., (Wisdom Publications, 2009). Copyright © 2009 by Urgyen Sangharakshita. Reproduced with permission from The Permissions Company, Inc., on behalf of Wisdom Publications, www.wisdompubs.org. **Santideva:** *A Guide to the Bodhisattva Way of Life*, translated by Vesna A. Wallace and B. Alan Wallace (Snow Lion, 1997). Reproduced with permission from Shambhala Publications. **Sogyal Rinpoche:** *The Tibetan Book of Living and Dying*, edited by Patrick Gaffney & Andrew Harvey (Rider, 2008). © 1993 by Rigpa Fellowship. Reproduced with permission from Random House Group Ltd and HarperCollins Publishers. **A. Sumedho:** *The Four Noble Truths*, (Amaravati Publications, 1992). Reproduced with permission from Amaravati Publications. **Bhikkhu Thanissaro**: *The Four Noble Truths: A Study Guide*, (Access to Insight, Legacy Edition, 2013) © 1999 Metta Forest Monastery. Reproduced with permission from Metta Forest Monastery. **Thich Nhat Hanh:** *The Heart of Buddha's Teaching*, (Parallax Press, 1996. Paperback edition 1999, 2015 Random House). Reproduced with permission from Parallax Press. **Thich Nhat Hanh:** *The Miracle of Mindfulness*, (Rider, 2008). © 1975, 1976 by Thich Nhat Hanh. Reproduced with permission from Beacon Press and Penguin Random House LLC. **Thich Nhat Hanh:** *Old Path, White Clouds: Walking in the Footsteps of the Buddha*, (Parallax Press, 1991). Reproduced with permission from Parallax Press. **Tzu Chi Foundation:** *Mission Statement: The Vow of Tzu Chi Commissioners*, (Tzu Chi Foundation, 2016). Reproduced with permission from Tzu Chi. **United Nations**: *The Universal Declaration of Human Rights*, http://www.un.org/en/universal-declaration-human-rights/ (United Nations, 1948). Reproduced with permission from United Nations. **B. Daizen Victoria**: *Zen at War*, (Rowman & Littlefield Publishers, 2006). Reproduced with permission from Rowman & Littlefield. **T. Zopa**: *The Wish-Fulfilling Golden Sun of the Mahayana Thought Training*, (Nepal Mahayana Gompa Centre, 1973). Reproduced with permission from Lama Thubten Zopa Rinpoche.

We have made every effort to trace and contact all copyright holders before publication, but if notified of any errors or omissions, the publisher will be happy to rectify these at the earliest opportunity.

The publisher and authors would like to thank Dr Debbie Herring for reviewing this book, the Pali Text Society for helping to source the scriptural quotations, and Deborah Weston for help and advice across the AQA GCSE Religious Studies series. We would like to thank Munisha for contributing to and reviewing the book.

Index